MAPPING THE THIRD SECTOR:
Voluntarism in a Changing Social Economy

MAPPING THE THIRD SECTOR:
Voluntarism in a Changing Social Economy

JON VAN TIL

The Foundation Center

Library of Congress Cataloging-in-Publication Data

Van til, Jon.
  Mapping the third sector.
  Bibliography: p.
  Includes index.
  1. Voluntarism—United States.   I. Title.
HN90.V64V36   1988   361.3'7   88-3610
ISBN 0-87954-240-3

For Ross and Claire, who also like words and maps

CONTENTS

Preface

Voluntary association has existed since the emergence of civilization itself. In pre-industrial Britain, for example, such activity took place on the grounds of the Commons — that land in each village on which all members of the community could feed their stock and meet with their neighbors as custodians responsible for the preservation of that land. The Commons later became enclosed, or privatized, as we would say today, and the boundaries of Anglo-American society changed significantly. The Commons did not disappear, it was restructured; and as the reach of other institutions — governmental and economic — became extensive, the Commons receded in both prominence and significance.

The Commons exists today, as Roger Lohmann has observed, as "self-defining collectivities of voluntarily associating individuals operating jointly outside of markets and households and independent of the state." In such collectivities men and women gather for purposes other than private gain or the compulsion of law. It is within these commons — in neighborhood associations and interest groups, in houses of worship and secular places of contemplation, in nonprofit organizations and social clubs — that people communicate across the chasms between different life experiences and create meaning and value for their lives. It is in these modern commons that people learn the arduous joys of sharing what is good within the complex web of contemporary society.

Today, voluntary action — human endeavor not motivated by private gain or compulsion of law — generally is perceived to occur within a voluntary, philanthropic, nonprofit, independent, or third "sector," both for the convenience of discussion as well as the necessity of legislation. The depth and breadth of this "voluntary action" demand its systematic examination, but its scope and diversity continue to make this study problematic. Voluntary action takes many forms and cannot be circumscribed accurately by a single rubric; it is a process whose diverse nature makes it hard to "put your finger on" the sum of its effects at the same time that it offers the hope of community outside of institutional definitions.

This book reviews historical and contemporary models of voluntary action in order to clear the way for one that does not rely solely on a sectoral view of society; it implies the need for a new conception of how to preserve, extend, and experience community in an age of privatism, power, and self-absorption. It is about our individual actions in this quest and about our perceptions of the organizations we form to advance an agenda of mutual caring and concern.

The medieval village has been supplanted by Spaceship Earth. The demands of contemporary life, collective and individual, emphasize that we have never needed a Commons more than we do today.

Acknowledgments

Portions of this book have previously appeared, in forms rather greatly revised in this presentation, in such journals as *Volunteer Administration, Social Policy,* and the *Journal of Voluntary Action Research.* A predecessor to Chapter 3 first appeared in John Harman's edited collection, *Volunteerism in the Eighties.* The pages on coproduction in Chapter 9 first appeared in my *Living With Energy Shortfall* (Westview, 1982). Some ideas presented in Chapter 10 were first published as a paper, of which Trudy Heller was senior author, that appeared in the collection edited by Mel Moyer, *Managing Voluntary Organizations.* Several other sections were first presented at the 1983 and 1987 Spring Research Forums of INDEPENDENT SECTOR, and my thinking on voluntarism's future emerged from writings I did for the National Forum on Volunteerism in 1980. Finally, the practical thoughts on building partnerships offered in Chapter 9 were developed initially in collaboration with Ronald Lippitt, whose death in 1986 left a void in the study and practice of voluntarism that will be impossible to fill.

Many colleagues have read parts of this manuscript in many forms. Among those who have been helpful in advancing the several sections of this work are David Horton Smith, Louis A. Zurcher, Jr. (whose untimely death in 1987 deprived me of yet another friend and colleague), John D. Harman, Larry Moore, Trudy Heller, Ivan Scheier, Virginia Ann Hodgkinson, Susan Ostrander, Stuart Langton, William Van Til, Wayne Rydberg, Mme. Dan Ferrand-Bechmann, J. Roland Pennock, Michael O'Neill, and Stephen R. Block.

My students in the Policy Seminar on "The Structure of the Voluntary Sector" in Rutgers University's Graduate Program on Public Policy (Camden campus) offered helpful comments on this book as it took form. Research papers prepared for this seminar by Mark Solof and Ellen Smith influenced my thinking in crafting parts of Chapters 4 and 9, respectively.

A research grant from Rutgers University permitted the travel to Britain and France that underlies my reflections on the experience of those countries with voluntary sector development. A Rutgers sabbatical freed the writing time required, and the University of Colorado at Boulder provided a reflective location for that writing. My particular thanks in these regards go to Provost Walter K. Gordon of the Rutgers/Camden campus, and Prof. Paul Wehr, Chair of the Sociology Department at the University of Colorado at Boulder.

I am deeply grateful to Maurice G. Gurin, who suggested upon reading some of the manuscript that it might be of interest to The Foundation Center. Rick Schoff, Assistant Director of Publications at The Foundation Center, edited the manuscript and guided its revision. Rick was as helpful and constructively demanding an editor as any author could wish to have.

Finally, be it noted that my family engaged in few of those long-suffering behaviors so graphically chronicled by other authors. My wife, Trudy Heller, made sure that I didn't plagiarize from the sections of our joint work that were hers, and excused me from none of the joint child-rearing responsibilities we have undertaken to assume, whatever the urgency of the manuscript's needs. And Ross and Claire, accustomed to seeing their parents engaged in the process of writing, continued to assume that the more difficult skills in life were the ones they were at the time learning. Throughout, however, my family provided me what seems consistent with my own needs as a writer: a lively life at home. I appreciate them all for that, and more as well.

PART I
Voluntary Action

Introduction

We have created in our complex society three separate institutional worlds. We define them as different from one another. We create separate places in which to learn about them. We prepare for careers within them by learning what seem to be very different skills.

One of these institutional sectors, that of business, commands 80% of our economy (Hodgkinson and Weitzman, 1984). Often viewed, as by Calvin Coolidge, as the "business of America," this sector occupies most of the attention of the science of economics and is the focus of a very large applied academic focus, "business studies."

Second in size, the governmental sector weighs in at about 14% of the economy's bulk. Its importance subject to cyclical forces, this sector is sometimes reduced to Hobbes' watchman (providing for domestic and international security) and is at other times invested with a far wider reach in the provision of human betterment. Government is studied by the discipline of political science and is the focus of the applied academic disciplines "public policy" and "public administration."

The third sector, sometimes called the "voluntary" or "independent" or "nonprofit" sector, constitutes the remaining 6% of the national economy (and accounts for 9% of total national employment). Commonly defined as residual, its scope extends into many corners of our society. No single academic discipline, however, exists for its study, although its study has most frequently occupied many sociologists. No applied discipline has emerged in universities for the preparation of individuals for careers in the voluntary sector (although one seems at present to be emerging).

This book aims to explore the interrelationships of the three sectors in an era of fundamental institutional change. In it, the suggestion is made that, when the three sectors are viewed as separate but related components of a single structure—a political–economic society—important functions of the voluntary sector begin to appear, perhaps with more clarity than if that sector were studied in isolation. This book, then, is aimed toward improved understanding of the roles of the three sectors in their joint societal embeddedness, with a particular focus on the role of the voluntary sector.

The role of the third sector has been seen as one of both articulating and mediating the crucial boundary between the state and the economy in contemporary society. In such a view, voluntarism provides a unique contribution to the sustenance of modern societies. In this book, I shall probe both of these expansive claims. One competing hypothesis claims that nonprofit organizations may be simply one more way of doing business in an organizational society, and that view merits review as well.

The task of examining the meaning of voluntarism in contemporary society requires, first, clearly identifying the matter at hand for study. Thus, the two chapters in Part I present prevailing images of voluntary action, develop a glossary of terms for their comprehension, and identify a variety of perspectives from which the world of voluntary action may be approached.

Voluntary action research is an interdisciplinary field to which practitioners of many disciplines have contributed. The chapters in the later parts of the book review major contributions by historians, political scientists, sociologists, anthropologists, and policy scientists, among others, to the study of voluntary action. The end of the study ideally leads to a truly interdisciplinary perspective, and that task begins with a consideration of definitions of the field.

1

Defining Our Terms:
In Search of "Volunt ... ism"

We lie, as Emerson said, in the lap of an immense intelligence. But that intelligence is dormant and its communications are broken, inarticulate and faint until it possesses the local community as its medium.

—John Dewey, *The Public and Its Problems* (1927, p. 219)

Individual voluntary action is that which gives personal meaning to life. It is that which one freely chooses to do either for enjoyment in the short term and/or from commitment to some longer-term goal that is not merely a manifestation of bio-social man, socio-political man, or economic man.

—David Horton Smith, Richard Reddy, and Burt Baldwin (1972, p. 163)

INTRODUCTION

The implication that the voluntary sector has a key role to play in modern societies does not reflect the conventional scholarly assessment of its role. The *third sector* seems aptly named in terms of the significance customarily accorded it. It tends to be the least attended in American studies. It is often confused with the other "private institutions" of the business world, or it is dismissed as the locus of mere "do-gooding."

Consider the residual terms in which this institutional sector is commonly defined. Writing from a corporate background, Theodore Levitt (now the editor of the *Harvard Business Review*) notes, first, that "conventional taxonomy divides society into two sectors—private and public. Private is business. Public is presumed to be 'all else.' " But "all else" is too broad a concept, Levitt asserts. It leaves an "enormous residuum," which he proceeds to call "the Third Sector." This societal arena is host to "a bewildering variety of organizations with differing degrees of visibility, power, and activeness. Although they vary greatly in scope and specific purposes, their general purposes are broadly similar—to do things business and government are either not doing, not doing well, or not doing often enough" (Levitt, 1973, p. 49).

Of all the terms commonly used to describe this sector, only *voluntary* and *independent* are not essentially derivative, though even they are not wholly free of derogatory implications. The term "independent sector" implies a judgment of putative freedom from something else, suggesting several questions for consideration: independent of what? and what of the implication of dependence? On the other hand, the term "voluntary" is clouded by the diverse uses of the term both in the vernacular and in scientific language—uses as diverse as "freely willed" in philosophy to "unintentionally sown" in botany—not to mention its quixotic military application and its physiological meaning as a bodily reflex under conscious control.

Clearly it is necessary to attend to language and its many meanings if we are to make sense of this subject. Thus, it is necessary to examine the principal concepts used when voluntarism is studied, beginning with the individual act of volunteering, which forms the basis of most concepts in this field.

Volunteering may be identified as a helping action of an individual that is valued by him or her, and yet is not aimed directly at material gain or mandated or coerced by others. Thus, in the broadest sense, *volunteering* is any uncoerced helping activity that is engaged in not primarily for financial gain and not by coercion or mandate. It is thereby different in definition from work, slavery, or conscription. It differs from employment in that it is not primarily motivated by pecuniary gain, although much paid work includes *volunteering*; it differs from conscription in that it is unpaid and uncoerced; and it differs from slavery in that it is not coerced.

Volunteering may be extended beyond the purely individual, and it may also take the form of a group activity. Thus, the informal, spontaneous, individual act of the motorist aiding an accident victim and the formal participation of a volunteer meeting with a parolee as part of an organized program are both acts of *volunteering*. Actually, there are two dimensions involved here, one varying between individual and group activity, the other varying between structured and unstructured activity. As depicted in Figure 1, the contexts of *volunteering* involve a range of activities, all of which are uncoerced, not primarily aimed at financial profit, and oriented toward helping others—and possibly oneself, as we shall see later.

Volunteering, as defined here, is similar to but somewhat less broad in definition than *voluntary action,* as defined by David Horton Smith, Richard Reddy, and Burt Baldwin in the second of this chapter's introductory quotations. By that definition, individual *voluntary action* may include an extramarital affair, a chess game, or the composition of a book of verse—in short, anything that feels good or meaningful and that is not biologically compelled, politically coerced, or financially remunerated. Smith and his colleagues proceed to note (1972, p. 167) that a more limited concept may be desirable:

Voluntary action directed at the long-range betterment of society and the general welfare may be the "best" kind of voluntary action in the eyes of most people. But there are many other important kinds of voluntary action phenomena, even if not clearly aimed at the general welfare—for example, riots, wildcat strikes, fraternity hazing, shoplifting for "kicks," "bingo parties," "social drinking," and perhaps even watching TV.

With ruthless logic, Smith and his associates bring us to the precipice of a real dilemma. As founders of the Association of *Voluntary Action* Scholars, they recognize that a world of behavior, seemly and unseemly, public and private, is encompassed by the term *voluntary action*. But from the perspective of a leader of, say, the National Center for *Voluntary Action* (to take the name of a prominent organization of the 1970s, now renamed), it is doubtful that such actions as "bingo parties" will generate enthusiasm, and it is nearly certain that opposition will greet such voluntary actions as shoplifting, rioting, and extramarital affairs.

Resolution of this dilemma may be achieved by two means. First, the concept of *voluntary action* might be defined in the narrower way, removing those actions not directed at long-range betterment and the general welfare. Simultaneously, the concept could be recognized to be broadly descriptive in nature, and not be referred to in value-charged ways. When speaking of *voluntary action* as a good thing, a term with a clear ideological content could be used. (Later in the argument, I shall suggest that *freedom* might be as good a word as any for this value.)

This usage seems conventional. Thus, it is awkward to speak of an individual volunteering to drink with the boys at the corner pub, or volunteering to spend an evening watching TV, although these are clearly forms of voluntary action that we celebrate among the joys of freedom. But thorny issues remain in defining *volunteering* as that form of *voluntary action* that involves helping. Helping whom? How?

Smith and his colleagues sought to get around the issue by identifying as the " 'best' kind of voluntary action in the eyes of most people [that] directed at the long-range betterment of society and the general welfare." A slightly different view is suggested by Herta Loeser, who gives a central place to "the free giving of one's time and talents for work deemed socially or politically beneficial" (1974, p. 1). Ivan Scheier (1982) takes a third view, preferring the concept of "helping" as a central one, and urging individuals to adapt its meaning as they choose.

I tend toward Loeser's and Scheier's positions for a starting point. By focusing on the volunteer's act as involving free giving for work "deemed beneficial," Loeser removes from the volunteer the rather ponderous responsibility of determining that an act is aimed at the "long-range betterment" of society. Clearly much may be of value in the short run as well.

And, even more important, her definition leaves room for the recognition that *volunteering* may be very much in the self-interest of the volunteer him/herself. Some forms of *volunteering* begin from an explicit basis of self-help, and almost all forms may contribute to individual goals of career exploration and development, sociability, and other forms of personal enhancement.

A third prominent concept may now be introduced: *voluntary associa-tion*. This concept refers to forms of behavior that are organized and that are directed at influencing broader structures of collective action and social purpose. A *voluntary association* is a structured group whose members have united for the purpose of advancing an interest or achieving some social purpose. Theirs is a clear aim toward a chosen form of "social betterment." Such an association is directed in its aims beyond the immediate enjoyment of fellowship and consummatory group activity; it links the group in some direct way to the larger society.

Thus, groups like neighborhood associations seeking to restrain crime or to encourage the cleaning of streets are *voluntary associations* by this iden-tification; so are church-based organizations that seek to provide for school prayer and civic organizations that aim to improve a city's economic cli-mate; and so are groups of volunteers who hope to reduce family abuse by means of direct service and legislative advocacy. Such organizations are vol-untary in a dual sense: much of their human resources are contributed by members as volunteers, and they are nongovernmental, nonprofit, and nonconsummatory—and thus are clearly located in the "voluntary sector" of society.

Voluntary associations are more structured and formal than *voluntary action* and *volunteering*. They are the organized vehicles of the third sector. Many *voluntary associations* are informal in their structure and convene to advance purposes that range from political protest to the provision of social care and service. Prominent among the contemporary ranks of *voluntary associations* stands a subcategory that is governmentally identified as pub-licly chartered tax-free organizations. This group, called *nonprofit corpora-tions,* is certified to perform a wide range of charitable functions in society, and in return for their tax-free status they are required to provide public accounting of their actions. *Nonprofit corporations* are themselves divided into a number of categories, including *philanthropies,* which provide support to other nonprofit groups, and service-providing nonprofit organizations.

These, then, are the principal actors who inhabit the "third," "independ-ent," or "voluntary" sector: all of us who engage in *voluntary action;* most of us who *volunteer;* and those who join with others in *voluntary associa-tions* or *nonprofit corporations.* The behavior of these actors takes place in the broader societal milieu of organizational life and forms the empirical data for the study of voluntary action. These concepts are empirical (or positive) and reflect the concrete behavior of major actors.

Associated with each of these forms of action is a normative component —a concept that lends moral or ideological support to the phenomenon. These concepts may be identified as *freedom, volunteerism,* and *voluntarism,* respectively (the latter concept applying to both *voluntary associations* and *nonprofit corporations). Freedom,* as was argued above, is the normative concept that claims the goodness of *voluntary action. Volunteerism* is the normative concept that asserts the value of *volunteering.* And *voluntarism* is the normative concept that declares the worth of *voluntary associations* and their publicly chartered subtype, the *nonprofit corporation.*

As indicated in Figure 1, then, the third sector contains four major forms of actors, supported by three major ideological systems.

FIGURE 1.   BASIC CONCEPTS IN VOLUNT . . . ISM

	Individual action—not coerced, etc.	and deemed beneficial	and organized
Empirical	Voluntary action	Volunteering	Voluntary associations Non-profit corporations
Normative	Freedom	Volunteerism	Voluntarism

VOLUNTARISM IN THE AMERICAN EXPERIENCE

Our major concepts identified and defined, we can now proceed to explore ways in which they have been employed in the study of the varieties of voluntary action. The remainder of this chapter conducts this review by examining the ways in which voluntary action has been viewed throughout American history. Later chapters will extend this analysis into a variety of theoretical and empirical approaches taken by contemporary social scientists.

Let us now note, however, the long tradition that exists in American thought extolling the virtues of voluntarism. Voluntary action has been variously identified as a "natural" act of virtue, a source of community, an antidote to loneliness, a building block of democracy, a source of social justice, and an efficacious method of problem resolution. These themes have recently been orchestrated by Brian O'Connell in his comprehensive collection, *America's Voluntary Spirit* (1983).

The following pages rehearse a number of strong and telling voices, voices of scholars, philanthropists, and social change agents.* A unifying theme of this choir is that a strong bond exists between voluntarism and societal virtue.

A Natural Act

Various arguments have been presented to indicate that voluntarism is built directly into the fabric of social life. Scientist Warren Weaver, for example, points to the widespread presence of cooperative behavior among animal species, and observes that "altruistic behavior is an invention of nature herself" (p. 6). And physician Lewis Thomas, arguing from a sociobiological position, claims "a biological mandate for each of us to do whatever we can to keep the rest of the species alive" (p. 25). "Altruism," writes Thomas, "in its biological sense, is required of us" (p. 26).

The voluntary spirit is seen by others to reside in the very core of human existence. Gordon Manser and Rosemary Cass point to the power of the theme of "one common humanity, of the basic dignity and worth of all persons without exception" in inspiring voluntary acts (p. 21). Andrew Carnegie noted the importance of bending "the universal tree of humanity a little in the direction most favorable to the production of good fruit under existing circumstances" (p. 100). And writer Erma Bombeck describes a nightmare of the day the volunteers didn't: "I fought in my sleep to regain a glimpse of the ship of volunteers just one more time. It was to be my last glimpse of civilization . . . as we were meant to be" (p. 28).

A third aspect of the naturalness of voluntarism derives from its place in the kinship system. By preserving one's kin, one literally preserves oneself. Thus, as Thomas explains, the combat marine throws himself on the live grenade in order to protect the remainder of his family, his platoon, from danger (p. 24).

Finally, the Divinity is often cited as reinforcing such natural tendencies toward the voluntary mode of action. Historian Merle Curti notes that "Jewish, Catholic, and Protestant doctrines and practices have been central

---

* All references in the remainder of this chapter, with the exception of that to Schindler-Rainman and Lippitt (1975) and Simon (1957), are to selections from the O'Connell reader (1983).

in the development of philanthropy in America" (p. 165). "There is a time," Puritan leader John Winthrop asserted, "when a Christian must sell all and give to the poor as they did in the apostles' times; there is a time also when a Christian, though they give not all yet, must also give beyond their ability" (p. 31). To William Penn, "True Godliness" enables people to live in the world, and "excites their Endeavors to Mend it" (p. 38).

Penn's Quakerism, like Calvinist prescriptions, encouraged moderation. But unlike Calvinism, it suggested the application of economic surplus to the dedication of benevolent and humanitarian purposes. The performance of such good works was, wrote Cotton Mather, "an incomparable pleasure" (p. 40). Additional religious benefits derived from remaining in grace (Winthrop, p. 32), showing gratitude to God (Benjamin Franklin, p. 43), and contributing to social harmony (Robert Bremner, p. 40).

Building Community Through the Evolution of Cooperation

A second justifying theme found in the American literature emphasizes the positive contributions voluntarism provides for cooperation on the community level. Tracing the origins of cooperation through the progress of societal types from hunter-gatherer to industrial-urban societies, Manser and Cass note that "men and women had to cooperate just to survive in the face of hostile environments" (p. 10). Feudal society provided for help for individuals in need, generally without requiring detailed scrutiny of the particular conditions that bred the need. Informed by a Roman Catholic conception of poverty as virtue, and charity as responsibility, medieval voluntarism was provided in church and court.

The rise of Protestantism, and particularly its Calvinist variant, was accompanied by the transfer of some welfare responsibilities from community to state. The particulars of the predestination ideology of the Calvinists, combined with the loss of priestly intermediation to the Deity, gave rise to a harsh judgment of those in worldly need, who were thereby signed as morally fallible. Only those impoverished by conditions clearly beyond their personal responsibility were deemed worthy of public or private assistance, and government was called upon more and more to make the fateful determination of the degree to which the impoverished were deemed deserving of aid. With the Industrial Revolution, state care began to replace voluntary care for the needy, and with its development came the emergence of a variety of reform and protest movements.

In the "New World," Daniel Boorstin writes, it is not sufficiently recognized that "*communities* existed before governments were here to care for public needs" (p. 131). However, the concepts of community developed by the Puritans were employed eloquently to justify inequality and the selective award of philanthropic support, the needy drawing its lion's share. The familiar quote from Winthrop (p. 32) shows the closeness of the connection between inequality and community in this view:

> We must delight in each other, make other's conditions our own, rejoice together, mourn together, labor and suffer together: always having before our eyes our commission and community in the work, our community as members of the same body.

Curti (p. 37) addresses the same theme: "Differences in condition existed, not to separate and alienate men from one another, but to make them have more need of each other, and to bind them closer together 'in the bond of brotherly affection.' And those differences, important and essential though Winthrop believed them to be, seemed less significant to him than 'our community as members of the same body.' "

In practice, individualist Protestant concepts of self-help and self-reliance were deemed the proper basis for voluntary giving by Benjamin Franklin, who led in the establishment of "a free library, the Pennsylvania Hospital, and the Academy, which later became the University of Pennsylvania. He founded a volunteer fire department and developed plans for cleaning and lighting the streets of Philadelphia" (Curti, p. 18).

Self-help remained a central theme in American philanthropy. Writing over a century after Franklin's activities, Andrew Carnegie (p. 105) noted that, "In bestowing charity, the main consideration should be to help those who will help themselves; to provide part of the means by which those who desire to improve may do so; to give those who desire to rise the aids by which they may rise; to assist, but rarely or never to do all. Neither the individual nor the race," concluded Carnegie, "is improved by almsgiving." John D. Rockefeller (p. 113) echoed the same American theme when he stated: "The only thing which is of lasting benefit to a man is that which he does for himself. Money which comes to him without effort on his part is so seldom a benefit and often a curse."

The American legacy of giving placed its greatest emphasis upon aiding the deserving, and its insistence on individual pride rendered the entire philanthropic transaction problematic. To be sure, Emerson could wax eloquent on the need to "let our affection flow out to our fellows," and urged that "The state must consider the poor man, and all voices speak for him" (p. 51), while McGuffey envisioned the spread of goodness and concern from family to society (p. 61).

But reality never approached rhetoric, as even McGuffey's Mr. Goodman realized. Questioned about how to find the occasions to prove his benevolence, he replied: "if they are so distant that he cannot reach them, or so vast that he cannot grasp them, he may let a thousand little, snug, kind, good actions slip through his fingers in the meanwhile; and so, between the great thing that he *cannot* do, and the little ones that he *will not* do, life passes, and *nothing* will be done" (p. 61).

Despite Booker T. Washington's assertion that many donors "seem to feel, in a large degree, that an honour is being conferred upon them in their being permitted to give" to work they come to view as their own (p. 66), and Carnegie's claim of the responsibility of the rich to dispose of their wealth within their lifetime, an ambivalence continued to surround the philan-thropic enterprise. An Aesopian language, and even culture, developed to surround the philanthropic act, well captured by Curti's telling of Carnegie Foundation head Francis Keppel's conversation with a college president "who on one occasion announced that he had not come to ask for anything that day. 'How much is it,' asked Mr. Keppel, 'that you don't want to ask for?' " (p. 169).

Values of individualism, contesting with those of community and cooper-ation, have tended to prevail in the American experience. Thus, some have argued that what voluntarism provides is not the vision of community pro-vided by Winthrop, no matter how eloquently quoted by contemporary political leaders,* but rather the search for meaning in individual lives. This theme is also a major one in the literature under review.

Building Habits of the Heart

The phrase is Tocqueville's, and it has been amplified in the recent literature by Bellah and his associates (1985). The problem identified is the quality of human interaction in an individualistic nontraditional society. In Tocque-ville's analysis (p. 55): "Feelings and opinions are recruited, the heart is enlarged, and the human mind is developed only by the reciprocal influence of men upon one another. I have shown that these influences are almost null in democratic countries; they must therefore be artificially created, and this can only be accomplished by associations."

If community is rendered problematic by individualism in the United States, then does not the voluntary association provide a way to introduce its human connections and warmth as a by-product of the very coming together in association? This at least has been suggested by Dennis Wrong and a number of other observers of contemporary life, with their implica-tion that community is essentially a behavioral concept.

Max Lerner has probably been the most acute observer of the "con-trived" nature of associational "community" in contemporary America. It is the "social placing" of the American, he writes, "that defines his social per-sonality." In the voluntary association, "he can make his way as a person, by his qualities of geniality and friendliness, his ability to talk at a meeting or run it or work in a committee, his organizing capacities, his ardor, his public spirit. Here also he stretches himself, as he rarely does on the job, by work-ing with others for common nonprofit ends" (p. 82).

---

* In the 1984 Presidential campaign, both Ronald Reagan and Democratic convention keynoter Mario Cuomo used this quote prominently.

Participation in associations, Lerner contends, aids Americans in their fight against loneliness and isolation, cushions the urbanization process, and alleviates the tensions endemic to a competitive society. Such participation, thus, does not provide the sense of community offered by diminished kinship and neighborhood ties, but rather offers the closest thing to it available in modern society—a place where one can develop qualities not enhanced in any other milieu. It is a place in which we, to use Simon's (1957) terms, "satisfice" rather than "maximize." Thus, for many women, Lerner writes, the "club fills the emotional void of middle age, helping in the fight against loneliness and boredom" (p. 85).

At the heart of the voluntary impulse, Lerner asserts, is the desire to "join," to participate in "the sense of the mysterious and exotic . . . to belong to a secret order and be initiated into its rites, to be a part of a 'Temple' with a fancy Oriental name, to parade in the streets of Los Angeles, Chicago, or New York dressed in an Arab fez and burnoose, to have high-sounding titles of potentates of various ranks in a hierarchy: all this has appeal in a nonhierarchical society from which much of the secrecy and mystery of life has been squeezed out" (p. 84).

Thus, to Lerner, Tocqueville, and Bellah and his associates, the association serves as a survival tool of the lonely crowd, a place to turn to cope with the rigors of a society that espouses the value of community without successfully achieving or implementing it. Less grandiose than the two previous claims made for it, neither built into the beast nor its communities, it remains as an important claim. If established and accepted, the association as antidote to isolation and loneliness may help preserve other values claimed for voluntarism, including the support of democratic institutions.

Assuring Democracy

The contributions of voluntarism to democratic theory have been widely asserted, and Chapter 3 provides a more detailed examination of this relationship. Manser and Cass strike a central issue when they note the close relationship between voluntary and governmental activity: "one is struck by the extent to which [voluntary effort] has contributed to the developing and shaping of governmental services, and conversely, the extent to which governmental services have in turn tended to shape the direction of voluntary effort" (p. 12).

In 1974 the Commission on Private Philanthropy and Public Needs spelled out five "underlying functions" of voluntary groups that relate to the support of democracy: 1) "initiating new ideas and processes," 2) "developing public policy," 3) supporting minority or local interests, 4) overseeing government, and 5) "furthering active citizenship and altruism."

Many voluntary sector organizations and initiatives are directly related to the expression of citizen wants and needs. And the literature strongly asserts this connection. Eva Schindler-Rainman and Ronald Lippitt (1975) put it clearly:

> In a pluralistic and fragmented democratic social system, made up of many types of individuals and groups, a major requirement is that the system establish procedures to provide for full communication, or orderly confrontation and conflict resolution, and for the coordination and blending of the energies and interests of the disparate subgroups (p. 6).

Contributing to Social Justice

One critical democratic value, and one often not given top billing in the American variant of democracy, is that of social, or distributive, justice—the relatively equal distribution of rights, privileges, and rewards in society. Tocqueville saw the direct connection between an effective voluntarism and social–political equality when he announced that one most "precise and clear" law that rules in human societies: "If men are to remain civilized or to become so, the art of associating together must grow and improve in the same ratio in which the equality of conditions is increased" (p. 57).

A long reform tradition in American politics and voluntarism addresses directly issues of unequal justice and the maldistribution of income, wealth, and other resources in American life. The O'Connell reader features statements from leaders of the black, womens', Mexican American, and civil rights movements. These and other movements, sometimes working within the laws of society and sometimes violating them, have all been voluntary in their origins and principles.

The spirit of most of these movements is captured by the words of Mary McLeod Bethune:

> I see no cause for discouragement, in viewing the years ahead. Democracy in this country is neither dead nor dying. As every mother knows, the pangs of childbirth are keenest just before the child is born. If our hurts are great, now; if our country is torn with controversy over the expansion of social responsibility, over the acceptance of civil rights, it is because a new and more powerful democracy is being born, to serve more greatly the people of all races, of this country, and of the world (p. 212).

Viewed as the support of minority rights, the quest for social justice has been a strong theme in the history of American voluntarism. But support of economic equality has been more greatly tempered, and generally emerges as support for the values and institutions of "equality of opportunity." Thus the Commission on Private Philanthropy and Public Needs sees as vital functions of voluntary action "overseeing the marketplace" and "bringing the sectors together." The first function allows a "critical gaze," the organization of competing services, and a certain detachment, according to the

Commission. Nowhere in the Commission's discussion, however, are themes of "regulation" or "public ownership" raised as options to this oversight.

The Commission also spoke warmly of voluntary efforts to provide "services that the government is constitutionally barred from providing" and of "giving aid abroad." Such activities may redress broader structural inequalities, but this pursuit is rarely articulated as a goal of voluntary action.

The American legacy is ambiguous and ambivalent when it comes to the advocacy of inequality. Consider Emerson, who follows that call, quoted above, of the state's responsibility to heed the man, with a clear statement of the principle of equality of opportunity: "Every child that is born must have a just chance for his bread." This statement is then followed by the more egalitarian admonition, "Let the amelioration of our laws of property proceed from the concession of the rich, not from the grasping of the poor. Let us begin by habitual imparting. Let us understand that the equitable rule is, that no one should take more than his share, let him be ever so rich" (p. 51). While the last modifying clause would not have been added by a Marxist, Emerson may be pardoned for not forgetting that the rich, like the poor, we seem to have always with us.

Assure the Efficacious Solution of Problems

The third sector has also been identified in its own supporting literature as a place in which work is productively performed. Manser and Cass (p. 12) point to the way "that both individual service and social reform are necessary if we are to solve the myriad social problems with which we find ourselves confronted."

The voluntary sector specializes in "making the world better" (p. 66) by managing the change process expeditiously. It provides for the rapid exchange of information (p. 19), an intelligent and efficacious process of redistribution (p. 114), and a forum for the discussion of problems that leads toward their resolution (p. 19). The "cost-effectiveness" of the sector is enthusiastically noted by John D. Rockefeller (p. 114): "We must always remember that there is not enough money for the work of human uplift and that there never can be. How vitally important it is, therefore, that the expenditure should go as far as possible and be used with the greatest intelligence!"

AND JUST A POSSIBILITY THAT THINGS ARE MORE COMPLEX

In the pages of the O'Connell compendium, from which the previous sections of this chapter have been drawn, there is scarcely a sour note in the sweet choruses that are sung. Only Cornuelle (p. 280), in an otherwise enthusiastic paean, notes that all is not always well when the choruses of voluntarism start to sing. His discord is brief, but telling:

> Sometimes independent action shows itself in ugly, perverse ways, as when the Ku Klux Klan organizes a vigilante force to terrorize negro Americans or the Minutemen drill grimly in their cellars. But more often, it moves with a soul-stirring magnificence, as when Dr. Tom Dooley hurriedly raised money to finish his hospital in the Laotian jungle before cancer drained his life away.

There does appear to be a strong tendency in the literature of voluntarism to find what one seeks. Thus both conservative and change-oriented writers identify a wide range of organizations and activities that embody their particular conceptions of what voluntary action should be and what it can accomplish. Their writings catalogue manifold experiences and tend toward the conclusion that the type of voluntarism advocated by the author is massively strong and clearly the wave of the future.

The result is an apparent ambiguity in the American literature on voluntarism, an ambiguity reflected in our estimations of the motivation of volunteers and of the efficacy of voluntary associations. The nature of this characteristic of American voluntarism is probed in the next chapter.

2

Mixed Messages:
The Ambiguous Legacy of
American Voluntarism

Measured by the active goodwill, efforts, time, and talents of millions of persons and by its impact on society over the sweep of history, voluntary effort represents the unfolding of humanity's highest and noblest impulses.

Gordon Manser and Rosemary Cass, *Voluntarism at the Crossroads*
(1976, p. 16)

Essentially, NOW believes that service-oriented volunteerism is providing a hit-or-miss, band-aid, and patchwork approach to solving massive and severe social ills which are a reflection of a social and economic system in need of an overhaul. More than this, NOW believes that such volunteering actually prevents needed social changes from occurring because with service-oriented volunteering, political energy is being used and will increasingly be used, to meet society's administrative needs.

National Organization for Women, "NOW Task Force on Volunteerism"
(1975, p. 73)

INTRODUCTION

We Americans have never quite believed the oft-cited quotation from Emerson, in which he claims as one of the most "beautiful compensations" in life that "no man can sincerely help another without helping himself." Rather, we have struggled with ideas of self-denial and altruism in a quest to find what Richard Sennett (1978) would call a "purified identity" for volunteering. We seem to need to sustain and balance in our lives and values both the self-sacrifice of the volunteer and the avariciousness of our pursuit of economic self-interest.

The intellectual historian will be required to help us fully understand our eagerness to accept the theory of the "invisible hand" in economics, while we are so uncomfortable with it when it comes to voluntarism. Perhaps it is the Manichean side of the Protestant Ethic, or perhaps a yearning for a

golden age of simplicity and goodness. Whatever its origins, recent work by
Burton Yale Pines and Harry C. Boyte illustrates the tension.

Pines (1982) studies the movement commonly identified as "rightist" or
"conservative." He prefers to call this movement "traditionalist," noting
that it embodies:

> a faith in conquering frontiers and building better societies, in political
> democracy and market capitalism, in a federal system that protects the
> residual powers of the states and local communities and in public ritual
> that enthusiastically celebrates patriotism. It is the struggle on behalf of this
> traditionalism that is providing a bond for what in most respects remain
> quite separate phenomena. By marching in the same general direction
> along a common front, they constitute a loose, informal movement that is
> changing the way that America poses and answers questions of public
> policy (Pines, 1982, p. 20).

Boyte (1984), on the other hand, finds Pines' traditionalism mere rightist
fluff: "From the typical conservative point of view, themes such as family,
neighborhood, community, religion and the American heritage are honored
too often largely in the breach. They become rhetorical buzzwords . . . easily discarded whenever such values conflict with the 'real world' concerns of
the marketplace and private property" (p. 12). To Boyte, what is most
authentic in the world of voluntarism are those actions that follow Martin
Luther King's democratic and populist dream, which:

> held forth the hope that ordinary people could take their lives in their
> own hands. It affirmed the dignity of a great pluralism of heritages and
> communities—even those of southern segregationists, faith in whose
> redemption, and positive features, Martin Luther King never abandoned.
> And it grounded a vision of change in our nation's finest traditions and
> values, the strands he believed offered an alternative possibility to bigotry,
> unbridled individualism, greed and violence.

One author's set of heroes are thus the other's victims of ignorance.
Moreover, each author sees his protagonists advancing traditions and values
that are quintessentially American. Pines's heroes are the managers of a utility company as they develop a videotape refuting charges brought against
them by media radicals from "60 Minutes," corporate leaders who seek to
introduce "economic education" and "free-enterprise chairs" into schools
and colleges, economists who advocate the rolling back of governmental
regulation of business, politicians who seek a return to "basics" in education, pro-family activists who oppose the Equal Rights Amendment and
abortion rights, religious leaders who promulgate the fundamentalist "faith
of our fathers," and criminal justice reformers who seek stiffer mandatory

penalties for offenders. His villains are the members of the "New Class," who deal professionally "full time with words and other symbols of ideas" (Pines, 1982, p. 321). Such intellectuals—professors, clergymen, journalists, bureaucrats, planners, researchers, and social workers among them—

> promote views shaped greatly by the counterculture—hostility to capitalism, rejection of economic growth and contempt for the middle-class values of hard work, discipline, individual restraint, deferred gratification and social propriety. A special villain is technology, excoriated for ravaging the environment and squandering resources. . . . Above all, the New Class opposes capitalism and its private enterprise corollary (Pines, 1982, p. 322).

On the other hand, Boyte's heroes are the citizen-activists on the West Side of St. Paul who sought to prevent their neighborhood from conversion to an industrial park, the citizens' coalitions of Massachusetts who sought to restrain a waste-dumping corporation in Lowell from illegal and damaging chemical disposal, the residents of the Jubilee Partners Christian communal farm in Georgia who seek to develop alternative technologies and to house refugees, the tenant organization in the Cochran Gardens public housing project in St. Louis which developed a multitude of services for residents, the Center for Independent Living which provides empowerment and services for disabled members, and the Communities Organized for Public Service (COPS) in San Antonio which spearheaded a widespread shift in power from old moneyed families to the ordinary citizen in that city. Those who seek to block progress are seen by Boyte to include "the centers of corporate power behind the Reagan presidency" and "conventional notions of 'progress,' 'success,' and unbridled individualism" (1984, p. 219).

To Boyte, the core of the matter is to return to the truths of populist democracy, particularly as embodied in the social movements of the 1880s and 1890s. The core values of this experience involve "breaking up concentrated wealth, decentralizing power, dispersing ownership, and grounding it in community life" (1984, p. 215). To Pines, on the other hand, the public interest is found in "defending the free marketplace from government or special interest interference" (1982, p. 315) (to cite a "major task of conservative legal groups"). Community and market, then, are key values to Boyte and Pines, respectively, and adherence to them provides an entirely different conception of voluntarism—its nature, aims, and meaning in society. Both see their protagonists as deeply rooted in American traditions and values; both find them following deeply held personal and religious convictions; both see in the triumph of the movements they study the achievement of the American dream.

The outcome of the struggle between the two forces seems clear to Pines: "liberalism today looks and acts like a movement in retreat, a dynamo burned out. As the right generates a torrent of ideas, liberals huddle, confer, caucus and grope in workshops for new thoughts and concepts. But they simply are not coming. Liberalism indeed seems like a dynasty fast losing the Mandate of Heaven. On the ascendancy is traditionalism, challenging liberalism on every major front and ending the liberal monopoly of the agenda-setting process" (1982, p. 331). Boyte also agrees that the agenda is changing, and he quotes at length from COPS organizer Ernesto Cortes in his conclusion:

> What is democracy? How does it operate in a technological culture? There has to come out a vision which is relevant to this culture, this situation, that is decentralist and pluralist. These organizations don't have the answers. What we have is the beginnings of a process. There has to be a recreation of an agenda for the United States. What will be exciting will be to see that agenda put together, with everybody participating. . . . Where it might take us, how fully it might prevail in the face of the enormous forces that move against it in the modern world, is an open question. We will all be involved, however, in the answer (Boyte, 1984, p. 219).

The tensions between the conceptions of voluntarism provided by Pines and Boyte dramatically demonstrate the breadth of the voluntary sector and the way in which parts of it emerge as more appealing than others to the interpreter. As Cornuelle puts it:

> The Third Sector is a rich stew of organizations, formal and informal, good and bad, sensible and sentimental, imaginative and conventional. The variety of purposes of independent organizations is staggeringly diverse. . . . Nor are their aims consistent. For example, there are agencies that provide abortion services and actively promote their use, while others try to discourage abortion and lobby for its abolition. Some independent organizations seek government support; others reject it. . . . Sometimes their methods are simplistic and naive; sometimes they are highly complex and sophisticated. The forms and functions of independent action in America are so diverse that any generalization about the abilities and possibilities of the Third Sector is bound to be misleading (1983, pp. 156–158).

Nonetheless, Pines and Boyte join the mainstream of literature reviewed in the previous chapter by joining in the praise of voluntarism. That mainstream posits the existence of an "independent sector" freed from the constraints of profit and politics (though possibly at their service); it claims an effectiveness in the identification and resolution of problems by voluntary organizations; and it describes a motivational clarity to the acts of countless philanthropists. The work of Pines and Boyte thereby assumes a common point of departure that underlies many studies of the "non-economic" motivation of the volunteer. It poses what we may now identify as a problem for study: how can we understand why it is that the volunteer does what he or she does? Why do some of us, at least, "sincerely try to help another"?

"CHANGING MOTIVATIONS": THE REPORT OF THE FILER COMMISSION

Working in the mid-1970s, the Commission on Private Philanthropy and Public Needs (commonly identified as the Filer Commission, after its chairman, John Filer) recognized with clarity and sensitivity the ambiguous legacy of volunteering in America: "Personal sacrifice for the community good has probably always been esteemed," it wrote, "and, in some eyes suspect —and underlying motivations have perhaps always been complicated" (1975, p. 62).

In its discussion, the Filer Commission ranged over the history of giving from tribal society through the Middle Ages and Puritan America. Particular attention is paid to the thinking of Cotton Mather and Andrew Carnegie in their review. Mather is viewed as articulating "an exceedingly broad philosophy of giving and one that covers the wide spectrum of motivations that have been and often still are attributed to giving." Carnegie, on the other hand, is seen to have focused on the ways in which conspicuous giving by "administrators of surplus wealth" could contribute to the philanthropist's own rise to prominence in his community and nation.

The Filer Commission proceeds from its historical review of the motivation of giving to an almost entirely institutional analysis. The institutionalization of philanthropy receives detailed attention in its study, as does the emergence of the state as a "major 'philanthropist.' "

The Commission directed little attention to the current disposition of Americans toward giving and volunteering. Although it commissioned a study of "non-economic motivational factors in philanthropic giving," it cites only at one point (p. 62) any contemporary research, and then only parenthetically (a finding introduced with the observation that "some social scientists feel" that there is not as much individual volition involved in giving "as we might pretend"). The lonesome finding is that the Commission's survey finds that 30 percent of higher income givers feel pressured into giving more than they would otherwise choose to.

The curious treatment of this datum by the Commission speaks both to its uncertainty in interpreting social science and its hesitation in confronting the ambiguous legacy of volunteer motivation. There is a faint derogation in the observation that some social scientists "feel" about a matter on which "we" (the Commission?) "pretend."

The Filer Commission clearly finds itself on firmer gound when it addresses institutional change or economic data, and the remainder of the report is based almost entirely on such research. The behavioral sciences, having been given their parenthesis, receive no further attention on the question of motivation in the pages of the Commission report.

WHAT RECENT RESEARCH TELLS US
ABOUT THE MOTIVATION OF VOLUNTEERS

The motivation of giving and volunteering is a topic not unlike the weather: everybody talks about it, but few give it systematic study. For the purposes of this chapter, I have reviewed every article published in the *Journal of Voluntary Action Research* for a discussion of the motivation of voluntary action. This review, encompassing papers published over a 12-year period in the major international journal in its field, yields a manageable number of papers for individual review. Additional material on motivation research may be found in a number of major recent publications, and these are selectively reviewed in this section.

A grand total of 20 papers focusing on the motivation of voluntary action were published in the first twelve volumes of the *Journal of Voluntary Action Research*. These papers have varied widely in their theoretical and methodological approaches, as well as in the types of voluntary activity they have investigated.

The first of the 20 articles, for example, is a brilliant application of Maslow's celebrated "hierarchy of human needs" to the question of volunteer motivation. The author, the distinguished community educator Malcolm Knowles, noted that "institutional volunteerism has been structured in this country, on the whole, on fairly low-level and static assumptions" about why people volunteer (1972, p. 27). In Maslow's terms, Knowles argues, organizations usually cast their appeals in terms of needs for safety, belonging, and esteem.

"What," Knowles asks in this seminal article, "would volunteerism in America (or elsewhere) look like if it were structured around self-actualization as its motivational mode?" And he answers: it would involve both service and learning; it would be developmental; it would provide growth for the volunteer; it would treat clients as collaborators in mutual self-development, and not mere objects of service; and finally, it would place volunteering at the center of a national education enterprise, rather than at the periphery of the national welfare enterprise (p. 28).

Knowles concludes:

> My prediction is that if service-oriented volunteer programs were to be organized around this developmental concept of motivation: (1) individuals would enter into volunteer service in an ego-extending frame of mind; (2) they would see the field as offering a rich variety of resources rather than as

a set of parochial fiefdoms; (3) they would relate to volunteer agencies and their clients as partners in a process of mutual change and development; and (4) they would engage in volunteer service as an aspect of a lifelong process of continuing self-development (p. 29).

Knowles's focus on the self-enhancing aspect of giving sets a useful context for discussing a range of later studies that have focused on just what it is that one "gets" from volunteering.

In a dramatic demonstration of Knowles's point regarding the institutionalization of low-level motives in appealing to volunteers, sociologist Richard Ofshee and five research colleagues studied the motivation of participants in Synanon, an intentional community initially formed around goals of drug rehabilitation. Three catagories of motives are found to explain the attraction of new members to Synanon: (1) direct ties to a present resident of the community; (2) attraction to the "social movement aspects of Synanon (the drug-free environment or the communal life-style)"; or (3) the search for help with a personal problem, be it the need for "simple companionship" or the alleviation of emotional distress (Ofshee et al., 1974, p. 69). Only the second category approaches the level of self-actualization, and that in the dubious context of a "total community."

David Gottlieb (1974), in a study of volunteering in a very different context, that of what motivated VISTA volunteers, finds a similar mix of motives. "Females, Gottlieb's data indicate, tend to be more altruistic than male volunteers; and younger volunteers, particularly females, are most likely to view VISTA as a relevant and useful activity—an activity which allows one to get away from it all and at the same time provides an opportunity for learning about oneself and contemplating one's future" (p. 4). Males, on the other hand, more often cite motives of "escape"—"to get away from what I was doing"—in explaining their volunteering.

John Flynn and Gene Webb, in a study of women volunteers in Kalamazoo, Michigan, lent further credence to the "multiple motives" explanation. "When asked what had led the participants to work on policy campaign issues, responses centered upon the primary beneficiary of their own participation. Almost one-half of the actors indicated that 'self-oriented' needs were served by their activism." However, the same women also spoke of the importance of "self-maintenance needs" such as the need to keep busy or to "escape," and self-actualizing goals such as self-education and personal growth (Flynn and Webb, 1975, p. 140).

These studies, each of which indicates that motivational multiplicity is the usual pattern among volunteers, lead to the conclusion so clearly drawn by Gidron (1977), that, "contrary to common beliefs which relate volunteer work solely to altruistic motives, people have both other and self-oriented reasons for volunteering." The implications of this motivational multiplicity include, Gidron writes in another article (1983, p. 32), "that in order to be satisfied, a volunteer needs, above all, a task in which self-expression is possible—a task which gives the volunteer the opportunity to develop abilities and skills, a task which is seen as a challenge, a task where achievements can be seen."

Organizationally, Gidron continues, his findings "imply that the work conditions should enable the volunteer to receive from the job what it has to offer. The volunteer should not have to waste precious time getting to work, looking for tools, arguing with officials about what to do and how to do it. These findings call for clear policies on the role of volunteers in the organization and the means to implement these policies."

The research summarized above, then, leads to the first of several summary propositions regarding what we do know about volunteer motivation. This proposition is:

1. *People volunteer for multiple reasons, among which are their own personal and social goals and needs.* The discovery of the "nonaltruistic" volunteer in the mid-1970s led to the application of theories of rational self-interest to the world of volunteering. Thus in 1975, Peter Gluck applied "exchange theory" to the study of volunteers in an urban political organization. Gluck (1975, p. 104) summarized this theory as follows:

> The theory is based upon the following basic assumptions: 1) individuals have a variety of needs, drives, and goals which they seek to attain; 2) some of these can best be achieved within the context of organizational participation; 3) organizations need some mechanism to influence the behavior of their activists.

Gluck proceeded to distinguish between two dimensions of motivation: on the one hand he found two sets of "objects of incentives," self- and other-regarding motives; in a second dimension he distinguished between tangible and intangible rewards. Only among one group of political activists, those who were young and college-educated, did Gluck find substantial expression of the other-oriented motives. Most of the political volunteers he studied were in it for themselves (1975, p. 107).

More recently, exchange theory has been employed by Phillips (1982) to understand how volunteers evaluate their continuing participation. Studying hosts of a "Fresh Air" placement program for city children, Phillips finds that host motivation develops in predictable stages. In stage 1, "exposure to the idea that one might be a host," altruistic motivation clearly prevails. In stage 2, "preliminary decision to be a host," altruism is mixed with "egoistic" motives as arrangements begin to be made for a two-week visit by a child. Stage 3, "final decision to be a host," brings the commitment to a family decision, typically made on the basis of benefits (companionship, exposure to a different life-style) perceived from hosting. In stage 4, the child actually comes for the visit, and altruism returns to prominence as a motive, particularly when expectations are not met, and the visit turns out to be more difficult than anticipated. In stage 5, the family decides whether to invite a child for the following summer. Here the question of the degree to which the visit fulfilled the mixed altruistic–egoistic motivations of the family becomes critical. The logic of exchange theory—that pluses must outweigh the minuses if an action is to be undertaken—was stated formally in economic terms by Stinson and Stam (1976) in their "Toward an Economic Model of Voluntarism." The two economists conclude that citizens facing the decision of whether to volunteer in local governmental programs make that decision "based both on the amount of satisfaction derived from [the] volunteer work and the shadow wage, or tax savings, obtained from having the service provided from volunteers rather than paid professionals" (p. 58).

The applicability of exchange theory to the study of the decision to volunteer suggests a second generalization from the literature:

2. *The individual who volunteers typically does so only after weighing alternatives in a deliberate fashion.* Sharp's paper (1978) usefully identifies three major forms of incentives that may motivate volunteers: material (e.g., goods or a service); solidary (e.g., status, enjoyment, or sociability); and expressive (e.g., the chance to act out certain values).

Sharp concludes that different motivational configurations seem particularly suited to different organizational challenges. Thus, if citizens are volunteering to "coproduce" a desired outcome with officials (say by organizing a neighborhood crime watch), the appeal to solidary incentives is most successful. But if advocacy (protest, legislative change) is the goal, two alternative models seem most viable. One focuses on adversarial politics— here material motives seem most effective in generating volunteering. A second advocacy style involves achieving an advisory credibility, and here solidary motives are most prominent.

A similar finding emerges from the study of a midwestern opera guild, the "Angels," as studied by Marlyn and Richard Wilmeth (1979). Two distinct groups of participants are found within the single organization: "one very pointedly instrumental and the other, probably more typical group, an instrumental-expressive one" (p. 24). The instrumental group is older, and evinces an "almost religious" dedication to the advancement of opera, and to the role of volunteers within that mission. One member put the matter clearly to the Wilmeths: "The reason for the success of the Opera is the people who kept up the public interest before the "Angels" decided it was SOCIALLY fun and ruined it!" (1979, p. 24).

The papers by Sharp and the Wilmeths suggest a third important lesson that may be drawn from the studies reported in the *Journal of Voluntary Action Research:*

3. *That the realm of voluntary action itself is a complex and many-faceted one, in which different organizational tasks appeal to different motivational forces.* Laurie Davidson Cummings illustrates this third law in her study of can and bottle recyclers (1977). She finds that recyclers are often "one-timers" responding to a small cash return from their recycling. Nonetheless, the recyclers, when asked about their reasons for recycling, overwhelmingly cited the need "to help the environment." Cummings observes that "recyclers, perhaps like other volunteers, believe that altruistic rather than economic incentives should be given as the major reason why they volunteer" (p. 154). Cummings's work suggests that the ideology of giving may mask the more "real" motives of self-interest. Perhaps, one may be tempted to conclude, such realism also must force a reassessment of the vaunted American willingness to participate in voluntary action.

Greta Salem addressed this issue in her study of local political participation in Chicago (1978). "There is a popular tendency to presume that apathy is an innate characteristic of American citizens who prefer to focus on private rather than public affairs. However, another explanation is possible" —the system may not provide adequate opportunities for the development of participatory skills and culture (p. 18).

Salem's study of Chicago's 44th Ward Assembly lends substance to the structural explanation. Given the chance to participate, Salem finds urbanites actively engrossed in local decision-making. Some volunteers become even more dedicated to their activity, as Ross's memoir on the New Left movement of the 1960s indicates. Ross (1977) writes: "Through personal ties which legitimately carry affective expression, primary groups . . . offer a series of secondary gains which support movement participants emotionally and help to mold them intellectually. Primary groups become the locus of an individual's collective orientation" (p. 149).

The observation of Louis Zurcher (1978) that many voluntary roles are "ephemeral" (i.e., transitory, ad hoc in nature) gives further fullness to the nature of voluntary participation in complex society. Those who work together—in disasters, in bowling groups, or in the Naval Reserve—all move quickly into and out of roles that take on great meaning and structure for them. The participant may be active in several forms of action, each with a fulsome structure and culture within the context of the "ephemeral role."

What, then, of altruism as a motive for volunteer service? Is it merely one more "ephemeral role," to be discounted as so much ideology? Or does it form one, albeit of many, force that continues to impel people to participate as volunteers?

Jessica Jenner (1982) addresses this question in her study of women volunteers in a national organization. She carefully distinguishes between three major motivating configurations (pp. 30–31):

- PRIMARY. "Volunteer work is my main career or work activity. . . ."
- SUPPLEMENTAL. "Volunteer work is a supplement to the other parts of my work life."
- CAREER INSTRUMENTAL. "Volunteer work is a way to prepare me for a new (or changed) career, or to maintain skills and contacts in a career I am not actively pursuing at this time."

Just about three in five of the volunteers studied by Jenner fitted the "supplemental" category, the others being evenly divided between the remaining categories. For the supplemental volunteers, motives of community service, association, and personal growth were almost equally prevalent. Jenner draws the conclusion from her study that "altruism and self-actualization were about equally important motivators. For organizations this suggests that not only must the cause be worthy, but the role played in the organizational context must also be meaningful" (1982, p. 35).

In a comprehensive review of the role of altruism as a motivator of voluntary action, David Horton Smith (1981) finds "literally no evidence to justify a belief in some 'absolute' form of human altruism, in which the motivation for an action is utterly without some form of selfishness" (p. 23). Smith concludes that:

> The essence of volunteerism is not altruism, but rather the contribution of services, goods, or money to help accomplish some desired end, without substantial coercion or direct remuneration. It is the voluntariness and unremunerated character of volunteerism that is distinctive. . . . Altruism is a variable both among volunteers and among voluntary organizations. Failure to admit this constitutes a failure to face human social and individual reality (p. 33).

Natalie Allen and William Rushton (1983) put Smith's concepts to a rigorous empirical test. They review all available studies of the altruism of volunteers, and conclude that the concept of the "altruistic personality" is a valid one. Thus, community volunteers "appear to have more positive attitudes toward themselves and others and, as such possess greater feelings of self-efficacy. Compared to non-volunteers, these individuals can be characterized as being more emotionally stable."

From these studies, we may also draw a fourth major conclusion, to wit:

4. *Concern for others, while not always purely altruistic, remains an important motivating force for much voluntary action.* Anderson and Moore (1978), in a study of Canadian volunteers, see altruism as the leading motive of those who perform voluntary action. "It appears that people do volun-

teer for a variety of reasons but that the humanitarian motive—to help others—and the desire to feel useful and needed quite consistently outweigh other reasons given" (p. 120). If pure altruism does not exist, it is not the case that altruism has lost its appeal. It remains a critical force in the motivation of those who practice voluntarism.

One further point may be derived from the literature, and it harkens back to Salem's observation regarding the ways in which structures may retard active participation. In a remarkable pair of papers that appeared in the 1980 Special Issue of the *Journal of Voluntary Action Research,* Jone Pearce and David Adams explored two little-studied facets of voluntary organizations.

Pearce examined the ways in which volunteers often seek to avoid leadership roles. Comparing the rates at which leadership is sought in employing, as against volunteer, organizations, Pearce finds that few rewards are available to the volunteer leader. She concludes that if "voluntary organizations are to remain viable, they must find ways to increase the attractiveness of leadership positions" (p. 92).

Adams explores another structural factor within many voluntary organizations—their tendency to segregate volunteers into "elite" and "lower" roles. Studying a Red Cross chapter, Adams finds that what board members do and what serving volunteers do are quite different tasks. Moreover, the two rarely meet, nor is there much mobility between their separate organizational roles. Voluntary organizations seem quite able, Adams suggests, to create miniature class systems within themselves, or at least to reflect the class divisions prominent in the world beyond.

The research of Pearce and Adams implies that we carefully attend to the structural realities that form the societal context of giving and volunteering. This theme, that voluntary action is itself a social activity highly dependent upon the "turbulent environment" of today's social realities, was a central one in the significant research that emerged from the National Forum on Volunteerism (Rydberg and Peterson, 1980).

Writing for this forum, Gordon Manser (1980), with his customary acuity, observed emergent patterns of volunteer development:

> Many volunteers have transferred their loyalty from so-called traditional organizations to small, neighborhood or block groups, where cause and effect, (effort and outcome), are more closely linked and more manageable. Others, especially younger people, have moved into cause and advocacy groups as a reaction to the powerlessness of politics (p. 6).

The interaction of fast-changing social currents and the "multiple motives" of volunteers (recognized as demonstrated fact by all the consulting writers to *Volunteerism in the Eighties*—Ivan Scheier, Gordon Manser, Harleigh

Trecker, and myself [Rydberg and Peterson, 1980])—is well summarized by Manser:

> On the one hand, enlightened self-interest includes a desire to make a significant impact on a community problem. On the other hand, it includes a desire to have an experience which is meaningful in terms of one's personal career or skills goals. Because this represents a symbiotic balance between altruism and self-interest, volunteers thus motivated are found to be highly committed and responsible in their work. They also have greater expectations from the organizations for which they work. At the same time, volunteers may tend to have more commitment to an issue than to an organization. If the organization does not live up to the volunteer's expectations, the volunteer will move to another interest and another organization (p. 7).

Above shifting organizational challenges and opportunities stands our inability, as a society and as a planet, to assure our own survival. The late Harleigh Trecker put the matter powerfully in his essay for the National Forum on Volunteerism (1980):

> Perhaps of greater significance than anything else is our failure as a people to articulate, enunciate and work for common national and international goals. One searches in vain for any agreement on the need for a universal quality of life goal meaningful to most people. No doubt four decades of life under the "balance of terror" approach of the great powers in their defense structure has had a subliminal effect on people. Unconsciously, "survival" is the real, though not necessarily spoken goal. If this is true, it is lamentable, because it eliminates, or at least delays, the immense opportunities for world betterment and more satisfying lives for humanity (p. 37).

Trecker's observation that our failure to deal with issues of planetary survival retards our ability to create a voluntary society suggests the wording of our final generalization from the literature:

5. *The motivation to give and to volunteer is shaped and constrained by broader social realities, and particularly by the omnipresent reality of world chaos and destruction.* This generalization goes far to explain the success of the "nuclear freeze" movement in recent years, as well as the continuing prominence of narcissism in American culture. After all, if the world can end at any moment in a frenzy of nuclear destruction, it often seems to make just as much sense to ignore the possibility as it does to try to do something about it, or anything else.

The rapid shift in the ways authority and power are viewed and exercised in the modern world suggests the importance of looking directly at those issues.

ALTRUISM AND SELF-INTEREST IN AMERICAN VOLUNTARISM

Five major findings have emerged from this literature review: first, that the motivation of volunteers is a multi-faceted process; second, that volunteers weigh their options deliberately; third, that the realm of voluntary action is itself complex and many-faceted; fourth, that concern for others persists as a motivating force; and fifth, that the motivation to volunteer is constrained by broader social realities.

These conclusions suggest that what people do in many voluntary sector organizations is different, in significant part, from what people do in other institutional sectors. It does make a difference to act from a concern, at least in part, for the well-being of others. The difference is not absolute, but it is a difference. The volunteer is not wholly unlike the employee, but the volunteer is different from the employee. And that difference is important enough to justify analyzing society in terms of the distinctiveness of voluntary action, if not in positing a wholly "independent" sector.

It is also clear that conceptions of voluntarism are affected by prevailing intellectual currents. As social movements wax and wane, however imbued with images of particularistic gain for the solidary group in question, they are surely affected by the dominant societal images of self-absorption or collective gain. If the president of the day were to use the rhetoric of voluntarism to mask an effort to repeal the welfare state, one would not be surprised to see the black, native American, and women's movements teaching their members to "dress for success" and to "go for" the "it" of private gain. If, on the other hand, that president were to continue to spend a day a month in volunteer house-construction activity for inner-city poor families, one might expect a rise in concern for the black poor, the homeless, and the single mother on the part of the appropriate particularistic movements, if not their formation into a single coalition for social and economic justice.

The ephemeral roles of voluntary action are easily molded to fit the prevailing intellectual climate of the day. What in one era is felt as a cultural imperative to contribute to society in another era may become an act of unpaid apprenticeship useful in providing a "leg up" in the rat race toward admission to medical school or political life. When voluntarism begins to appear on résumés, and to be counted as work experience, it is a signal that some overarching societal principle is beginning to emerge.

Interpreting these shifts requires consideration of underlying forces at work in society. It is clear that volunteering is affected by deeper forces of structure and change, although the literature reviewed barely begins to address these questions. Nevertheless, questions foreshadowed by the work of Pearce (1980), Adams (1980), and the consulting writers to the National

Forum on Volunteerism (Rydberg and Petersen, 1980) may be asked—questions that confront the impact of vast and seemingly uncontrollable social forces upon the decisions that each of us make as we plan our daily lives and actions. These questions are those of how we each choose, and how our institutions select, between the forces of narcissistic self-indulgence and those of realistic societal reconstruction, of how we might relate ourselves both to persons and to the societal forces.

Richard Sennett (1978) has shown us, in the brilliant corpus of both his sociological and literary work, how important it is for us to make this dual connection. He has also shown us how particularly difficult that connection is, for we are the heirs of a Protestant Ethic that has confounded our sense of social responsibility. Sennett explains why (p. 334):

> Worldly asceticism (the denial of gratification for the purpose of validating the self—the hallmark of the Protestant Ethic) and narcissism have much in common. In both, "What am I feeling?" becomes an obsession. In both, showing to others the checks and impulses of oneself feeling is a way of showing that one does have a worthy self. In both, there is a projection of the self onto the world, rather than an engagement in worldly experience beyond one's control.

In our patterns of giving and volunteering, most Americans surely remain heirs to the Protestant Ethic. We perform our community service with the same stolid quest for respectability with which we play out our economic and family lives. And, if Sennett's surmise is indeed correct, we give and volunteer ourselves with the narcissist's wish to avoid confronting forces beyond our control.

Here we come face to face with the limits of contemporary voluntarism and its inability, in many cases, to deal directly with issues of distribution and inequality, corporate and governmental irresponsibility, war and peace. Like the narcissist, paralyzed by the fear of missing an experience that may prove to be gratifying—and like the ascetic, aiming desperately to interact only with those forces that will validate self-worth—we tend to limit the range of our volunteering to what is safe, respectable, and consonant with the limits of our economic and political lives.

Action at the frontier of motivational studies, then, consists of searching for and nourishing the courage to create and to act upon visions of voluntary action that meet the challenges of a world in flux. And it is the role of voluntarism in that very "real" world to which our attention is directed in the chapters that form the second part of this work.

PART II
Mapping the Third Sector

Introduction

The three chapters that form Part II seek to "map" the third sector in contemporary society. By "mapping," I mean to present in topographic terms images of voluntary action in its relationship to other important institutionalized activity in modern society—activity conducted by governments, businesses, and households.

In Chapter 1, a celebratory literature on voluntarism was reviewed, a literature that suggests that such activity forms an independent sphere of social action, in which the best of the human spirit is applied to the resolution of common problems. Despite the overwhelmingly positive, and even "boosterist," nature of that literature, a counter-theme of ambiguity and ambivalence about the characteristics of some voluntary action was discerned. That ambiguity was examined in detail in Chapter 2, with its presentation of the Pines–Boyte debate and its review of contemporary studies of volunteer motivation.

The chapters in Part II pursue the diversity of perspectives on voluntary action by examining in some detail its roots in political and social theory. Chapter 3 looks at voluntarism in terms of democratic theory and finds five major traditions presenting themselves for analysis and evaluation. A specification of the ambiguity of voluntarism begins to emerge in this chapter, with different hesitations and enthusiasms relating to different conceptions of democracy. Here the variation may be explained in terms of differences in theoretical interpretation—democracy means different things to different people. In Chapter 4, on the other hand, different theoretical approaches to voluntarism are discussed. Here we begin to see that voluntary action looks different when different aspects of it are selected for study. And we also see that varying visions of the good society underlie vastly different images of the significance and potential of voluntary action in modern society.

An obvious and important question is presented by this diversity in approach, interpretation, and evaluation: is it possible to develop a single overarching and unifying theory of voluntary action—a multidisciplinary theory that articulates the role of voluntarism in society and guides the evaluation of its meanings and contributions? If yes, what is that theory and how can it be developed? If no, how shall we live with the multiplicities and perplexities of paradigmatic diversity that characterize the field?

Many books could be written in valiant effort to produce a unifying theory of voluntary action, and some strong efforts have been essayed. (Perhaps the bravest recent effort along these lines was made by Smith and Macaulay, [1980].) I am doubtful that such efforts can succeed, at least at this juncture in the development of voluntary action research. The reasons for this contention are essentially threefold. First, there is no paradigmatic agreement in contemporary social science about the nature and structure of major institutions and their interrelations. Second, the breadth of organizational purposes and functions in the voluntary sector is so great as to render problematic any unifying theory. And, third, the plethora of disciplines that approach the subject has retarded the development of comprehensive multidisciplinary theory and study.

My approach to the chimerical challenge of developing unified theory is to replace that task with the more elemental one of seeking to comprehend approaches to study and analysis. By mapping the third sector in relation to other institutions, I hope to demonstrate, first, that there is a reality and even a validity to the major paradigms prevalent in the field; second, that it is possible to think about the major forms of voluntary action in the same approach; and third, that a multidisciplinary perspective can, to a certain (though limited) degree, be achieved.

Beyond this pluralism, each reader bears the responsibility for selecting an image of voluntarism that meets the tests of individual value and preference. I, too, have such values and preferences and will articulate them in due time (largely in Part IV, but scattered throughout Part III as well). The task of the following three chapters, however, is to confront the diversity of ways in which voluntary action may be conceptualized and oriented. It is a rich and broad field that we study, and one that has been enlightened by much able thought throughout the years.

3

Democracy and Voluntary Action

In a pluralistic and fragmented democratic social system, made up of many types of individuals and groups, a major requirement is that the system establish procedures to provide for full communication, or orderly confrontation and conflict resolution, and for the coordination and blending of the energies and interests of the disparate subgroups.

—Eva Schindler-Rainman and Ronald Lippitt (1975, p. 6)

Democracy's "ideal-type" refers to . . . "voluntarism."

J. Roland Pennock (1979, p. 478)

INTRODUCTION

Voluntarism is not often discussed in terms of its contribution to democracy; it is customarily evaluated, as we saw in Chapter 1, in terms of the social services it provides to the needy and destitute or the satisfaction it engenders in the volunteer. Nevertheless, the individual decisions of millions of people to volunteer to perform actions they deem to be in the general interest surely has relevance to the development and maintenance of democracy, as Tocqueville noted in his oft-cited statement in *Democracy in America:*

> Among the laws that rule human societies there is one which seems to be more precise and clear than all others. If men are to remain civilized or to become so, the art of associating together must grow and improve in the same ratio in which the equality of conditions is increased.

This chapter explores interrelations between voluntary action and democracy. Many of these connections are familiar ones regularly explored in the social science literature: citizen participation in public policy implementation, participation in social movements, voting, and other modes of voluntary electoral participation. Others are more indirect, and come from service as a board member of a social service organization or as a participant in a neighborhood association.

Whatever the form of voluntary action, it has been contended that voluntarism serves as a school for democratic action and that it is central in the development and maintenance of a fully democratic society. This contention will be examined in the context of the varying forms of democratic theory, and then by consideration of the "two faces of voluntarism" identified in Chapter 2. Each of these tasks requires a working definition of democracy, and it is to that task that we now turn our attention.

DEFINING DEMOCRACY

It is difficult to arrive at a definition of democracy that will seem reasonable to most thoughtful persons, and it is nearly impossible to develop a theory of how democracy is institutionalized that will be accepted by more than a minority of political theorists.

Definitional efforts by political theorist J. Roland Pennock present a case in point. Pennock (1979) gives democracy a dual definition, one ideal and the other procedural. As an ideal, democracy is seen as "government by the people, where liberty, equality and fraternity are secured to the greatest possible degree and in which human capacities are developed to the utmost, by means including free and full discussion of common problems and interests" (p. 6). Procedurally, Pennock (1979, p. 7) views democracy as:

> "Rule by the people" where "the people" includes all adult citizens not excluded by some generally agreed upon and reasonable disqualifying factor, such as confinement to prison . . . or some procedural requirement, such as residency within a particular electoral district for a reasonable length of time before the election in question. "Rule" means that public policies are determined either directly by vote of the electorate or indirectly by officials freely elected at reasonably frequent intervals and by a process in which each voter who chooses to vote counts equally ("one person, one vote") and in which a plurality is determinative.

Pennock's precise and painstaking definitions of democracy as ideal and procedure are difficult to fault, comprehending as they do a vision of democracy as one of humankind's greatest social inventions. But these definitions are congenial with a multitude of theoretical forms for their implementation. Building largely on the work of Pennock, and that of Robert Putnam (1970), I identify five major forms of democratic theory for further discussion in this chapter: populism, idealism, pluralism, neo-corporatism, and social democracy.

Populism is a theory of democracy that empowers the many, and provides few limitations on their power. Idealism also involves rule by the many, but under prescribed constitutional limits. Neo-corporatism provides for control by elites, under constitutional empowerments. Pluralism, another elite theory in its conventional presentation, relies upon social arrangements for the limitation of power. The final type of democratic theory, social democracy, provides for rule for the many under limits of social arrangements.

Each of these forms of democratic theory provides a distinctive approach to the problems of institutionalizing the democratic vision in complex and large-scale societies like our own. We may now turn to a closer look at each form of theory.

FIVE FORMS OF DEMOCRATIC THEORY

Populism

Populist visions of democracy are among the easiest to conceptualize, and the most difficult to organize, in societies as complex as our own. Most simply, populist democracy is that of the town meeting, the referendum and recall, the long ballot, and the theory of participatory democracy. As a historical movement in U.S. society, populism has featured the voluntary action of farmers joining the Grange and citizens flocking to the support of William Jennings Bryan. More recently, populism has taken the form of environmental concern, preservation of farmland, and evangelical preservation of traditional moral standards (Boyte, 1980, p. 65). Populism involves a belief in the importance of decision-making by all members of a constituency, direct and unmediated, on those issues of most central concern to the constituency.

Populism, in contemporary democratic theory, stands almost as a critical perspective on other forms of democracy, particularly pluralism. Pennock (1979) notes that such direct democracy approaches "voluntarism" as a political ideal, maximizing cooperation and minimizing domination (pp. 476–477). But populism is rarely presented as a "realistic" theory of democracy, for reasons that are not difficult to fathom. It is exceedingly difficult to conceive of democracy actually working in a large-scale complex society without the establishment of any limits to power beyond participation in majority votes. Even in small communities dedicated to decentralized and participatory ideologies, the limits of participatory rule are quickly felt, as Rosabeth Moss Kanter (1972) notes in her study of communes:

> Even in anarchistic communes that reject any formal organization or demands on members, informal group pressure still constitutes a powerful influence for conformity, and members often report a great unease at "letting down the group," that is, failing to live up to the standards of the community (p. 233).

Perhaps the search for limits in the communal experience reflects the weakness of populist theory as a base for contemporary society. In any case, the populist critique of elite forms of democracy seems to drift into the development of idealist democratic theories. When power is limited only by the vigilance of its holders in continuous session, the burdens of democracy become insupportable.

Idealism

Idealism is one of those "polysemic" terms that plague readers and creators of social science; that is, it is one term with many meanings. In political theory, idealists are those descendants of Aristotle, T.H. Green, and Rousseau who view the polity as the locus of dialogue and mutual enlightenment. For the idealist, political participation is, as Robert Paul Wolff (1968) put it, the establishment of one's place in a:

> . . . rational community. It is an activity, an experience, a reciprocity of consciousness among morally and politically equal rational agents who freely come together and deliberate with one another for the purpose of concerting their wills in the positing of collective goals and in the performance of common actions (p. 192).

Idealists are those democratic theorists who view politics as providing a genuine community in which people fulfill themselves by performing the humanizing activity of political participation. Politics, in the idealist vision, is not mere bargaining and the advancement of the self-interests of individuals and groups; rather, it becomes a process of mutual education and the creation of community.

On the local level, contemporary idealists like Philadelphia's Edward Schwartz seek to create community and neighborhood organizations in which a full range of issues are resolved in the context of mutual discussion and dialogue. Nationally, theorist Theodore Lowi (1969, pp. 313–314) has called for the creation of "juridical democracy," in which public administration and public law are fused in the creation and production of rights, justice, and legitimacy. In Lowi's theory, constitutionalism becomes the basis of the ideal community.

Idealism is a theory of reflection, intellect, and the refinement of institutions. But how well does it reflect the realities of human motivation as they confront the political system? In particular, how does idealism transform personal interests into the advancement of the general good? Building on the critique of idealism as impossibly rational, the pluralist perspective has sought to explain how democracy "really works."

Pluralism

Another polysemic term, pluralism in the context of democratic theory refers to the balance and competition among groups and their interests in political society. The core of the pluralist vision was powerfully expressed by Durkheim (1958):

A nation can be maintained only if, between the state and the individual, there is intercalated a whole series of secondary groups near enough to individuals to attract them strongly in their sphere of action and drag them, in this way, into the general torrent of social life (p. 28).

To the pluralist, the individual is preoccupied with personal concerns and interests—economic, family-based, religious, and ideological. As a citizen, the individual is hardly eager to participate in dialogue and communal determination. Rather, he or she must be "dragged into the torrent" of the political process. This participation is seen by the pluralist as best accomplished by means of the voluntary association.

A theory greatly elaborated in American political science by Arthur Bentley, David B. Truman, and Robert A. Dahl; in political sociology by Robert Nisbet, William Kornhauser, and Seymour Martin Lipset; and in economics by A.A. Berle, Gardner Means, and John Kenneth Galbraith—pluralism has tended to focus on the need to preserve the autonomy of the major societal sectors (polity, economy, associational, and cultural) in decision-making, and on the preservation of multiple centers of power in each of those sectors. Attention has also been paid to the quality of the civility and decisions produced by multiple and cross-seaming membership patterns.

The tendency of some influential pluralists to conclude that the actual participation of citizens is of secondary importance has led many to reject pluralism. Idealism and populism draw more consistently on a more active concept of citizenship than mainstream pluralist thought, as do many theorists who hold to the social democratic perspective.

Social Democracy

The critics of pluralism ruled the roost in the political thought of the 1960s and the 1970s. They probed relentlessly the weaknesses of the pluralist vision, contending that pluralism is elitist and inegalitarian in its point of departure, insufficiently aimed toward the provision of justice in its quest to balance interests, ignorant of the bureaucratic realities of many less than "voluntary" associations, and destructive of the ties of political community. Further, they have argued, the claims of some pluralists that the theory describes decision-making in America are both overblown and wrong: rather than balancing institutional interests, American political society demonstrates an overarching power of corporate decision-making.

The weight of the attack on pluralism has seen a resurgence both of contemporary idealism and, to an even greater degree, of theories of social democracy in contemporary political thought. Such theories tend to retain much of the pluralist vision, but they seek to extend it in a fashion that moves the theory toward a central focus on participation, the reduction of inequality, and the special role of the state in assuring democracy. Theorists of social democracy contend that pluralism has not been presented in a sufficiently radical cast. By forging a union between key points of socialist, idealist, and populist political perspectives, a new and reformist theory of democracy has been developed—one that became highly prominent in academic writing on U.S. political society in the 1970s.

Social democrats claim that the problem of pluralism in America is that it has not been extended with sufficient vigor to counter the criticism that it prescribes a quiescent political system in which the interests of the wealthy dominate. The cure for ailing American democracy, these theorists argue, is more democracy. As Gar Alperovitz, one of the most searching of these thinkers, has written:

> To review and affirm both the socialist vision and the decentralist ideal is to suggest that a basic problem of a positive alternative program is how to define community institutions which are egalitarian and equitable in the traditional socialist sense of owning and controlling productive resources for the benefit of all, but which can prevent centralization of power, and finally, which over time can permit new social relations capable of sustaining an ethic of individual responsibility and group cooperation upon which a larger vision must ultimately be based (pp. 64–65).

A major challenge of a positive program, therefore, is to create "commonwealth" institutions, which, through decentralization and cooperation, achieve new ways of organizing economic and political power so that the people (in the local sense of that word) really do have a chance to "decide" (Alperovitz, 1973, pp. 64–65). Social democracy, Alperovitz argues, provides the most direct path to Pennock's "rule by the people"—distant as that vision appears from the realities of power and decision-making in contemporary politics.

Neo-Corporatism

Political theories, like old soldiers, appear never to die, but fade in and out as the moods and circumstances of history dictate. The democratic theory whose intellectual star waxed in the 1980s is neo-corporatism, a theory most intellectual historians had consigned to the dustbin of discarded ideas, particularly after Mussolini's disastrous flirtation with the concept in fascist Italy (cf. Gross, 1980).

Yet now we encounter the "new corporatists," armed with the contention that the concerns of pluralism are passé, and that contemporary political realities involve a balancing of the only three interests that matter in the worlds of power: business, government, and labor. Moreover, these latter-day descendants of Saint-Simon and Cole argue that the balance of power has slipped into the hands of government bureaucrats, who have become the key brokers of societal power as they arrange "understandings" between business and labor that determine the rate of inflation, the level of unemployment, and the general fate of the interlinked and complex contemporary political economy.

In the words of Streeck and associates (1980), leading students of contemporary corporatism:

> the corporatist hypothesis proceeds from the assumption that social integration and economic exchange in advanced industrial societies are not "naturally" accomplished and maintained through the aggregation of the independent decisions of individual actions in the market but rather have to be produced by political arrangements at the societal level (p. 29).

In their assertion that such organization is required of business, as well as labor organizations, neo-corporatists depart from conventional pluralists, who view business as operating in the context of the market and bargaining in the political sector.

VOLUNTEERING IN DEMOCRATIC THEORY

It follows from the conceptual work of Chapter 1 that volunteering and the ideology that supports it includes the following distinctive behaviors:

- Service volunteering, aimed at the alleviation of distress and the enhancement of quality of life of those population groups identified as being in need of such service
- Self-help volunteering, aimed at the advancement of those sharing a common interest, perspective, or life experience
- Grassroots volunteering, aimed at the clarification and advancement of interests of citizens at the local level of social–political organization.

By focusing on these quintessential forms of volunteering, the following discussion will exclude from analysis the major forms of institutional "voluntary association," such as philanthropic organizations, labor unions, trade associations, consumer organizations, professional associations, civic associations, and ethnic–cultural associations, as well as political parties and associations. Thus we focus on the acts of individual volunteering as democratic behaviors, rather than on the work of the formal organizations that draw sustenance, at least in part, from voluntary energies.

By examining forms of voluntary action not generally thought to be centrally relevant to democratic theory, it is my intention to illustrate connections that have not been clearly established in either the voluntary action research or the political science literature. If a close relationship can be discerned, a wide range of empirical and normative approaches is open to the student of voluntary action.

The literature that will be examined in this section has been selected from major studies of U.S. political society by political scientists over the past generation. These statements are both empirical and normative in their focus; that is, they seek to describe the nature of contemporary political society, and they also aim to interpret and evaluate this society. Studies have been selected to include major statements about each of the five forms of democratic theory.

Neo-Corporatism and Volunteering

To the neo-corporatist, the major value of volunteering is found in the tax savings it engenders, and not in its strengthening of democracy. The theory centrally focuses on those forms of organization that advance economic interests at the level of collaboration among elites. Such economically inspired activity, however important, is neither voluntary nor democratic— in that it is remote from the rule of the people. Citizen participation plays a role in restoring traditional values of respect and decency in this theory, but the citizen activist is seen as preferring the pleasures of private life to the rigors of social politics (Pines, 1982).

A distinctly neo-corporatist tinge characterized the administration of Ronald Reagan, although the governmental and, especially, the trade union partners were viewed as considerably junior to the corporate interest. A key Reagan advisor, Edwin Meese, succinctly expressed the low value citizen participation was given by the Reagan team. When asked if citizens would be encouraged to participate in the shaping of a new foreign policy, he replied: "Yes, every four years" (quoted in Wolin, 1981, p. 4).

Contemporary U.S. versions of the theory have also been most prominently presented as normative by "neo-liberal" investment banker Felix Rohatyn. The neo-corporatist ideology abounds in discussions of "public–private" partnerships, and these discussions (as well as the packaged "deals" they lead to) also demonstrate the general absence of either citizen participation or voluntary action. Neo-corporatist theory prescribes a decision-making system in which the leaders of business and government meet as formally designated agents of their organizations to decide the great issues of economic policy, social distribution, and general welfare. The perspective of this theory, and the residual role it provides for the individual citizen (voter and trade union member) suggests that the theory stands somewhat removed from the "rule by the people."

Lawrence Goodwyn (1978) has commented critically on the neo-corporatist ideology:

> Today the values and the sheer power of the corporate America pinch in the horizons of millions of obsequious corporate employees, tower over every American legislature, state and national, determine the modes and

style of mass communications and mass education, fashion American foreign policy around the globe, and shape the roles of the American political process itself" (p. 322).

An examination of the work of President Reagan's Task Force on Private Sector Initiatives illustrates the neo-corporatist approach to voluntarism. Wrapped in a mantle of glorification of the concept, two major themes were emphasized: first, that voluntarism is a major source for the provision of social services, and second, that decision-making in the voluntary sector should be the prerogative of a variety of "public–private partnerships." The task force came up remarkably short of suggestions for accomplishing its goals. Task force member Richard Cornuelle (1983), a writer and former corporate official, noted that Reagan's statements on volunteerism often "carelessly" appeal "to a faith that was lost fifty years ago." And, he added, "Reagan's desperate midterm suggestion that each business hire one unemployed person, a pathetic caricature of what must be done, was greeted with the derision it deserved" (p. 177).

In the hands of neo-corporatist thinkers like George Gilder (1981) or E.S. Savas (1982), neo-corporatist theory advocates the "privatization" of public services, positing the development of private economies for the provision of formerly public goods. Building on the disenchantment with the bureaucratic state as service-provider, an influential contemporary critique of government has developed. The claim is forwarded that the state cannot perform as well as the market in certain activities, and that its role should be narrowly circumscribed. As bluntly put by British economic writer Arthur Seldon (1980), "Government is not the dependable cure for economic ills but the invariable cause. Private enterprise works with the grain of human nature; socialism works by frustrating it through coercion" (Summary).

In such a view, voluntary action becomes part of an expanded "private sector," facilitating the reduction of public social service expenses and calling upon the volunteered contributions of individual donors and actors. On grounds of both morality and efficacy, the superiority of the corporation and the voluntary agency has been asserted. Harry Hogan (1981), for example, has argued that corporations and voluntary organizations, in an era in which religion has declined, are the major bastions defending us from the perils of "Statist Humanism." Therefore, the "private sector institutions of business and voluntarism must now not only develop a new moral base, but also recapture a leadership position from the state" (Hogan, 1981, p. 96).

Volunteering in Populist Theory

As already mentioned, populism tends in American theory to be a point of departure for criticism rather than a fully developed guidance theory for democracy. From the populist perspective, service volunteering would appear to be of little salience, but grassroots action and self-help may be seen as central.

If the role of voluntarism in populism is to be understood, it is the work of historians who have studied specific social movements that will be of greatest use. Thus Saloutos and Hicks write, in *Twentieth Century Populism* (1951), of the agricultural movement in the Midwest in the first four decades of the 20th century, chronicling the organization of agricultural interests into cooperatives and associations. The central thread of the populist movement is found in their work to involve the organization of citizens' economic associations in the search for direct governmental rule, and the replacement of monopoly rule (p. 33).

Reviewing a more recent experience, that of McCarthyism, Michael Rogin (1967) concludes that the late Senator's support did not consist of a "right-wing populist movement." Rather, "McCarthy was supported by the activities of a party that emphasizes free enterprise, achievement, and individual responsibility. The politics of these people seems more sensibly explained by their preoccupations with achievement and failure than by their populist concerns" (p. 251). Rogin concludes that the prevailing tendency to identify the McCarthy movement as populist can be explained in terms of the inability of pluralist theory to focus directly on specific issues in political life (p. 261).

But the most far-reaching examination of populism as citizen democracy in action emerges from the historical analysis of Lawrence Goodwyn (1978). To Goodwyn, the Populist revolt of the 1870s saw the flowering of democratic voluntarism, and was then followed by a period of severe restriction by pervasive corporate power that continues to the present. Populism, Goodwyn writes, "cannot be seen as a moment of triumph, but as a moment of democratic promise. It was a spirit of egalitarian hope, expressed in the actions of two million beings—not, in the prose of a platform, however creative, and not, ultimately, even in the third party, but in a self-generated culture of collective dignity and individual longing" (p. 295).

The links between populism and volunteering are clearly shown by Goodwyn when he notes that the core vision of populism was:

> . . . a profoundly simple one: the Populists believed that they could work together to be free individually. In their institutions of self-help, Populists developed and acted upon a crucial democratic insight: to be encouraged to surmount rigid cultural inheritances and to act with autonomy and self-confidence individual people need the psychological support of other people. . . . The Populist essence was . . . an assertion of how people can ACT in the name of the idea of freedom. At root, American Populism was a demonstration of what authentic political life can be in a functioning democracy (Goodwyn, 1978, pp. 295–296).

Contemporary populist theorist Harry Boyte (1980) has noted that voluntary participation may open "free social spaces that, under certain conditions, can turn into breeding grounds of insurgency" (p. 63). And economist–sociologist S.M. Miller (1985) states that while "neo-populism" is plagued by "contradictory tendencies within its ideology," it does have the advantage of being a "locally oriented, democratic alternative to centralized socialism. . . . It does so by allowing us to be aware that traditional values and institutions can be and are part of a progressive, radical outlook" (p. 3). But Frank Riessman's warning (1985) is worth consideration: "The new progressive populism will have to tread a careful path, avoiding the errors of democratism and over-response to the moment, while attempting to redress the imbalance that has been produced by big institutional power, particularly big business" (p. 2).

Volunteering in Idealist Theory

Idealists focus their democratic theory on the role of dialogue in the building of political community. The British idealists T.H. Green, Bernard Bosanquet, and Mary Parker Follett saw voluntary action as a central aspect of the good society. Unlike Rousseau, they tended to view dialogue as capable of being engendered within both political institutions and voluntary ones.

Several influential contemporary idealists—most prominently Sheldon Wolin and T.J. Lowi—fault voluntary action for its particularism. Lowi (1969) proclaims the virtues of constitutional democracy and observes that private bureaucracies accrete around the provision of volunteering, and require public observation and regulation:

> Life in the cities would be hard to imagine without the congeries of service and charitable agencies that, systematically, keep our streets clean of human flotsam and jetsam. Of growing importance are the family service agencies, agencies for the elderly, for adoption, and for maternal and child care, all of which in turn draw financial support from still other (e.g., Community Chest, United Fund) agencies that are still more tightly administrative. To repeat, all such groups naturally possess potential political power, but only occasionally are politicized. The rest of the time they administer (p. 38).

With a more ruthless pen than idealists like Robert Pranger (1968), Lowi comes to view voluntary action as a threat to democracy, rather than its embodiment, as pluralists are wont to contend. Thus:

> . . . there is the proliferation of groups—"do-gooders" groups—manifestly dedicated to ministering to one problem or another of socialization or

social control. Between church school and public school, almost nothing is left to the family, clan, neighborhood, or guild—or to chance. Even sandlot baseball has given way to Little Leagues, symptomatic of an incredible array of parental groups and neighborhood businesses organized to see that the child's every waking moment is organized, unprivate, wholesome, and, primarily, oriented toward an ideal of adjustment to the adult life of rationality that comes too soon (Lowi, 1969, p. 37).

If the point has not yet been fully digested, Lowi puts it even more bluntly: "All of the larger voluntary associations, as well as most of the smaller ones, have given up their spontaneity for a solid administrative core" (pp. 37–38). The voluntary sector is handmaiden to a repressive and less than fully democratic society: it requires the "tempering" of the "excesses of pluralism" (Wolin, 1960) and the distrust of interests and groups (Lowi, 1969, p. 296).

Contemporary idealists, it may be concluded, tend to distrust volunteering and volunteerism for their linkages with other forces of bureaucratic and administrative power. Only when legitimated by the active will and voice of the people does the organized voluntary impulse come to be valued by the idealist.

Volunteering in Pluralist Theory

Pluralists frequently write of the contributions of service volunteering, self-help, and grassroots action—and they find little to fault in these approaches, though their emphases vary among the three forms. Service volunteering, when it is discussed by pluralists, is generally valued for its participatory contributions rather than for the service outcomes it provides. In this respect, it is the associational aspect of volunteering that is most central to pluralists. Thus, Berger and Neuhaus (1977) write that: "Associations create statutes, elect officers, debate, vote forces of action, and otherwise serve as schools for democracy. However trivial, wrongheaded or bizarre we may think the purposes of some associations to be, they nonetheless perform this vital function" (p. 34).

Writing from the perspective of long experience in the development of volunteering, Eva Schindler-Rainman and Ronald Lippitt (1975) note that volunteering "not only represents a significant contribution to the volunteer's own psychological health and self-actualization. Volunteering offers many experiences necessary to democratic personality development" (p. 15). Volunteering, to Schindler-Rainman and Lippitt, is an important form of participation in democratic society, and it is to be valued for gains it provides to both individual and society. Similar themes echo in the work of other pluralists (see Kornhauser, 1959, p. 76; Nisbet, 1962, p. 266; Truman, 1951, p. 101; Berle, 1959, p. 150).

The case for self-help is made even more strongly by many pluralists.

Berger and Neuhaus (1977), for example, note the way in which self-help activities allow the fulfillment of public policy. They cite "the growth of the women's movement, which in some areas is effectively challenging the monopolistic practices of the medical establishment." They go on to suggest that the "ideas of such people as Ivan Illich and Victor Fuchs should be examined for their potential to empower people to reassume responsibility for their own health care. Existing experiments in decentralizing medical delivery systems should also be encouraged with a view toward moving from decentralization to genuine empowerment" (p. 39). Nisbet (1962) writes of the contribution of mutual-aid associations in the nineteenth century to the development "of both security and freedom—security within the solidarity of associations founded in response to genuine needs; freedom arising from the very diversity" of associations and their relative autonomy (p. 266).

As for grassroots organizing, the pluralist literature is largely devoid of explicit discussion of it. Kelso (1978) does treat the matter directly when he writes of the centrality of "issue-publics" in pluralism, noting that such an "interest-public may be a loosely knit group of people who are troubled about a particular problem in their local neighborhood" (p. 62).

The pluralists, thus, value each form of volunteering, but in an order of preference: first, self-help; second, service-volunteering; and third, grassroots action. This order may be explained by their historic preference for order and civility as outcomes of pluralist decision-making. Service volunteering is not usually seen as central to decision-making processes by pluralists, but grassroots organization is often seen as a way of shortcutting more established paths to participation, and thereby of threatening the orderly workings of the pluralist system. The specter of mass society remains, in the eyes of pluralists, a central threat. Therefore, any form of direct action is viewed with a wary eye.

To the critics of pluralism, however, the theory appears flawed by its bias toward established interests. Pluralism in this view is seen as a system dominated by special interests and pressure groups, one that relegates the individual citizen to a level far inferior to that assigned established groups. Such a system is denigrated as the "corporate liberalism" of a "broker state," as Alperovitz and Faux (1984) put it.

Volunteering in Social Democracy

The three forms of volunteering under discussion are generally valued positively by social democrats as well, although, as for the groups already discussed, there are definite shadings among their preferences.

Service volunteering is the most controversial in the social democratic view. Amitai Etzioni (1968), to take a supportive example, speaks positively of the contributions of "service collectivities," organizations in which

"service to others and a societal cause is a central value (p. 539). Gar Alperovitz (1973) writes of the benefits that flow from cooperative activity:
"voluntarism and self-help can achieve what centralized propaganda cannot—namely, engender group involvement, cooperative enthusiasm, spontaneity" (p. 80). And Michael Lerner (1973) notes that the spirit of
volunteerism is not entirely foreign to the new democratic theory, though
not its highest priority: "it is good to put iodine on scratches, but iodine will
not cure a malignant tumor. Obviously, a situation in which people are
starving or suffering under intolerable conditions cannot be analogized by
minor abrasions; hence the revolutionary movement takes on the struggle
against poverty, for adequate food, free and adequate health care, and for
welfare rights as high priorities" (p. 240).

Marcus Raskin (1971) comes closest among the social democrats to a
negative position on service volunteerism when he writes:

> Suppose I distribute food to the poor at Thanksgiving time. In itself this is
> not a bad act—but only because I feel good in the process. I am looked at
> as being good because I fulfilled a role of being good. But the facts are
> otherwise. There is no sense of equality or association between me and the
> one who gets the good, the object of my affection or need. There is also
> the perverse reinforcement of scarcity and my role as giver in that act. I
> help the taker reinforce the colonized reality. I am the representative of the
> hierarchic other now reaffirming the object state of the taker-beneficiary
> (p. 220).

The social democrats are far less cautionary when they consider self-help.
Gartner and Riessman (1974), leading students of self-help, point to the
contribution of "alternative institutions," many of which operate on the
basis of volunteer participation. They particularly focus on such institutions, as organized by young people, which "have been involved in service
giving and service receiving in the area of tutoring and a great variety of
youth-serving endeavors—runaway houses, crash pads, free clinics, book-
stores, educational reform projects, cooperatives, hot lines, vocational and
educational clearing houses, peer counseling groups" (p. 85). Seen as ways in
which consumers and service receivers can be united, volunteerism can be
part of a socialist strategy of transformation and reorganization, Gartner
and Riessman imply. Self-help appears to be even more strongly supported
in the social democratic tradition than by the pluralists. Social democratic
theorists see the positive functions of self-help in the black ghetto and
youth communes (cf. Alperovitz, 1973, p. 90), in consciousness-raising
groups, health collectives, and womens' caucuses (cf. Lerner, 1973, pp.
214–215).

The attractiveness of self-help to social democrats may reflect the belief
that such "small groups," to use Lerner's phrase, may easily develop into

independent centers of political consciousness and action in times of social change. This faith in decentralized and spontaneous social action also underlies the social democrats' enthusiasm for grassroots movements. Michael Harrington (1968) writes directly of the need to take America's "most cherished conservative myth seriously: that the 'grassroots' should be a spontaneous, natural locus of political life. To make this old saw come true will take a radical reorganization of local and regional government in America—and therefore a frontal assault on the bastion of undemocratic, conservative power" (p. 111).

Other social democratic thinkers also write strongly of the contributions of grassroots groups (see Lerner, 1973, p. 248; Litt and Parenti, 1973, p. 249; Alperovitz, 1973, p. 93; Raskin, 1974 p. 258). Raskin notes that such groups may have the "political effect of withdrawing legitimacy from the colonizing apparatus" of state and large institutions, while providing a chance for its participants to embrace their humanity of developing "projects" for the restructuring of political society along more fully democratic lines. And Walzer (1983, p. 318) writes of the vigilance of citizen action that is the price of both liberty and equality in such a society. It is this view of democracy as continuing struggle by means of citizen volunteering that marks the social democratic perspective.

CONCLUSION: THE TWO FACES OF VOLUNTARISM

This chapter has reviewed the role of volunteering in five contemporary forms of democratic theory, and has found that volunteering is central to two variants (pluralism and social democracy), is highly relevant to a third (populism), is viewed rather negatively by a fourth (idealism), and is seen as a substitute for governmental action by a fifth (neo-corporatism). These findings are summarized in Table 1.

TABLE 1. VOLUNTARISM AND FIVE CONTEMPORARY FORMS OF DEMOCRATIC THEORY

| | | Type of Volunteering | |
Form of Democratic Theory	Service	Self-help	Grassroots action
Populist	0	+	+
Idealist	−	0	0
Pluralist	+	+	+
Social Democracy	+	+	+
Neo-corporatist	+	0	−

Symbols: − = negatively valued; + = positively valued; 0 = no opinion.

Conclusions about the role of volunteering in democratic theory must be conditioned by remarking that they depend upon, first, the form of democratic theory, and, second, the type of volunteering. Variation is far wider among forms of democratic theory in relation to volunteering than among forms of volunteering as viewed from democratic perspectives. There is a tendency for evaluations of service volunteering, self-help, and grassroots participation to be relatively consistent across particular interpretations of democratic theory.

More important, the work examined in this chapter suggests that voluntarism is a two-sided phenomenon when held to the criteria of democratic theory. On the one hand, it contains those elements of social action so highly valued by pluralists and populists—the direct action of citizens (mediated through group action, the pluralists insist). On the other hand, however, voluntarism also contains structures that inhibit the dialogue of idealist forms of democracy and the equity that is the desired outcome of social democratic forms. Voluntarism is the citizens' association *and* the special interest group, the discussion group *and* the Klan chapter, the peace group *and* the cult. The legacy of voluntarism is ambiguous in democracy, but it is hardly less settled than the contemporary landscape of democratic theory itself.

Throughout this and the previous chapters, I have noted this dual legacy. Despite the enthusiastic literature reviewed in Chapter 1 describing the contribution of voluntary action to social process, the contributions of voluntary sector organizations are often viewed as ambiguous, as was seen in Chapter 2. In the present chapter, several perspectives critical of voluntarism have been identified as existing in the realm of democratic political theory.

It seems indisputable that voluntarism is often interpreted through perspectives of political ideology. The divergences in the perspectives of Boyte and Pines, rehearsed in Chapter 2, show clearly how a democratic populist perspective differs from that of a neo-corporatist conservative. Similar shadings, often just as dramatic, emerge in this chapter from the perspectives of democratic socialism, pluralism, and idealism. Forms and instances of voluntarism highly valued from one perspective are seen as perverse or misguided by those who hold a divergent perspective. Few interpreters choose to value equally all forms of voluntarism in their estimation.

Indeed, some have come to view voluntarism as a realm of human endeavor possessed of two faces, one progressive and positive, the other regressive and negative. While the second face is rarely confronted by those who write glowingly of voluntarism, it may be discerned in the works of serious scholars who have attended to its study. Summary statements presented by two distinguished voluntary action researchers, David Sills and David Horton Smith, may be taken as cases in point.

Sills (1968) identifies a number of functions of voluntary organizations for individuals and society. The individual functions are social integration and training in organizational skills. The societal functions are mediation, integration of subgroups, affirmation of values, governing, initiating social change, and distributing power. These lists consist of positive functions, but Sills also discusses in his review article several problematic organizational processes that characterize many associations, such as "minority rule" and "goal displacement."

Offering a similar list of functions of voluntary action, Smith (1973) balances a discussion of ten positive contributions (discussed later in this book, in Chapter 6) with an analysis of the negative side of voluntary action, as well. To quote at length:

> For every one of the ten types of impact we have noted, there can be negative consequences in certain circumstances and with regard to certain values. Thus, when voluntary associations experiment with new social forms, the failures can often be harmful to specific people and organizations. When alternative definitions of reality and morality are offered, these can be evil as in the case of Nazi Germany and its ideology as generated by the Nazi party, a voluntary association. When voluntary groups focus on the play element, their fun can become mischievous as in the case of the boys' gang that wrecks a school "just for kicks." When social clubs provide a warm and close sense of belonging to their members, they can also create deep dissatisfaction in people who would dearly like to belong but are excluded from a particular club or kind of club.
>
> In the same way, voluntary groups striving to preserve some beliefs or values from the past may be holding on to anachronisms that would be better left to the pages of history books. Clubs whose members chase around seeking flying saucers and little green men from Mars might more profitably spend their time and energy elsewhere with more satisfying results. Organizations that arouse the full potentials of black people—who must then go out into the real world and face a harsh reality of bigotry and discrimination—may or may not be doing them a favor. The kinds of systemic corrections being suggested by cause-oriented and advocacy groups may not be conducive to the greatest number. Economic self-interest voluntary groups often tend to ignore the public interest in favor of an exclusive and selfish private interest. And the latent potential of the voluntary sector can be mobilized to do evil as well as to do good for one's fellow man (Smith, 1973, pp. 397–398).

Smith's reminder that the legacy of voluntary action is a mixed one clearly implies the need to develop evaluative criteria for this form of human endeavor. But is it possible that a hybrid conception of democratic theory might emerge, one that finds room for the corporation and the community, the State and the group? In such a vision might be found the central aspects of the idealist's dialogue, the pluralist's flourishing of group life, the social democrat's focus on distributive justice, the populist's community life, and even many neo-corporatists' sense of institutionalized responsibility. In what Etzioni (1968) has called the "active society" and Alperovitz and Faux

(1984) the "pluralistic commonwealth," after all, stand many elements of the vision of a transformed society, a vision that includes many, though not all, of "the basics" to which Pines's "traditionalists" (1982) seek to return and most of the changes advocated by Boyte's community advocates (1984).

Bellah and his associates (1985) articulate such a traditional, religious-inspired vision of voluntarism in the conclusion to their study of the contemporary American character:

> Above all, we will need to remember our poverty. We have been called a people of plenty, and though our per capita GNP has been surpassed by several other nations, we are still enormously affluent. Yet the truth of our condition is our poverty. We are finally defenseless on this earth. Our material belongings have not brought us happiness. Our military defenses will not avert nuclear destruction. Nor is there any increase in productivity or any new weapons system that will change the truth of our condition.
>
> We have imagined ourselves a special creation, set apart from other humans. In the late twentieth century, we see that our poverty is as absolute as that of the poorest of nations. We have attempted to deny the human condition in our quest for power after power. It would be well for us to rejoin the human race, to accept our essential poverty as a gift, and to share our material wealth with those in need (pp. 295–296).

Contemplating the blending of a variety of democratic themes as a third sector mission implies that the major theoretical perspectives may be less impervious than Alford and Friedland (1985) suggest. But this contention requires a familiarity with other than political perspectives on voluntary action, and this perspective is essayed in the next chapter.

4

Voluntary Action and Society: A Survey of Theories

A society composed of an infinite number of unorganized individuals, that a hypertrophied State is forced to oppress and contain, constitutes a veritable sociological monstrosity.

—Emile Durkheim, *Professional Ethics and Civic Morals* (1958, p. 28)

INTRODUCTION

The question of which social science has best advanced the study of voluntary associations is a matter of some controversy (Powell, 1987, p. xii). Political theorists, as shown in Chapter 3, have contributed importantly. In the behavioral sciences, sociologists, anthropologists, and psychologists have attended to specialized topics in this field, with the attention of sociologists particularly guided by a long tradition of scholarly concern in that discipline. Social welfare scholars have maintained a considerable interest in the subject. Recently, economists, lawyers, and students of public policy have entered the field with both theoretical and empirical studies.

Voluntary action is central to a number of dominant theoretical perspectives in social science. Writing at the turn of the century, Emile Durkheim, following in the steps of his countryman Alexis de Tocqueville, gave a major role to associations in his theories of social structure. The observations of Max Weber and Robert Michels, contemporaries of Durkheim, illuminated aspects of organizational reality in the voluntary sector. Karl Marx, while never a voluntarist, nevertheless left an implicit theory of voluntarism that is as critical as it is incomplete. And, in the 20th century, social theorist Talcott Parsons saw the voluntary sector performing basic functions of "integration" in society.

Contemporary journals of sociology contain a large number of articles on various aspects of voluntary association structure and behavior. While generally seen as an interdisciplinary field, voluntary action research has been most actively performed by sociologists over the past quarter-century.

However active sociologists have been in the study of voluntary action, this area of interest by no means represents the central focus of the discipline. The voluntary sector, unlike the polity or economy, has not given rise to a separate scholarly discipline for its study (e.g., political science, economics). Sociologists who have specialized in voluntary action research often complain of the marginality of the field, at least in their colleagues' perception. However valid these complaints, the fact remains that the field has been central in the thought of many of the foremost developers of the sociological tradition.

Anthropological studies of voluntarism, while less numerous, have also been conducted, and a sub-specialization in voluntary action research may be discovered in that discipline. Reviewing that tradition in 1968, Michael Banton notes that associations seem to be linked to the emergence of new forms of economic activity, and also provide a means of preserving values and sociability in times of rapid change. From the anthropological perspective, associations provide a bridge across the troubled seas of the present, a bridge that builds on the values of the past while it reaches toward the anticipated gains of the future (cf. Anderson, 1971; Bradfield, 1973; and Wallace, 1961).

Psychological studies of voluntary action have largely been confined to studies of motivation, but of these there are a rather large number. Allen and Rushton (1983) note the existence of an "increasingly voluminous experimental literature on human altruism" (p. 36), and a beginning exploration by psychologists of altruism in real life.

The more recent efforts by scholars in economics, law, and public policy to develop theories and empirical studies of voluntary action is discussed later (see Chapter 6). But in any case, this chapter (and those that follow) will not essay a comprehensive review of any single disciplinary literature; rather, here I seek to focus on questions of central interest to a consideration of the relations between the third sector and other sectors. Specifically, themes of central interest to the present study are addressed: the problem of the "two faces" of voluntarism, the connections between voluntary action and other forms of institutional action, and the presumed independence of the third sector. These problems are considered in the present chapter within the context of classic problems in voluntary action research—each identified with the theorist who most clearly posed the problem. An understanding of these problems will assist, I contend, in the understanding of the ambiguous legacy of voluntarism in modern society.

The five problems to be examined are associated with the central concerns of Tocqueville, Michels, Weber, Parsons, and Karl Marx, respectively. Each of these concerns was illuminated by the theorist in question, and each remains to puzzle and inform contemporary students of voluntary action. These problems are considered in the remaining sections of this chapter.

THE TOCQUEVILLE PROBLEM:
CAN ASSOCIATION RESTRAIN BENIGN DESPOTISM?

The first classic problem in the field of voluntary action research derives from the work of Tocqueville and his sociological descendant and country-man, Emile Durkheim. We have considered it above as the problem of social and political pluralism.

To Tocqueville, the basic problem facing modern societies is the building of consensus. Faced with the demise of the old hierarchical order, and the leveling occasioned by the rise of democratic politics, Tocqueville "sought to assess whether such democratic societies would be able to maintain free political institutions or whether they might slip into some new kind of des-potism" (Bellah and associates, 1985, p. 36).

It is the fear that democracy might prove a temporary societal form, prone to give way to a seemingly benign and yet irrevocable despotism of the "mass" that troubled Tocqueville. Durkheim would later identify the socio-psychological root of this condition as "anomie," the inability to connect societal goals with means to achieve them.

To both Tocqueville and Durkheim, the solution to the problem lay in the building of intermediate associations, groups that permitted individuals to transcend the gentle bonds of individualism, and to participate in the reali-ties of contemporary social living. Durkheim put the matter graphically in the sentence cited at the head of this chapter. On the same page, he offered his prescription for hyperindividualism and the untrammeled state, already quoted in Chapter 3, to the effect that the individual requires being dragged into the "general torrent of social life" by voluntary associations (1958, p. 28).

THE MICHELS PROBLEM: IS OLIGARCHY INEVITABLE?

The Tocqueville problem is essentially a societal one, addressing the inter-relations of large organizations and the patterns of their connections. The Michels problem, on the other hand, pertains to voluntary organizations and their own internal structure. Michels posited as a central characteristic of the turn of the century German Social Democratic Party he studied the separation of their members into two internal classes: leaders and masses. He notes that those who assumed leadership in the party acquired both inside knowledge and the love of power and its accompanying privileges. As Orum (1978) interprets Michels, such leaders "try to co-opt future leaders from among the rank-and-file members and thus, to prevent members' free choice in the selection of their future leaders. They also create further posi-tions within the leadership ranks, multiplying the benefits that can be obtained from holding office and simultaneously further insulate them-selves from contact with and influence by the rank and file" (p. 257).

Michels's "iron law of oligarchy"—"who says organization says oligarchy"—has been widely accepted in the study of political organizations. Thus Lipset, Trow, and Coleman (1956) sought to test the iron law in a study of the International Typographical Union, and countless political sociologists have pointed to the applicability of the law in other modes of organization (cf. Orum, 1978). Students of voluntary organization have generally assumed the applicability of the law to many quintessential voluntary groups, as well.

Michels's law is more often referenced than tested, however, and contemporary organizational studies of voluntary action have cast it in a rather different light. When a distinction is made between what contemporary voluntary action researchers call a "PSNPO"—a paid-staff nonprofit organization—and a wholly volunteer-based organization, the iron law does not appear universally applicable. Indeed, Jone Pearce (1980) has contended that Michels's law does not apply at all to many volunteer-staffed organizations. Rather, her studies find that the very act of leadership in a volunteer organization can be problematic in itself, since the costs of exercising leadership in such organizations clearly outweigh the immediately perceptible gains: ". . . in voluntary organizations leadership brings more labor, no more real autonomy than any volunteer has, and little of the reward and coercive power available to most employee leaders. . . . When volunteers have little to gain and much to lose by assuming active leadership roles in their organizations, it certainly is in many members' self-interest to maintain a rank-and-file role" (p. 90).

The Michels problem can rather clearly be specified in modern society. The iron law applies most directly to those organizations in which rank-and-file assume more highly paid positions upon (s)election to them, and in which they enjoy considerably heightened privilege as a consequence of their new rank. The law applies less well to many contemporary corporations, including universities, in which the costs of advancement may be more apparent than the gains. For example, the tenured faculty member, privileged in the possession of a moderate teaching load and a number of hours to pursue research and writing on a schedule of his or her own construction, may find the assumption of the responsibilities of a dean distasteful, involving as they do long hours, shorter vacations, heavy paperwork, and the loss of autonomous scheduling opportunities. Similarly, a study of management trainees in the AT&T corporation found a declining level of the "motive to manage" in the 1970s, leading the authors to ask, rather plaintively, "who is going to run our corporations in the future?" (Howard and Bray, 1980, p. 26).

If the Michels proposition does not universally apply in the realm of paid employment, it seems even less broadly applicable to the volunteer organization that is without paid staff, as Pearce's work (1980) so dramatically demonstrates. Yet Michels is not wholly inapplicable to the voluntary sector. Countless voluntary organizations at all societal levels do not demonstrate shared and revolving leadership patterns, but rather become the bailiwick of a single dominant leader. Specifying the conditions under which oligarchy emerges remains an important issue on the agenda of applied behavioral scientists.

THE WEBER PROBLEM: CAN THE PERILS OF BUREAUCRACY BE AVOIDED BY THE VOLUNTARY SECTOR?

The Michels problem is in many ways a subunit of a broader problem, that of the organizational structure of modern society. Viewed as involving the increasing dominance of bureaucratic principles of organization in society, this issue is most closely linked to the work of Max Weber.

Alford and Friedland (1985) have identified this problem as involving the "managerial perspective" on society. The unit of analysis in such a view is the organization, seen to "have a significant degree of autonomy from society and the individual and group relations" that compose the organization (Alford and Friedland, 1985, p. 5). The managerial perspective involves a heightened awareness of "interorganizational networks," organized structures of power, and a pervasive conflict between centralization and fragmentation (ch. 1).

Students of American life have often noted the resistance of voluntary associations to the bureaucratic principle. Focusing on the breadth and significance of informal organizational patterns, they have asserted the importance of neighboring, familism, and other interactional patterns. Donald and Rachelle Warren (1985) have identified a widespread system of "problem-anchored helping systems" that allow most Americans access to unpaid counseling, home care, and other assistance. Their studies show that these informal patterns of assistance far outweigh the services of formal organizations in terms of the frequency of their use.

Such informal patterns of help-seeking and help-giving differ from those involved in formal organizations in several ways. As Hoch and Hemmens (1985) explain: "people conceive of informal helping within the context of ongoing social relationships. Unlike organized help in which the function defines the boundaries of the social relationship between the help giver and the recipient, informal help is defined by the qualities of the social relationships within which helping occurs" (p. 5). Such informal help tends to be reciprocal, rather than one-way, and may be seen to "compose the basic fabric of social life in households, communities, and organizations" (p. 5).

Formal organizational theory (cf. Knoke and Prensky, 1984), on the other hand, takes a very different position. When it considers voluntary organizations, it gives central attention to the rising professionalism of voluntary organizations, and it sees that professionalism as a response to the weakened effectiveness of amateurism in American voluntarism. Pearce (1980) and Rothschild-Whitt (1979) note that many factors render effective volunteering problematic, including the widespread difficulty of volunteer-based organizations to secure effective leadership (Pearce, 1982). Formalizing and professionalizing the voluntary agency is informed by the desire for efficacy, but it may lead to a rigid and bureaucratized structure, as Adams's study (1980) of a Red Cross chapter clearly indicates.

Kirsten Gronbjerg (1982) has documented the increasing similarity between many voluntary organizations and public sector organizations. Reflecting the social forces at play in a mass society, the voluntary sector, according to this view, responds directly to the claims for universal eligibility for social services. Gronbjerg contends that these pressures create a special niche for voluntary sector organizations, leading them to focus on providing supplementary, "quality of life" services, such as health, family, and educational services. Further, Gronbjerg contends that specialization of clients—by age, ethnicity, and religion—continues to be a central aspect of voluntary organization structure and service.

Contemporary forces at work in the environment external to voluntary organizations impel such organizations toward models that are bureaucratic and increasingly corporate in form, if not in spirit. As Kramer (1985) puts it:

> At least for the remainder of the 1980s, in their relationships to their government and profit-making counterparts voluntary agencies will be confronted with the related dilemmas of entrepreneurialism and vendorism, both of which have an exceedingly high potential for goal deflection. . . . Not surprisingly, with reductions in their governmental income, many voluntary agencies have been attracted to the prospect of earning funds not dependent on grants or contributions. The launching of a subsidiary business enterprise has been described as the "hottest area of nonprofit funding" and includes thrift and gift stores, restaurants and catering services, periodicals and mail-order services, housing and real estate syndication, cable TV franchising, and nurseries and garment factories (p. 388).

Alford and Friedland (1985) note that, in the managerial view of society, the concept of "voluntary association" becomes replaced by that of "organization" (p. 449). In such an "organizational society," the distinctions between private and public, profit and nonprofit, are greatly lessened. All organizations, be they voluntary, corporate, or governmental, are seen to follow the same laws of organizational domination and competition. All come to be seen as "enterprises," ultimately dependent upon their ability to secure an economic niche capable of sustaining them.

From the organizational perspective, the tendency for voluntary organizations to become more bureaucratic in form and more dependent upon the sale of their products in practice is to be expected. For such are also the expectations placed upon contemporary governmental programs (with the single exception of the military) and economic enterprises themselves (including those industries like nuclear energy and defense contracting, which are themselves sustained by their privileged role with relation to the state).

Questions of inter-institutional relations form the Parsons problem, which is considered later in this chapter. For now, the important question to note is that of the bureaucratization of the voluntary sector—the degree to which it becomes subject to societal-wide laws of institutional survival and demise. And these laws are fundamentally Darwinian, rewarding those organizations that have chosen their patrons well. Whether the favored product is planes for military, electricity generated from nuclear plants, or the latest militarized childrens' toy, it brings profit to its producers if it can achieve the support of a mass market or a wealthy patron.

In such a society, the nonprofit organization increasingly takes the form of a tax-free business, organizing itself around "profit centers" and divesting program elements that do not lead to its organizational growth and survival. If such "loss centers" involve persons with profound personal and economic needs, there is a special sense of regret. But bills must be paid, and the shrunken welfare state cannot be expected to perform at levels it achieved in the days before the great economic transformation of 1973.

Neil Gilbert (1983) explains that, "Although the voluntary sector generates a significant volume of service, there is little evidence that it possesses the inherent capacity to move far beyond current levels of activity or to compensate in any reasonable degree for decreased public spending in the social market" (p. 133). In this respect, the bureaucratization of the voluntary sector occurs along with the straightening of class lines in society. The Weber problem, then, develops in a close dance with what concerns us next, the Marx problem.

THE MARX PROBLEM: DO VOLUNTARY ORGANIZATIONS POSE THE RIGHT QUESTIONS?

The centrality of economic power and control in society is the focus of the Marx problem. In this holistic societal perspective, labor and capital struggle with each other in a contradictory and unstable relationship maintained only by class power. Either the dominative hegemony of the state–capital relationship maintains itself, or a radical transformation occurs in which labor takes revolutionary control of society.

The role of the voluntary sector has not been seen as a central problem by Marxists. From this perspective, as Alford and Friedland note (1985),

"Explosions of participation—in the voting booth, in the factories, or in the streets—are treated as manifestations of societal contradictions" (p. 5). A somewhat fuller examination of the Marxist approach to voluntary action is essayed in this section, one that leads to the fundamental question this approach raises for the activist: are the right questions being addressed?

In attempting to investigate Marxist views on voluntary association, one is immediately confronted with a seeming contradiction: while Marxists have historically accorded voluntary associations—revolutionary parties, political movements, cooperatives, etc.—a central role in the struggle to achieve socialism, analysis of the voluntary sector's role within capitalism are notably absent from the Marxist literature. Part of the reason for this neglect apparently results from the emphasis that has been placed since Marx's day on the relations of production as the primary determinant of capitalist society and as the necessary focus for attempts to transform that society. Yet even for neo-Marxists, who have attempted to assert a more prominent role for the state and cultural institutions in the maintenance of class relations, the role of the voluntary association is largely taken as a given, undeserving of detailed analysis. One is thereby left to attempt to draw inferences from concepts in the literature that posit space within the social structure for voluntary associations or that assume their existence, in order to construct a Marxist analysis of voluntary association.

Building on Marxist concepts of domination in the social and political spheres, one can postulate a role for voluntary association that corresponds to various functional types of associations. Fraternal, cultural, and religious organizations may be seen to play roles in the reproduction of labor and to provide compensation for feelings of alienation; philanthropic and social service organizations may be seen to maintain a dependent reserve army of labor; and political organizations can be viewed as serving to legitimize existing social relations.

Add to these roles of associations Gramsci's concept of "hegemony," (cf. Adamson, 1980) or ideological domination, and one sees that while the state performs its task of maintaining hegemony, it also assumes important supportive functions to sustain capitalists and the capitalist process. This requirement would appear to suggest an important role for institutions that can carry out state functions while not creating increased demands on state (and ultimately capitalist) finances and that can influence the expectations of workers about their rights. While not directly recognized by neo-Marxist writers, voluntary sector organizations, given their involvement in nearly every aspect of social life and their ostensible independence from both business and government, appear uniquely suited to fulfill such a role.

Drawing on classical and neo-Marxist concepts, the beginning outlines of a Marxist theory of voluntary action may now be discerned. Three general characteristics of voluntary associations may be identified, all of which may be seen by Marxists as useful for the maintenance and support of capitalist relations.

First, because they are dependent on outside funding, the programs and activities of voluntary associations can be controlled or influenced by members of the ruling class. Marxist instrumentalists have pointed to the mechanisms of this control. Of particular importance are the large foundations established by corporations; they have played an important role in creating and supporting a wide range of voluntary associations. Roelofs (1985) has noted that foundations choose to fund organizations that engage in safe reformist activities while shunning those whose activities—such as promoting cooperative ownership—are inconsistent with the interests of the power structure. Through their funding of various research activities and think tanks, foundations also can "create, disseminate and sustain an ideology protective of capitalism; they can deflect criticism and mask or actually correct damaging abuses of the system" (p. 61). Ruling class members also dominate positions on the governing boards of major philanthropic institutions, not only directing these organizations but also reinforcing their elite status through activities of "conspicuous leisure," to use Veblen's (1934) phrase.

The subservience of voluntary associations to the interests of the capitalist class is furthered by another characteristic of the voluntary sector—the use of unpaid volunteers. Since volunteers provide unpaid, and to the Marxist, often gratuitous, labor, they are seen as unlikely to have a deep interest in the setting of organizational goals. Their lesser stake in the organizations makes them less likely to organize around interests or grievances. If they eventually do advance to paid work, volunteers are likely to fall prey to the indoctrination of organizational values and be disinclined to mount internal organizational challenges or external campaigns regarding social power. The high turnover in grassroots volunteers, due in great part to the lack of remuneration, gives paid staff justification to limit the influence of participants over fundamental organizational policy—further constraining the possibilities for debate within the voluntary sector on goals and activities that might challenge aspects of capitalist domination.

A final characteristic of voluntary groups relevant to the maintenance of capitalist relations involves the fragmentation within the voluntary sector. What liberals hail as pluralism in the sector, Marxists argue is a fragmentation that prevents effective class-based organizations from developing to challenge the system. The fragmentation is perpetuated by piecemeal funding that leads groups to address isolated issues or service discrete sectors of the population rather than allowing them to confront problems on a system-wide basis. The precariousness of funding for voluntary associations reinforces the fragmentation by limiting the scope of issues that groups are able to address and their ability to organize large numbers of workers.

Moreover, the fragmentation serves to create a marketplace of groups competing with each other in promoting the ethic of self-interested individualism—a crucial part of capitalist hegemony.

Building on these three major elements, the Marxist theory of voluntarism would surely note that social service organizations develop as an adjunct to the family providing for social reproduction and in controlling the reserve army of the unemployed. Fraternal/cultural organizations play their role in social reproduction by filling leisure time with "sterile diversions" (Gorz, 1967, p. 118). Among these diversions may be included consumption of the mass media and its messages, participation in organized religion, problem-solving in self-help groups, and the celebration of patriotic rituals. Political organizations, finally, serve to marginalize subversive groups and channel others into "safe" activities. System challenges are blunted by reformist groups, and politics becomes harmless of ruling interests. "It is in the interest of the elite," writes Roelofs (1985), "to have every type of 'disadvantaged' person join a separate organization; each neighborhood, block or backyard to have its own revolution" (p. 87).

Despite their central focus on the power of the ruling class to retain hegemony, most Marxists retain the belief that radical change will eventually occur. Gorz (1967) views the labor movement as the instrument of puissant change: the "autonomous power of workers—in the large enterprises but also in the cities, towns, public services, regional bodies, and cooperatives, etc.—prepares the way for a dialectical progression of the struggle to higher and higher levels," leading to the replacement of dominant capitalist relations (p. 10). As long as the efforts of workers are directed toward the achievement of autonomous powers, Gorz is confident that the forces of cooptation and hegemony can be countered and eventually vanquished.

Other Marxists are even more optimistic about the role of voluntary associations in creating change. Dreier (1980), to take one instance, argues that alternative worker-based organizations such as producer and consumer cooperatives and employee-owned enterprises constitute "socialist incubators" that can provide participants, and eventually the entire society, with instruction in practical socialist solutions to the problems of modern capitalism. Even organizations advancing reformist goals, he argues, can be seen to further socialist struggle by "providing large numbers of people with the self-esteem, self-confidence and opportunity to 'make history'—to wrest some control over their lives in a concrete, strategic and confrontational way" (p. 34).

The development of a Marxist theory of voluntarism is clearly an important intellectual requisite, if the sociological vision is to be presented fully and completely to the problem of the three sectors and their interrelations. The outlines of such a theory have been deduced in this section, but much further work might be undertaken to both flesh out such a theory and subject it to test. The Marxist approach provides the student of voluntarism with a crucial challenge: confronting with brutal honesty the role of voluntary associations in sustaining privilege, inequality, and injustice in the contemporary political economy. The right questions to ask, the Marxist asserts, are not those aimed to foster voluntarism; rather, they are those directed at the way various forms of voluntarism restrain critical thought and decisive action. On the basis of such a critical perspective, the Marxist contends, those forms of voluntary action that will ultimately usher in a new age can be identified and nurtured. The right question from this perspective is that of the meaning of the voluntary act for the future of the political economy.

THE PARSONS PROBLEM: WHAT IS THE STRUCTURE OF INTERDEPENDENCE?

The 20th century sociological theorist Talcott Parsons (1966) saw society as structured around the provision of four basic functions: adaptation, goal-attainment, integration, and latent pattern-maintenance (or culture). The great institutions of society—1) the economy, 2) the state, 3) the voluntary, and 4) church, home, and family—were seen to develop, respectively, around the four basic functions. Parsons developed a macro-societal theory around these four functions and their related institutions.

Of greatest interest to the present study, Parsons observed that each institution relates to each of the others. The currency may be power, or influence, or money—but in each case the major institutional sectors of society are in active relationships with one another. From the Parsonian perspective, a sector may dominate over another, but it should not be seen to be "independent" of another.

Parsons's perspective is vital in identifying the links between the three major sectors that concern us in this work: economy, state, and association. In Chapter 9, these links are probed in greater detail, following the leads provided for their study by Parsons. For the present, however, it should be noted that this topic has received the careful study of a number of contemporary social scientists.

To take one exemplary study of this sort, James G. Hougland and Jon M. Shepard (1985) have probed the "structural pressure" placed on corporate managers to encourage volunteering among their employees. Probing Bartolomeo Palisi's (1972) contention that: "Any person who participates in any group does so because of some type of social pressure," they note that community service is often advocated within corporations as part of a strategy to improve the local "business climate." By examining the voluntary participation of a sample of corporate managers, Hougland and Shepard find that the variables of organization size and company policy toward participation do affect the voluntary action of managers. But other variables also affect this action, including the degree of interest in local affairs held by the manager. Hougland and Shepard (1985) conclude:

> Few middle-level managers can afford to ignore company expectations when making decisions about participation in voluntary organizations, but company expectations and structural constraints do not determine all aspects of managers' voluntary participation. As a result, it is likely that few leaders of voluntary organizations can afford to ignore the preferences and interests of their members when making decisions about their organizations' policies and practices. For this reason, the concept of voluntarism, while hardly pure, remains important for understanding the dynamics of many important organizations.

Another perspective on the relations between economic and voluntary life emerges from classic studies of American philanthropy, which emphasize the limits of the philanthropic impulse and capacity. Bremner, for example, concludes his historical study (1960) with the observation that:

> Americans had a long experience in founding voluntary agencies to perform tasks which individuals could not accomplish alone and which public bodies, for one reason or another, were not able to undertake. They had long experience with charity, too. They knew that charity was subject to abuse, by the giver as well as the taker, and that the most effective and acceptable form of benevolence was not endless, soul satisfying almsgiving but sensible efforts to help people become independent and prepared to work out their own destinies (p. 186).

Gaylin and his associates (1978) and Bakal (1979) echo similar themes. However serious the problems of Americans, philanthropy and charity will only address some of them, and those only incompletely.

If voluntary sector organizations are to be seen as partly autonomous, and partly influenced by corporate structures, they also relate to political organizations in a similar way. Studying service organizations in Chicago, Kirsten Gronbjerg (1987) finds four major patterns in relationships between government and voluntary sector organizations. She identifies these patterns as cooperation, accommodation, competition, and symbiosis (or "mutual exploitation"), and notes that each set of relationships has become more politicized in recent years. Primary among the determinants of government–voluntary relationships that she finds are the following: the nature and history of the public mandate; the fiscal interaction; resource dependency; institutional character, and the strength of the involvement of private sector providers.

The last factor listed by Gronbjerg pertains, of course, to the private economic sector. Its inclusion suggests that the interdependence of government–voluntary sector activity involves the private sector as well. In the conclusion of her paper, Gronbjerg notes the increasing adoption of "proprietary management styles" by nonprofit organizations and predicts the emergence of a smaller and more specialized role for nonprofits as cooperative inter-sector relations are increasingly replaced by accommodation, competition, and symbiosis (p. 78).

Studying the impact of citizen organizations of government, Knoke and Wood (1981) see social influence associations playing "a major part in the nation's political life," by shaping collective decisions, mobilizing latent social resources, and affecting decision-makers (p. 190). Indeed, the power of such associations, when targeted upon specific policy changes, often seems to overwhelm conceptions of deliberative democracy, such as those of the idealist and populist theorists examined in Chapter 3.

The associational relationship to the state gives rise to another two-way facing problem. On the one hand is the recognition of citizen impact, through groups, on government policy and action—surely a desirable aspect of democracy. On the other hand threatens the dark side of direct democracy, replete with the blue smoke and mirrors of "special interests," political action committees, and direct mail. Knoke and Wood (1981) describe the threat well:

> Special interest organizations have proliferated in recent years to the point of subjecting the legislature and executive at all levels of government to almost continual pressure to accede to narrowly focused objectives. . . . The result is a real threat that minority special interests will triumph over wider' societal values (pp. 191–192).

Posed in the way we have considered the Parsons problem thus far, echoes of previous problems resound: questions of citizen power as seen by Tocqueville; matters of elite dominance as seen by Michels; issues of bureaucratization as viewed by Weber; issues of economic domination of the state as seen by Marx. That is, the problem is seen as one of major institutions engaged in transactions with each other—the corporation's buying power with money, the state's asserting power by regulation, the association's claiming power by participation, etc.

But the problem is seen in a different light by those, like Sharkansky (1979) and Musolf (1983), who see a fundamental blurring in the roles of the major societal institutions. Looking at a series of governmentally created corporations (Comsat, "Fannie Mae," Amtrak, and Conrail), Musolf (1983) identifies them as "Private-for-Profits," and notes that these corporations are given freedoms that go far beyond that previously granted to "government corporations" (p. 10).

To Sharkansky, the situation has so changed the way we need to view the relationship between government and other major institutions that the probing question of his title, "Whither the State?", is suggested. Sharkansky (1979) contends, on the basis of a comparative study of the United States, Israel, and Australia, in which the margins of the state appear to be expanding while its core contracts:

> On the margins of the state are those bodies related to the core
> departments but with substantial grants of autonomy from them. The
> margins include some units clearly attached to the government even when
> they hire staff outside the framework of civil service and enjoy substantial
> grants of financial and managerial autonomy. Other bodies on the margins
> of the state may be responsible to both state and nonstate masters. Still
> other marginal bodies may be described as "entirely" private (e.g.,
> companies that contract with American governments). Even these "private"
> companies design or deliver important features of government policy and
> serve as extensions or surrogates, albeit somewhat autonomous ones, of
> core departments (p. 11).

If the contention that the number of inter-institutional transactions is increasing in modern society, such that the core institutions are more and more difficult to discern in a maze of interacting marginalia, then the Parsons problem of independence becomes problematic indeed. What is public and private when a policy involves a welter of "partnerships," and when corporations undertake initiatives in the name of "corporate social responsibility," not to mention "privatization," that were formerly deemed the work of the state? In such a clash of forces, voluntarism truly enters the arena of public policy and no longer stands at the edges of societal action.

5

Current Maps of the Third Sector

On the map of American society, one of the least charted regions is variously known as the voluntary, the private nonprofit, or simply the third sector.

—Commission on Private Philanthropy and Public Needs, *Giving in America* (1975, p. 31)

INTRODUCTION

The previous chapters have set the stage for an understanding of how voluntary action figures in modern society. The task of this chapter is to examine and advance conceptions of that configuration. By means of the examination and development of a series of "social maps," this chapter will seek to present in clear terms the structure of voluntary action in the modern postindustrial world.

THE TERRAIN OF THE VOLUNTARY SECTOR

The task of mapping the voluntary sector does not involve the employment of an esoteric, or even an established, social science methodology. Rather, I understand by this activity the rendering of images that reflect the institutional terrain of society, and I comprehend both the structure of institutional sectors and their points of interrelationship.

Such societal maps may be schematic or verbal, but their utility is dependent on certain tests. One test involves the descriptive characteristics of such maps: do they visibly represent a way of understanding reality? Another test deals with their representation of the relationships between institutions: do they show these patterns clearly? A third test pertains to the major functions of the institution analyzed: are they comprehended by the map? A fourth test involves the identification of problems and areas of conflict: are they signified and comprehended? And a final test relates to social changes: are they suggested by the map? In other words, does the map suggest the best routes for our journeys?

Probably the best way to understand what I mean by a map is to look at several that are extant in the literature. Earlier the work of Talcott Parsons was discussed (Chapter 4), and his identification of four major sectors in interaction forms a comprehensive societal map. But before the implications of his work are considered, let us look at the kind of maps that have recently been developed with a central focus on the voluntary sector.

A recent schematic effort by Russy Sumariwalla (1983) offers a point of departure (Figure 1). The problem this author confronts is the representation of the third sector. Should it be seen as truly independent from corporate and governmental structures? Or is it rather best linked with its fellow "private" sector, that of the for-profit economy? Sumariwalla presents two competing maps to represent these perspectives but does not select one or the other as preferred.

Alternative A, as seen by Sumariwalla, draws a fundamental distinction between "public sector or governmental entities," on the one hand, and "private sector or nongovernmental entities" on the other. Private sector activities are then substructured into "business" and "nonbusiness" categories, arriving at the identification of the three major sectors.

Alternative B, in distinction, begins by positing three parallel sectors, seeing the fundamental division as between "public," "business," and "nonbusiness-nongovernmental" activities and organizations. In both versions, the nonbusiness-nongovernmental (NBNG) sector is divided into two categories of organizations: "public interest entities" and "all other NBNG entities." Sumariwalla explains this distinction as contrasting the "totality of all those organized entities whose basic organizing purpose is to promote or advance some public, social or group good" with "those organized primarily to benefit its membership" (p. 186).

Paralleling the thinking behind Sumariwalla's Alternative B, Ralph Kramer (1984: 273) has derived a set of three parallel sector maps. Kramer's focus is on the delivery of personal and social services, and he identifies five possible relationships between the three sectors. These positions are reprivatization, empowerment, pragmatic partnership, governmental operation, and nationalization.

"Reprivatization," on the one hand, involves private-sector predominance in the delivery of social services. The role of the voluntary sector is an "alternative" in this situation. "Empowerment," on the other hand, sees the voluntary sector as the principal source of service provision, substituting for governmental or private delivery.

Kramer's last three maps all posit governmental predominance in the provision of services. "Pragmatic partnership," which Kramer (1981, p. 285) sees as the most likely map for the future, identifies the voluntary sector as a supplement or complement to service delivery. "Governmental operation" finds the government defining voluntary organizations as "obstacles" to

FIGURE 1: SUMARIWALLA'S MAP

Alternative Approaches to the Classification of Organizations

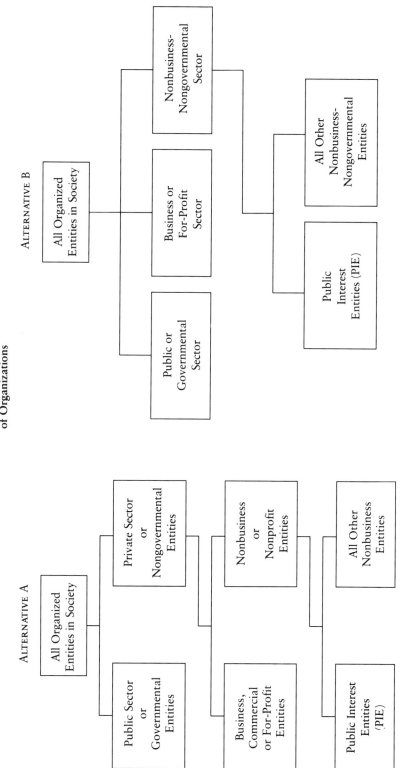

Source: Sumariwalla (1983) p. 188–189

FIGURE 2: KRAMER'S MAP

Alternative Sectoral Relationships in the Delivery of the Personal Social Services

Alternative Futures

ROLE OF VOLUNTARY AGENCY AS:	REPRIVATIZATION	EMPOWERMENT	PRAGMATIC PARTNERSHIP	GOVERNMENTAL OPERATION	NATIONALIZATION
	ALTERNATIVE	SUBSTITUTE	SUPPLEMENT COMPLEMENT	OBSTACLE	MARGINAL

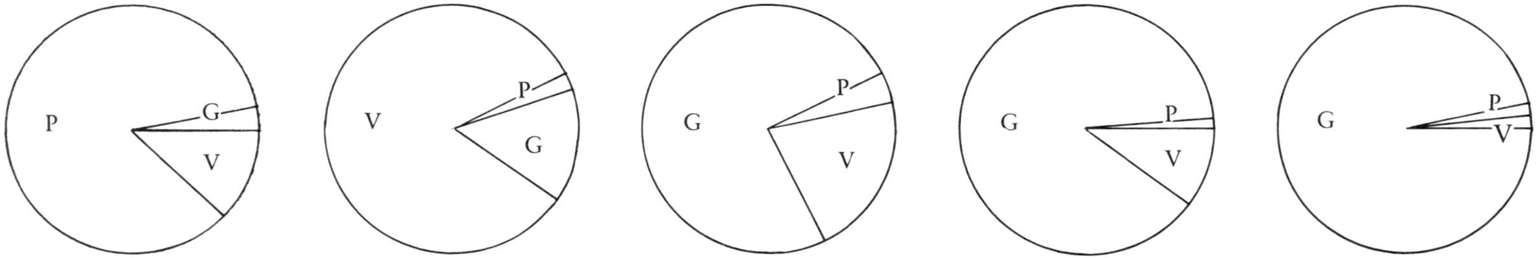

P = Profit-making organizations
G = Governmental organizations
V = Voluntary organizations

Source: Ralph M. Kramer, *Voluntary Agencies in the Welfare State*. Berkeley: University of California Press, 1984, p. 273. © 1984 The Regents of the University of California. Reprinted by permission.

effective delivery. And "nationalization" sees the voluntary organization treated as "marginal" to the provision of such services.

Another recent map was derived by philosopher Franklin Gamwell (1984), building on the earlier work of John Dewey and Milton Friedman. Gamwell presents three maps, each slightly different from the other. The first is built from Dewey's work, and it closely resembles Sumariwalla's Alternative A. In Gamwell's rendition of Dewey's work, the private for-profit sector is identified as "consumption-regarding," and the nonprofit sector as "community-regarding." The latter sector is then substructured into "nonpublic interest" and "public interest" categories.

Gamwell sees Friedman as constructing a map from a similar point of departure. Two nongovernmental sectors are identified: the "profit-seeking or commercial" and the "nonprofit or independent." Friedman diverges from Dewey's approach, however, when he identifies the nonprofit sector's two major components as the "charitable" and "public service" subsectors, respectively.

Gamwell proceeds to present his own map, which is closer to Dewey's than to Friedman's. Like the two others, however, it draws the first distinction between governmental and nongovernmental organizations. His second cut follows Edward Banfield's distinction (1963) between "private-regarding" and "public-regarding" organizations. The public-regarding category is then divided into organizations that are less inclusive and more inclusive. And the more inclusive public-regarding organizations are then split into those that are "nonpolitical-regarding" and those that are "political-regarding."

Gamwell's map, while it began with the assumptions of Sumariwalla's Alternative A, arrives at a strikingly different orientation. New boundaries are drawn that render the shapes of the previous distinctions between the three sectors much less precise. Gamwell (1984) describes this reconceptualization:

> ... this fundamental threefold division in the social order contrasts sharply with the common trilogy of governmental, profit-seeking, and nonprofit institutions. The common set of distinctions appears to find its theoretical foundations in some version of established liberalism ... The pivotal difference represented by Dewey and the present appropriation of his theory is that independent associations now constitute the telos of associational life (p. 150).

Gamwell attributes the primacy of independent associations to their congeniality with the comprehensive moral principle of the "maximal public ideal." The significance of nongovernmental associations is seen to follow "from the fact that voluntariness of association is an important aspect of freedom. . . . In short, independent associations are teleologically prior in

FIGURE 3: GAMWELL'S MAP OF ASSOCIATIONS

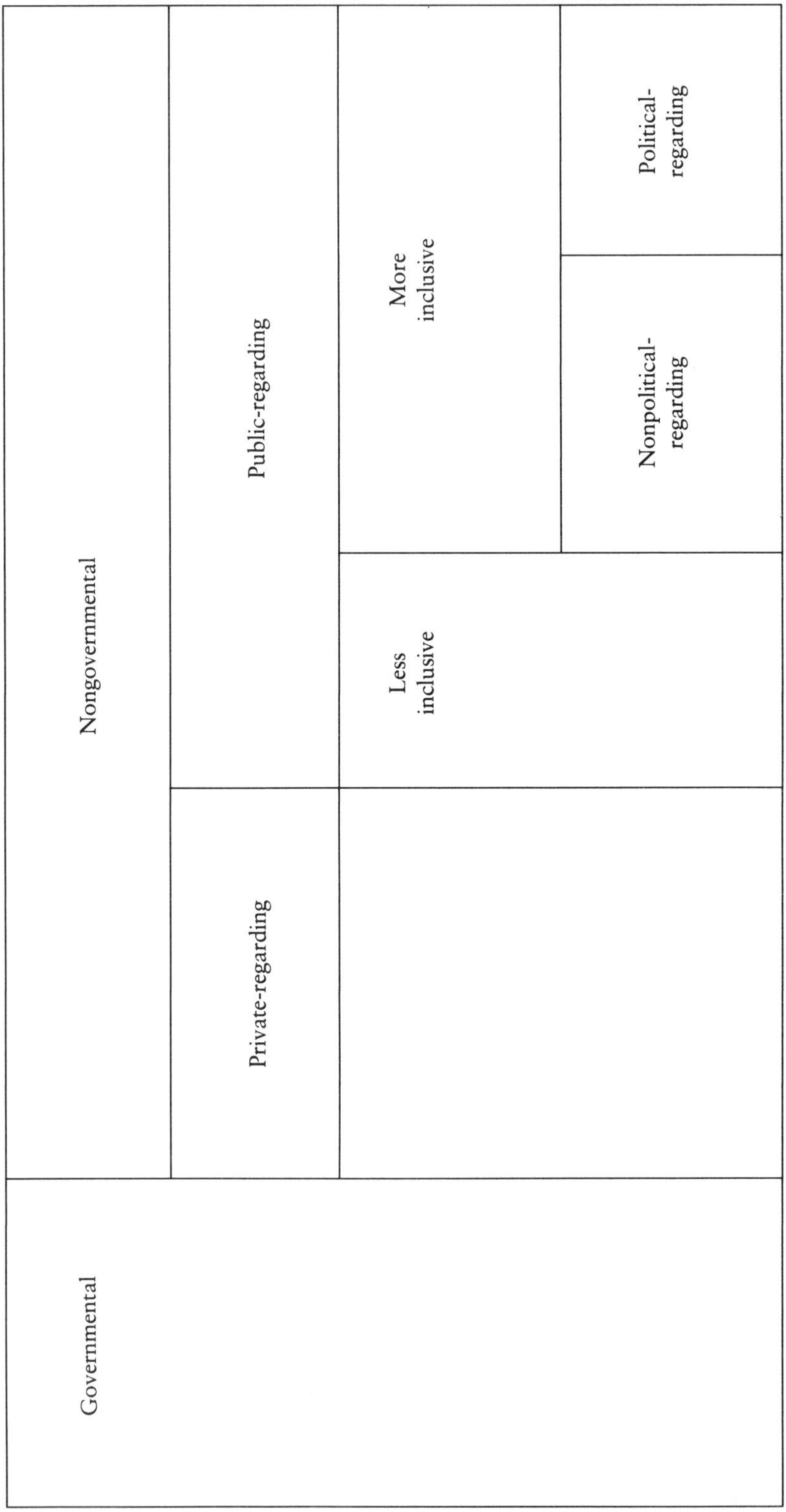

Source: Franklin I. Gamwell, *Beyond Preference: Liberal Theories of Independent Association.* Chicago: University of Chicago Press, 1984, p. 149. © 1984 The University of Chicago. Reprinted by permission.

the social order." Similarly, the more inclusive organizations are seen as "teleologically prior" to the less inclusive ones. However, no teleological priority is assigned on the basis of political- or nonpolitical- regardingness. Both types of organizations are seen to be of equal significance.

Gamwell essentially presents an idealistic theory of the social order, in the way in which we defined such theories in Chapter 3. In such a view of society, a certain class of associations emerges as of most central importance. This class is "significantly more narrow than the commonly designated 'third sector,' " Gamwell (1984) contends: "Many of the latter, e.g., health-delivery and social-service organizations, are private-regarding. Public-regarding associations, in other words, are designed to develop, in Dewey's phrase, 'the higher human capacities,' those activities in which individuals may pursue the public world for its own sake and, thereby, maximize it" (p. 150). Gamwell notes "a certain injustice" in ordering this special group of associations as the "third" sector: "At least in the sense that they are teleologically prior, public-regarding associations may properly be called the first sector of the human community" (p. 150).

THE USES OF SECTORAL MAPS

A comparison of the mapping efforts of Kramer and Gamwell illustrates the several uses of sectoral and societal maps. Obviously, the maps are different, and the importance of those differences should first be noted. Kramer identifies three parallel sectors, whereas Gamwell begins with two. Kramer aims to predict which model will be likely to dominate the future, whereas Gamwell seeks to identify the one that ought to prevail. Kramer seeks to analyze empirical differences between configurations of the three sectors; Gamwell questions if the common distinctions between the sectors have a continuing relevance.

Despite the differences between their efforts and the maps that they produce, the work of Kramer and Gamwell yields rich benefits for the voluntary action researcher. Kramer's work demonstrates the wide variety of possible relationships between the three sectors; each of these positions is a real possibility, he reminds us, and each needs to be studied and evaluated. Gamwell's work, on the other hand, opens the rich world of normative political theory to the purview of our subject; not all "third sector" activities are equal in value, he suggests. Indeed, those of most value are only a subsector of organizations, which are themselves important enough that they imply a reorientation of the way in which we view both society and the voluntary sector.

In light of the weightiness of the issues raised by the comparison of the Kramer and Gamwell models, the differences between Sumariwalla's two alternative models begin to fade. Both are essentially "three-sector" models that assume the primacy of the distinction between economic, political, and voluntary enterprise. And it is that very distinction that Gamwell challenges us to recast as he provides us a second set of maps to guide our exploration of the role of the voluntary in modern society.

Earlier in this chapter a set of tests for the uses of societal maps was suggested. Five criteria were identified for the development of such maps: adequacy of representation of reality; identification of interinstitutional patterns; comprehension of functions; identification of areas of conflict; and understanding and guidance of change. Application of these criteria to the models of Kramer and Gamwell suggests that each effort is of value. Kramer presents the powerful conventional "three-sector" map and identifies a number of interinstitutional patterns that have implications for change. Perhaps the least developed aspects of his maps involve their delineation of the functions of associations in the different situations, and in the guidance of appropriate change.

Gamwell, on the other hand, presents a suggestive if not fully delineated representation of societal reality, but he offers little illumination of interinstitutional patterns. He focuses on a specific set of voluntary sector functions and identifies a class of organizations that are of moral primacy in society. But conflict and prediction are not part of his effort, and his maps remain, in the final analysis, intriguing but incomplete.

Voluntary action researchers have most conventionally worked with three-sector maps such as those presented by Kramer and Sumariwalla. They have sought to identify a sector whose dimensions can be probed fully and comprehensively. In the service of this task, a number of classificatory schemes have been developed, most recently by Nelson Rosenbaum and Bruce Smith (1983), on the one hand, and by the National Center for Charitable Statistics (NCCS), on the other.

The NCCS (1986) system, of which Sumariwalla was the principal developer, works with 26 major categories of third-sector organizations, designated by "primary purpose, field of service, or type of organization." Each of these types is then further categorized on the basis of its major activity or program focus and its principal beneficiary. The result is a four-digit code, which allows for the identification of up to 67,600 different types of "Nongovernmental, Nonbusiness Tax-Exempt Organizations in the U.S. with a Focus on IRS Section 501 (c)(3) Philanthropic Organizations" (to cite the subtitle of the work). Figure 4 represents the exhaustive NCCS Taxonomy of Exempt Entities (1986).

The question arises of the degree to which such comprehensive typologies lend themselves to the kinds of distinctions Gamwell would have us draw. Once we are able to identify the several hundred principal types of organizations that inhabit the voluntary sector, how close have we come to

FIGURE 4: THE NATIONAL TAXONOMY OF EXEMPT ENTITIES

NTEE CODE	Entity by Primary Purpose, Field of Service or Type of Organization
A	**—ANIMAL RELATED**
A-00	Animal Related Not Elsewhere Classified (NEC)
A-01	Codes 01 through 20 describe functions activities
A-20	common to all Major Groups and are thus reserved and repeated under each Major Group
A-01	—Animal Related—Advocacy
A-02	—Consultation & Technical Assistance
A-03	—Equal Opportunity & Access
A-04	—Fund Raising
A-05	—Material, Supplies, Equipment, Building Provision (Gifts in Kind)
A-06	—Planning (Including Strategic Planning)
A-07	—Program Coordination (Similar/Several Agencies)
A-08	—Program Development
A-09	—Program Evaluation/Assessment
A-10	—Public Education (Increasing Public Awareness)
A-11	—Research
A-12	—Standards Setting/Accreditation/Monitoring
A-13	—Support Groups/Auxiliaries
A-14	—Training (Continuing Education—Staff/Volunteers)
A-15	Codes A-15 through A-20 are reserved for future
A-20	addition of common codes
A-21	Animal Exhibition/Show
A-22	Animal Population Control
A-23	Animal Protection & Welfare NEC
A-24	Audubon Society
A-25	Endangered Species
A-26	Humane Society
A-27	Wildlife & Wilderness Group NEC
A-28	Wildlife Sanctuary or Refuge
A-29	Zoo
B	**—ARTS, CULTURE, HUMANITIES**
B-00	Arts, Culture, Humanities Related NEC
B-01	For codes B-01 through B-20, see under
B-20	Major Group A. Titles are repeated
B-21	Architecture
B-22	Arts NEC
B-23	Ballet (Classical)
B-24	Cultural/Ethnic Awareness Group
B-25	Dance NEC
B-26	Folk Arts
B-27	Historic Preservation (Historical Site, Records, Reenactment, Monument, etc.)
B-28	Humanities NEC
B-29	Library, see under Education (G-29)
B-30	Local Arts Agency
B-31	Media Arts (TV, Radio, Film, Video)
B-32	Modern Dance
B-33	Museum Art Exhibit
B-34	Music NEC
B-35	Opera
B-36	Photography
B-37	School Band/Orchestra
B-38	Singing Society/Group
B-39	Symphony Orchestra
B-40	Theatre
B-41	Visual Arts
C	**—CIVIL RIGHTS, SOCIAL ACTION, ADVOCACY**
C-00	Civil Rights, Social Action, Advocacy Related NEC
C-01	For codes C-01 through C-20, see under
C-20	Major Group A. Titles are repeated
C-21	Defense of Human/Civil Rights
C-22	Elimination of Prejudice and Discrimination
C-23	Immigrants' Rights
C-24	Intergroup/Race Relations
C-25	Minority Rights
C-26	Pro-Choice
C-27	Right-to-Life
C-28	Voter Education/Registration
C-29	Women's Rights
D	**—COMMUNITY IMPROVEMENT, COMMUNITY CAPACITY BUILDING**
D-00	Community Improvement, Community Capacity Building Related NEC
D-01	For codes D-01 through D-20, see under
D-20	Major Group A. Titles are repeated
D-21	Community Coalition NEC
D-22	Community Neighborhood Development/Improvement
D-23	Jewish Federation
D-24	Junior League
D-25	United Way
E	**—CONSUMER PROTECTION, LEGAL AID**
E-00	Consumer Protection, Legal Aid Related NEC
E-01	For codes E-01 through E-20, see under
E-20	Major Group A. Titles are repeated
E-21	Consumer Protection & Safety
E-22	Legal Aid—Civil
E-23	Legal Aid—Criminal
E-24	Legal Aid/Public Defender NEC
E-25	Public Interest Litigation
F	**—CRIME & DELINQUENCY PREVENTION—PUBLIC PROTECTION**
F-00	Crime & Delinquency Prevention—Public Protection Related NEC
F-01	For codes F-01 through F-20, see under
F-20	Major Group A. Titles are repeated
F-21	Bail Assistance
F-22	Correctional/Parole
F-23	Crime Prevention NEC
F-24	Dangerous Weapons Regulation and Control
F-25	Delinquency Prevention NEC
F-26	Mothers Against Drunk Driving (MADD)
F-27	Offenders/Ex-Offenders Rehabilitation
F-28	Protection Against Neglect, Abuse, Exploitation
F-29	Protection Against Spouse Abuse
F-30	Transitional Care (Halfway House)—Offenders
G	**—EDUCATION/INSTRUCTION—FORMAL & NONFORMAL**
G-00	Education/Instruction—Formal & Nonformal Related NEC
G-01	For codes G-01 through G-20, see under
G-20	Major Group A. Titles are repeated
G-21	Adult Basic Education—Compensatory
G-22	Community College/Junior College
G-23	Continuing Education (Forums, Lectures, Panel Discussions, etc.)
G-24	Dropout Prevention
G-25	Education/Instruction—Formal Related NEC
G-26	Education/Instruction—Nonformal Related NEC
G-27	General Education Development (GED Certificate Program)
G-28	Kindergarten
G-29	Library
G-30	Nursery School/Early School Admissions
G-31	Parent Teacher Association
G-32	Post-Secondary/Technical School (Separately Organized)
G-33	Primary/Elementary School
G-34	Remedial Reading
G-35	Scholarships—Children of Employees
G-36	Scholarships/Students' Financial Aid
G-37	Secondary/High School
G-38	Special Education—Linguistically Handicapped
G-39	Special Education—Gifted
G-40	Special Education NEC
G-41	Undergraduate College
G-42	University, Professional School or Technological Institute
G-43	Vocational/Trade High School (Separately Organized)
H	**—EMPLOYMENT/JOBS**
H-00	Employment/Jobs Related NEC
H-01	For codes H-01 through H-20, see under
H-20	Major Group A. Titles are repeated
H-21	Employment Procurement Assistance (Including Bonding & Exemplary Rehabilitation Certification)
H-22	Employment Training (Including Apprenticeship)
H-23	Goodwill Industries
H-24	Homebound Employment
H-25	Sheltered Remunerative Employment/Work Activity Center NEC
H-26	Vocational Counseling
H-27	Vocational Rehabilitation
I	**—ENVIRONMENTAL QUALITY, PROTECTION & BEAUTIFICATION**
I-00	Environmental Quality, Protection & Beautification Related NEC
I-01	For codes I-01 through I-20, see under
I-20	Major Group A. Titles are repeated
I-21	Air Pollution Control
I-22	Energy Resource Conservation
I-23	Garden Club
I-24	Land Resources Conservation
I-25	Land Trust or Land Bank
I-26	Pesticides Control
I-27	Radiation Control
I-29	Solid Waste Management
I-32	Water Pollution Control
I-33	Water Resource Conservation
J	**—FOOD, NUTRITION, AGRICULTURE**
J-00	Food, Nutrition, Agriculture Related NEC
J-01	For codes J-01 through J-20, see under
J-20	Major Group A. Titles are repeated
J-21	Agriculture or Horticulture Group NEC
J-22	Commodity Distribution
J-23	Congregate Meals
J-24	Eatery, Agency/Organization Sponsored
J-25	Farmer's Cooperative Marketing/Purchasing
J-26	Free Food Distribution/Food Pantry
J-27	Groceries on Wheels
J-28	Home Meals/Mobile Meals
J-29	Soil and Water Conservation and Development
K	**—FOUNDATIONS; COMMUNITY, PRIVATE, OPERATING, OTHER GRANT-MAKING**
K-00	Foundations, Community, Private, Operating, Other Grant-Making Related NEC
K-01	For codes K-01 through K-20, see under
K-20	Major Group A. Titles are repeated
K-21	Community Foundation
K-23	Corporate Foundation
K-24	Gifts/Grants to Individuals (Other than Scholarships)
K-25	Private Non-Operating (Independent)
K-26	Private Operating
L	**—HEALTH—GENERAL & REHABILITATION (For Mental Health & Mental Retardation, see Major Groups M & N)**
L-00	Health, General & Rehabilitation Related NEC
L-01	For codes L-01 through L-20, see under
L-20	Major Group A. Titles are repeated
L-21	AIDS (Acquired Immunodeficiency Syndrome)
L-22	Alcoholism
L-23	Allergy Related NEC
L-24	Alzheimer's Disease
L-25	Ambulatory Health Center (Community Clinic)
L-26	Arthritis
L-27	Asthma
L-28	Autism
L-29	Birth Defects (March of Dimes)
L-30	Blindness
L-31	Blood Supply Related (Blood Bank)
L-32	Cancer
L-33	Cerebral Palsy
L-34	Communicable Diseases Control/Prevention NEC
L-35	Cooperative Hospital Service Organization
L-36	Cystic Fibrosis
L-37	Dental Care
L-38	Diabetes
L-39	Digestive Diseases
L-40	Disabled Persons; Promotion of Independence of (Easter Seal Society)
L-41	Emergency Health Transport (Rescue, Ambulance)
L-42	Epilepsy
L-43	Eye Bank
L-44	Family Planning (Planned Parenthood)
L-45	Group Health Practice (Health Maintenance Organization)
L-46	Health—Wellness Maintenance & Promotion (Health Screening, Health Fair)
L-47	Health Insurance (Medical, Dental, etc.)
L-48	Hearing & Speech
L-49	Heart Disease
L-50	Hemophilia
L-51	Home Health Care
L-52	Homemaker—Home Health Aide, see under Human Service, Other, Including Multipurpose (P-31)
L-53	Hospital, General—Medical & Surgical (Short Term)
L-54	Hospital, Specialty—Except Psychiatric (Long Term)
L-55	Hospital, Specialty—Except Psychiatric (Short Term)
L-56	Infertility Treatment
L-57	Intermediate Nursing Facility
L-58	Kidney Disease
L-59	Learning Disabilities
L-60	Leukemia
L-61	Lung Disease
L-62	Maternal and Child Health
L-63	Multiple Sclerosis
L-64	Muscular Dystrophy
L-65	Nursing NEC
L-66	Occupational Health Related
L-67	Optometry
L-68	Organ and Tissue Bank
L-69	Podiatry
L-70	Pregnancy, Termination
L-71	Prenatal/Child Birth
L-72	Rehabilitation—General
L-73	Rural Medical Facility
L-74	Sexually Transmitted Diseases NEC
L-75	Sickle Cell Disease
L-76	Skilled Nursing Facility
L-77	Specific Name Diseases/Disabilities NEC
L-78	Visiting Nurse Association
L-79	Voluntary Sterilization
L-80	Well-Baby Clinic

NTEE CODE	Entity by Primary Purpose, Field of Service or Type of Organization
M	**—HEALTH—MENTAL HEALTH, CRISIS INTERVENTION**
M-00	Health—Mental Health, Crisis Intervention Related NEC
M-01	For codes M-01 through M-20, see under
M-20	Major Group A-Titles are repeated
M-21	Community Mental Health Center
M-22	Drug/Other Substance Abuse
M-23	Eating Habits Related
M-24	Family/Patient Support Group (Mental Health)
M-25	Gambling Addiction
M-26	Hospital—(Mental Health Treatment)
M-27	Hot Line — Crisis Intervention
M-28	Mental Health Association
M-29	Mental Health Clinic
M-30	Psychiatric Care — General
M-31	Psychosocial Rehabilitation
M-32	Rape Victim Relief
M-33	Residential Treatment — Mental Health Related
M-34	Smoking Addiction
M-35	Suicide Prevention and Protection Against Physical Self-Harm
M-36	Transitional Residential Care-Treatment — Mental Retarded
N	**—HEALTH—MENTAL RETARDATION/ DEVELOPMENTALLY DISABLED**
N-00	Health — Mental Retardation/Developmentally Disabled NEC
N-01	For codes N-01 through N-20, see under
N-20	Major Group A-Titles are repeated
N-21	Long-Term Custodial Care
N-22	Retarded Citizens Association
N-23	Short-Term Residential Care
N-24	Special Day Care-Non-Residential Care — Mentally Retarded
O	**—HOUSING/SHELTER**
O-00	Housing Shelter Related NEC
O-01	For codes H-01 through O-20, see under
O-01	For codes O-01 through O-20, see under
O-20	Major Group A-Titles are repeated
O-21	Co-Op
O-22	Home Improvement and Repairs Assistance
O-23	Home Owners Association
O-24	Housing Development Construction
O-25	Housing Expense Reduction Support (Loans, Loan Insurance, Rent Supplements, etc.)
O-26	Housing Search Assistance
O-27	Low-Cost Temporary Housing NEC
O-28	Public Housing
O-29	Relocation and Allocation Under Renewal
O-30	Temporary Shelter for Homeless
P	**—HUMAN SERVICE, OTHER, INCLUDING MULTIPURPOSE (Also, Social Services — Individual & Family)**
P-00	Human Service, Other, Including Multipurpose (Also, Social Services — Individual & Family) Related NEC
P-01	For codes P-01 through P-20, see under
P-20	Major Group A-Titles are repeated
P-21	Adoption
P-22	American Red Cross
P-23	Catholic Human Services
P-24	Child Welfare NEC
P-25	Children's Home Society
P-26	Consumer Protection Association
P-27	Credit Counseling-Money Management
P-28	Day Care
P-29	Emergency Assistance (Food, Clothing, Cash)
P-30	Emergency Shelter Care
P-31	Family Life Education-Single Parent Management
P-32	Family Service Agency — Religious Auspices
P-33	Family Service Agency — Nonsectarian (Counseling — Individual/Family)
P-34	Foster Care
P-35	Foster Grandparents
P-36	Group Home
P-37	Homemaker-Home Health Aide
P-38	Hospice
P-39	Human Services — Other Religious Auspices
P-40	Human Services — Religious Auspices (General)
P-41	Information & Referral
P-42	Institutional Care
P-43	Jewish Community Center
P-44	Lutheran Human Services
P-45	Neighborhood Center-Settlement House
P-46	Parents Without Partners
P-47	Peer Counseling-Self-Help Group
P-48	Salvation Army
P-49	Seamen Center
P-50	Senior Center
P-51	St. Vincent DePaul Society
P-52	Transportation — Free or Subsidized
P-53	Travelers' Aid
P-54	Urban League
P-55	USO
P-56	Volunteers of America
P-57	YMCA
P-58	YMHA
P-59	YWCA
P-60	YWHA
Q	**—INTERNATIONAL/FOREIGN**
Q-00	International/Foreign Related NEC
Q-01	For codes Q-01 through Q-20, see under
Q-20	Major Group A-Titles are repeated
Q-21	Foreign Policy Research & Analysis
Q-22	International Education
Q-23	International Health
Q-24	International Peace & Security
Q-25	International Refugees Related
Q-26	International Relief
Q-27	International Social Service NEC
Q-28	International Student Exchange & Aid
Q-29	International Cultural Exchange — Promotion of Friendly Relations Among Nations
Q-30	United Nations Association
R	**—PUBLIC SAFETY, EMERGENCY PREPAREDNESS & RELIEF**
R-00	Public Safety, Emergency Preparedness & Relief Related NEC
R-01	For codes R-01 through R-20, see under
R-20	Major Group A-Titles are repeated
R-21	Civil Defense Emergency Preparedness
R-22	Disaster Preparedness and Relief
R-23	Fire Control and Extinction
R-24	Fire Prevention and Protection
R-25	First Aid
R-26	Public Safety and Control
R-27	Safety Education NEC
S	**—RECREATION, LEISURE, SPORTS, ATHLETICS**
S-00	Recreation, Leisure, Sports, Athletics Related NEC
S-01	For codes S-01 through S-20, see under
S-20	Major Group A-Titles are repeated
S-21	Amateur Athletic Association
S-22	Baseball-Softball (e.g. Little League)
S-23	Booster Club
S-24	Camping, Day, Overnight, Resident & Other
S-25	Group Home Center & Other Recreation Facilities (Park, Playground, etc.)
S-26	Country Club
S-27	Fair, County & Other
S-28	Hobby Club
S-29	Hunting or Fishing Club
S-30	Men's Club — Primarily Recreational NEC
S-31	Recreational Pleasure or Social Club NEC
S-32	School Athletics
S-33	Special Olympics
S-34	Sports Training
S-35	Swimming Club
S-36	Tennis Club
S-37	Variety Club
S-38	Women's Club — Primarily Recreational
T	**—RELIGION RELATED/SPIRITUAL DEVELOPMENT**
T-00	Religion Related/Spiritual Development Related NEC
T-01	For codes T-01 through T-20, see under
T-20	Major Group A-Titles are repeated
T-21	Association/Convention of Churches
T-22	Baptist
T-23	Buddhism
T-24	Catholicism
T-25	Church, Synagogue, Temple etc.
T-26	Confucianism
T-27	Coptic/Orthodox
T-28	Episcopalian
T-29	Evangelism
T-30	Hinduism
T-31	Islam
T-32	Jehova Witness
T-33	Judaism
T-34	Latter-Day Saints (Mormon)
T-35	Lutheran
T-36	Methodist
T-37	Missionary Activities
T-38	Presbyterian
T-39	Protestant NEC
T-40	Religious Group/Order NEC
T-41	Specific Religious Group/Order NEC
U	**—RESEARCH, PLANNING, SCIENCE, TECHNOLOGY, TECHNICAL ASSISTANCE**
U-00	Research, Planning, Science, Technology, Technical Assistance Related NEC
U-01	For codes U-01 through U-20, see under
U-20	Major Group A-Titles are repeated
U-21	Applied Research
U-22	Basic Research
U-23	Community Health & Welfare Planning
U-24	Public Policy Research
U-25	Research NEC
U-26	Science & Technology NEC
U-27	Science NEC
U-28	Scientific Research for Industry — Contract or Sponsored
U-29	Technical Assistance to Other Entities
U-30	Technology NEC
V	**—VOLUNTARISM, VOLUNTEERISM**
V-00	Voluntarism, Volunteerism Related NEC
V-01	For codes V-01 through V-20, see under
V-20	Major Group A-Titles are repeated
V-21	Voluntarism Promotion
V-22	Volunteer Bureau-Voluntary Action Center
V-23	Volunteer Recruitment and Referral-Placement
V-24	Volunteer Training and Supervision
W	**—YOUTH DEVELOPMENT**
W-00	Youth Development Related NEC
W-01	For codes W-01 through W-20, see under
W-20	Major Group A-Titles are repeated
W-21	Big Brothers
W-22	Big Brothers and Sisters
W-23	Big Sisters
W-24	Boy Scouts
W-25	Boys & Girls Club
W-26	Boys Club
W-27	Camp Fire
W-28	Catholic Youth Organization
W-29	Girl Scout
W-30	Girls Club
W-31	Key Club
W-32	4-H Club
X	**—RESERVED FOR NEW MAJOR GROUP (FUTURE)**
Y	**—SPECIAL INFORMATION NEEDS OF REGULATORY BODIES — MUTUAL MEMBERSHIP BENEFIT (SPECIFIC) & OTHER**
Y-00	Mutual Membership Benefit NEC
Y-01	For codes Y-01 through Y-20, see under
Y-20	Major Group A-Titles are repeated
Y-21	Benevolent Life Insurance Association — IRS Section 501(c)(12)
Y-22	Black Lung — IRS Section 501(c)(21)
Y-23	Board of Trade — IRS Section 501(c)(13)
Y-24	Burial Association — IRS Section 501(c)(13)
Y-25	Business League — IRS Section 501(c)(6)
Y-26	Cemetery Company — IRS Section 501(c)(13)
Y-27	Chamber of Commerce — IRS Section 501(c)(6)
Y-28	Corporation Financing Corporate Operation — IRS Section 501(c)(18)
Y-29	Credit Union — IRS Section 501(c)(14)
Y-30	Domestic Fraternal Societies and Associations —IRS Section 501(c)(10)
Y-31	Employee Funded Pension Trust (Created before 6-25-59) — IRS Section 501(c)(18)
Y-32	Fraternal Beneficiary Society, Order or Association — IRS Section 501(c)(8)
Y-33	Labor Organization — IRS Section 501(c)(5)
Y-34	Local Association of Employees — IRS Section 501(c)(4)
Y-35	Multiemployer Pension Plan — IRS Section 501(c)(22)
Y-36	Mutual or Cooperative Telephone Company — IRS Section 501(c)(12)
Y-37	Mutual Ditch or Irrigation Company — IRS Section 501(c)(12)
Y-38	Mutual Insurance Company or Association Other Than Life or Marine — IRS Section 501(c)(15)
Y-39	Pleasure, Recreational or Social Club — IRS Section 501(c)(7)
Y-40	Post or Organization of War Veterans — IRS Section 501(c)(19)
Y-41	Real Estate Board — IRS Section 501(c)(6)
Y-42	Supplemental Unemployment Compensation Trust or Plan — IRS Section 501(c)(17)
Y-43	Teachers' Retirement Fund Association — IRS Section 501(c)(11)
Y-44	Veterans Association Founded Prior to 1880 — IRS Section 501(c)(23)
Y-45	Voluntary Employees Beneficiary Association — IRS Section 501(c)(9)
Z	**—NONCLASSIFIABLE — TO BE USED AS A TEMPORARY CODE UNTIL INFORMATION IS AVAILABLE TO CLASSIFY ENTITY IN ONE OF THE MAJOR GROUPS A-Y**

Source: National Center for Charitable Statistics (1986)

distinguishing between those that approximate the "maximal public ideal" and those that do not?

It would appear that classification of voluntary sector organizations can proceed on grounds that are fundamentally empirical or grounds that are fundamentally normative. The NCCS has selected a task for itself that is based on what we identify in Chapter 11 as an "objectivist" methodology: NCCS aims to analyze the knowable world by means of concepts and categorization. Gamwell, on the other hand, works from an approach that is basically "subjectivist": he seeks to identify those qualities and activities that achieve a broader moral purpose, however related to whatever kind of organizational activity.

The question then becomes one of relating the two approaches. Is it possible that those organizations that are "teleologically prior" can be identified, or is such value rather randomly distributed throughout the organizational world, dependent upon such factors as individual commitment and situational opportunity? In the unraveling of that question, I suspect, lies the development of the most fruitful understanding of the role of voluntary action in modern society.

TOWARD THEORIES OF VOLUNTARY ACTION

I introduced Part II with a disclaimer about theories of voluntary action, noting that a single unified perspective cannot be developed in a time of paradigmatic diversity and uncertainty. One person's vegetarian delight, to update an ancient truth, is not another's image of an edible meal.

The best thinking in contemporary social science continues to identify the plausibility of competing theoretical paradigms for the understanding of the workings and meanings of major institutions, as both Burrell and Morgan (1979) and Alford and Friedland (1985) have so clearly demonstrated. And our own work in the previous chapters begins to suggest configurations and patterns as these paradigms affect the study of voluntary action.

Table 1 suggests a set of parallels between the major democratic theories examined in Chapter 3, the leading problems described in Chapter 4, and the various societal maps discussed in this chapter.

TABLE 1.   SOME PARALLELS IN VOLUNTARY SECTOR STUDIES

Democratic Theories	Leading problems	Maps
Neo-corporatism	Weber	Friedman
Pluralism	Tocqueville	Kramer
Populism	Michels	
Idealism	Dewey	Gamwell
Social democracy	Marx	
	Parsons	

Table 1 also suggests a number of points of correspondence between the work we have been examining, as well as several notable gaps. We have not yet identified a map of sectoral relations that corresponds to populist theory or the Michels problem of leadership. Nor have we found a map that corresponds to the theory of social democracy and the Marx problem of addressing the questions of economic control and power. Also, standing outside of the correspondences identified is the Parsons problem, which in actuality poses a challenge to each perspective—how to interrelate the varying sectors into a societal analysis.

Let us look at these five configurations, identifying them simply by number at the outset:

1. The first pattern coheres around a neo-corporatist theory of democracy, and focuses on the predominance of the large, bureaucratic organization in modern society. Moreover, the principal force is identified as the profit-seeking enterprise, with economics identified as the major concern of human beings in society. Voluntary organizations are viewed as a particular form of enterprise from this perspective, and volunteering is perceived as a value-linked, and inexpensive, surrogate for governmental action and responsibility.

2. The second pattern centers on the pluralist theory of democracy and places its central attention on the roles of interacting associations in society. The principal force in this conception is the concert of institutional actors, with each of the three sectors providing important parts in the symphony of the effective partnership.

3. The third configuration gives center stage to the citizen in struggle against the mega-institutions of corporate and governmental life. The drama here is one of confrontation against institutional injustice, with one part of the voluntary sector, that of independent citizen action, providing the leading role, and all other cast as "heavies."

4. The fourth pattern stresses the gains from a full and reasoned dialogue among citizens and leaders of the various societal organizations. Active citizen participation is given a central role, and distinctions are drawn between forms of action on the basis of their contribution to the goals of full democracy.

5. The fifth pattern places its emphasis on the reorganization of relations of power and economic control in society. Central is the reduction of the role of private ownership in corporate organization and political life. The voluntary sector is provided only an ancillary role in this conception, although various politically related voluntary organizations are seen to be central to the process of assuring productive social change.

The five patterns may be contrasted in a variety of ways. The role of the voluntary sector, to take one comparison, is strikingly less significant in models 1 and 5 than in the others. Model 1 is essentially an economic construction, and model 5 is primarily political; neither provides much of a role for either a voluntary sector or for voluntary action itself.

A second comparison finds models 3 and 4 emerging distinctly from the others: they involve a conception of voluntary action that allows it to reside in any institutional context, and not just in the "voluntary" sector. Indeed, of the five models, only the second posits an extensive sectoral contribution for voluntary action.

FIGURE 5: FIVE MODELS OF VOLUNTARY ACTION

Essentially derivative models	**Essentially sectoral models**	**Essentially action models**
1) Neo-Corporatist (essentially economic)	2) Pluralist (essentially organizational)	3) Populist (essentially direct action)
5) Social Democratic (essentially political)		4) Idealist (essentially informed action)

In a curious way, then, models 1 and 5 appear as mirror images of each other. Each finds one of the three sectors as the source of productive social action, and neither sees voluntary action as terribly significant. Of the three other models, one posits a three-sector partnership, and the other two seek to identify a pervasive contribution of voluntary action to all major forms of institutional action.

These distinctions now allow the assertion that societal maps pertaining to voluntary action fall into two major categories: on the one hand are the three-sector maps, each of which posits a particular relationship of dominance and significance among the sectors. On the other hand are the maps that accord primary significance to voluntary action rather than institutional structure as a principle of social action. The three-sector maps appear to be in closer accord with conventional images of voluntary action, both popular and scholarly. In this age of the organization, the tendency to view social reality in terms of the actions of concrete organizations is pronounced. And the division of the institutional world into economic, governmental, voluntary, and household seems both sensible and self-evident. This perception is surely further undergirded by the predominance of the pluralist paradigm in American academia, and the very division of the disciplines of the social sciences—one for the economy, one for government, and the interdisciplinary fields of voluntary action research and consumer economics for the others.

It is the alternative map, however, that we have seen recommended by Gamwell (1984). Here the central focus is not the institution, but rather the significance of the individual act. Volunteering and voluntary action, from this perspective, are forms of human action accorded a special level of meaning and significance in human affairs. Freed from the dominance of motives of profit or coercion, they offer individuals the chance to act in a truly self-determining and freely chosen manner: the worker to choose to put that extra something into the task to assure the quality of the product; the political leader to choose to make an extra effort to empathize with and speak for those not as privileged as himself or herself; the citizen to choose to declare in public media a deeply held opinion on a matter of local or global concern.

In this view, volunteering is a quality of participation, which at any time and in any institution empowers the individual and enriches the organizational setting in which that individual is sited. It may inform an effort to introduce workers' participation in (or control of) the corporate life of a company. It may inform the citizen's concern with the honesty and effectiveness of local government. It may inform the corporate leader's awareness that the rush toward international tension and war must be reversed if anything is to remain to be bought or sold.

Whatever its particular form and manifestation, it is a distinctive kind of human action, recognized by the clarity that surrounds its emergence. Trudy Heller (1986) has written of such moments as they suddenly appear in the most ordinary transactions of everyday business: "The dramatic quality of these meetings comes . . . not from any momentous decisions or action that turned the tide of the project. Rather it emerges from the completeness and richness with which the emotional life of the project was enacted and expressed" (p. 15).

Such voluntary action is a critical aspect of the behavior of the person who is genuinely alive. It may thus be seen as the hallmark of both the authentic person and the active society, as no mere appendage to the business of life, but rather as its very core.

SUMMING UP: A MAP OF VOLUNTARISM FOR OUR TIMES

The time has come for me to draw my own map, and to present my position regarding the choices drawn in the literature for voluntary action and its role in modern society. Thus far in this chapter we have seen a plethora of maps drawn and presented, conforming to the five-fold distinction between the democratic theories drawn in Chapter 3. That is, maps have taken on the distinctive cast of one of the following modes: neo-corporatist, pluralist, populist, idealist, or social democratic.

The work reviewed thus far in this chapter suggests that a somewhat different, though not unrelated, approach might also be fruitful. The area to be mapped is that of the voluntary structures of the quintessential Western society in relation to other major institutional structures. Perhaps it will be necessary to draw several different kinds of maps to understand fully the lay of the land. Natural scientists, after all, draw maps that are primarily topographic, primarily tectonic, or primarily meteorological. Social scientists may be advised to follow similar lines in their efforts.

A topographic map, analogous to the familiar map of land and ocean, rivers and nations, mountains and plains, places its central focus on boundaries. It is the size and location of the various countries that particularly concerns the readers of such maps, and these are the kinds of depictions that have been drawn along the lines of the two- and three-sector maps reviewed in this chapter. Here are the major institutions and their subcomponents, say Sumariwalla, Friedman, Dewey, and Kramer. Focus in more carefully on one sector or another and you will find some important distinctions to be drawn. And, adds the NCCS, look more carefully at the nations and you will see them composed of states and counties, subdivided into various comprehensible categories. This map is essentially a snapshot, a static portrait of one moment in societal time.

A second type of map, the meteorological, takes its particular interest in the climate and weather that characterize a particular area. Its social science analogy, perhaps a bit farfetched and certainly not without controversy, may be seen in the value-driven approaches of Robert Bellah and his associates (1985). Values move in determinable if not fully predictable patterns from coast to coast, or through the heartland. Like the "seasons" of life, they touch us all in recurring waves (some would say cycles) of fad and fashion. The force of changing values may not be great, but the cycles of change are not trivial.

A tectonic map, on the other hand, seeks to understand the forces that underlie the past, present, and future of the geography. Which underlying plates are moving in which directions? Which mountains will someday be sea floor? Where will the next range rise? Where will the new coastline be

located? Such maps, cast in terms of millions of years by geologists, are analogous to those drawn by social scientists in their efforts to comprehend the
vastly more rapid movements of societal change. Thus Weber identifies the
advance of bureaucratization in the third sector and elsewhere; Michels
notes the power of elite control of associations; Tocqueville charts the rise
of mass democracy; Marx seeks to chart the fundamental economic forces
that condition the responses of other major institutions; and Parsons identifies the interpenetration of institutions in modern society. In the maps
reviewed in this chapter, Kramer comes closest to adding a tectonic dimension to his three-sector map, but considerable work remains in understanding this aspect of voluntary action. An attempt to advance this work is a
major goal of the chapters in Part III of the present volume.

   In thinking about the three levels of societal reality, it should be remembered that it is individuals who act in society. As Giddens (1984) puts it,
individuals act with "agency"—motivation and capacity—as they perform
the acts that are the basis of social reality (p. 9). These acts are a basic part of
the "dual structuration" of society (again to use Giddens's term) in which
"underlying codes have to be inferred from surface manifestations" (p. 16).
The argument of this chapter is that those underlying codes come in three
forms, on the three levels already identified.

   I present, then, the outlines of a comprehensive map of voluntary action
in contemporary Western society. It is a map of three dimensions: surface,
atmosphere, and substructure. It begins with the identification of topography, and moves to its underlying tectonics, and adds on the crucial atmos-
pheric dimension. It is represented in a single conception in Figure 6.

   If we are to understand the role of voluntary action in contemporary
society, it will be by understanding its topographic, meteorological, and
tectonic structures and significance. The chapters in Part III develop and
elaborate these maps as they consider a number of prominent issues in the
voluntary sector.

FIGURE 6: A SCHEMATIC REPRESENTATION OF A COMPREHENSIVE MAP OF VOLUNTARISM IN CONTEMPORARY SOCIETY

I. TOPOGRAPHICAL STRUCTURE: THE MAJOR SECTORS
   A. Governmental

   B. Business

   C. Voluntary

      1. Public-regarding or charitable associations

         a. Nonreligious charitable service associations*
            1. Education and research
            2. Arts and culture
            3. Civic and social action
            4. Health service
            5. Human service
         b. Religious organizations
         c. Philanthropic and fundraising institutions

      2. Membership benefit associations

         a. Trade associations and unions
         b. Other private-interest associations
         c. Self-help groups
         d. Clubs
         e. All other nonpublic interest associations

   D. Household or Informal Sector**

II. METEOROLOGICAL FORCES AFFECTING THE CLIMATE OF VOLUNTARY ACTION

   A. Democratic values (Tocqueville)
   B. The spectre of privatism (Bellah)
   C. Cultural influences engendered by associational life itself (Durkheim)

III. TECTONIC FORCES AFFECTING THE STRUCTURE OF VOLUNTARY ACTION

   A. Bureaucratization (Weber)
   B. Mass democratization (Tocqueville)
   C. Power and oligarchical control (Michels)
   D. Economic concentration (Marx)
   E. The interpenetration of sectors (Parsons)

---

* See the National Center for Charitable Statistics schema (1986) for a fuller detail of these associational types.
** See Chapters 7 and 8 for a discussion of this fourth sector in contemporary society.

PART III

The Social Economy:
The Blurring of Sectoral
Boundaries

Introduction

Voluntary action, it should now be apparent, may be perceived appropriately from either of two basic points of view. On the one hand, it may be seen as the output of human organizations that are not directed primarily by the quest for monetary gain or conformance to legal mandate. And, on the other, it may be seen as individual or group activity not motivated primarily by biological imperative, economic gain, or authority and coercion.

The first point of view leads to a focus on institutional patterns within society, and particularly to the activity of nonprofit or citizens' organizations, structures that are central to the third, voluntary, or nonprofit sector. The second point of view directs attention to individual and group behavior, whatever its institutional context, which is informed by voluntary principles of meaning and commitment.

The distinction is fundamentally the one drawn in Chapter 1 between "voluntary association" and "volunteering." The voluntary association is organized, often under governmentally sanctioned charter, to achieve purposes deemed to be of public purpose. Or it is maintained, by the determination of its members and leaders, toward the achievement of such a purpose. Volunteering, on the other hand, is the commitment of individuals and groups to actions "directed at the long-range betterment of society and the general welfare" (Smith et al., 1972, p. 167).

In Chapter 1 a number of themes were identified from American rhetoric and letters that spoke of the positive contributions of volunteerism to American life. These themes are almost entirely cast in the language of the second perspective here under review—the perspective of individual and group volunteering. Whether perceived as a "natural" act of virtue, a source of community, an antidote to loneliness, a building block of democracy, or an efficacious method of problem resolution—it is the act of volunteering that is primarily valued in this tradition, and not the fact that the volunteering is organized within a certified voluntary association.

Similarly, the democratic themes identified in Chapter 3, and further analyzed in Chapter 5, are divisible into those that focus primarily on the principle of association and those whose central attention is on the quality of participation, whatever the organizational context. Neo-corporatism, pluralism, and social democracy take structured voluntarism most seriously; populist and idealist theories of democracy, on the other hand, place their central attention on the voluntary action of individuals and groups.

These organizing themes of democratic theory reflect as well the leading problems raised by the theorists whose work was reviewed in Chapter 4. The Weber, Tocqueville, Marx, and Parsons problems essentially focus on questions of structure, while the Michels problem centers on the process of individual and group participation in contemporary society.

These two impressions of voluntarism surely overlap each other, but are also distinct in their focus and emphasis. If the focus taken is on the voluntary association as organization, one succumbs to a state-certified definition of "nonprofit," and admits to analysis (and possible celebration) a wide range of organizations whose actual purposes are diverse and that are significant sources of paid employment. On the other hand, if the central focus is granted to voluntary action itself, the simplicity of the three-sector model is lost, and one runs the risk of becoming lost in a forest of individual acts which, however significant, are difficult to account for in their overall societal impact.

To be sure, a comprehensive model of social action would allow us to comprehend both every significant act of volunteering and the impact of each organization within the third sector. The achievement of a truly "synanthrometric" theory, as developed in outline by Smith (1980), would achieve this goal. Until such theory is implemented by social scientists, however, it will remain necessary to achieve perspective by choosing among competing perspectives or by developing hybrid perspectives to carry us to the desired point of analysis.

It is my argument that topography alone will not suffice if we are to understand the full significance of voluntary action. Volunteerism is itself a pervasive force for action, whatever its institutional context. And deep structural forces also affect and channel voluntary action, often providing it with the opportunity to make a difference in society. The chapters in Part III seek to show the way voluntary action fits in the contemporary "social economy" and how we can extend ourselves beyond the limits of an essentially topographical approach to the subject.

6

Toward a New Understanding

We can . . . describe (the economy) as a network of partnerships, corporations, unions, trade federations, cooperatives, and consumer organizations managed by human beings.

—Severyn Bruyn, *The Social Economy* (1977: xii)

INTRODUCTION

Important questions about voluntary action remain to be considered. How does thinking about voluntary action on the levels of topography, climate, and tectonics expand our understanding of it? How does its collective organization as independent relate to other major institutions? And how is voluntary action appropriately evaluated and judged for its value or contribution to society?

Questions of this sort require for clarification a solid theoretical base on which to stand. The shifting sands of contemporary ideologies offer neither sufficient firmness nor definition. And the mercurial patterns of financial support, whether philanthropic or grants-based, also inhibit the development of broad-based vision.

It is necessary, as sociologists of knowledge warn us, to be aware of the pitfalls of seeking that single best ("most objective") place to stand. In this modern age of public relations and media intrusiveness, we may all be, to some degree at least, the bearers, advertently or not, of some ideology or other. Perhaps the best we can do is to become aware of this baggage as necessary to our journey through life.

But if pure objectivity is elusive, and I believe it is, our sails need not be filled only by the prevailing ideological winds. We have resources to the task, and excellent ones, in the rich traditions of political and social theory probed in the previous chapters. Continuing to apply them to our study, we approach a perspective on individual voluntarism and the workings of voluntary associations.

JOHN DEWEY AND VOLUNTARISM:
THE BLENDING OF PUBLIC AND PRIVATE

If social science requires a point of departure to understand the nature of its primary institutions, I shall select as mine (acknowledging the inevitable arbitrariness involved), the authority of John Dewey. I make reference to his seminal study of institutional interrelations, *The Public and Its Problems,* written in 1927.

In his study, Dewey sought to make as clearly as he could the distinction between what is "public" and what is "private." He began by describing a conversation between two individuals, a transaction apparently private rather than public. But the distinction depends upon the consequences of the conversation, Dewey notes: "If it is found that the consequences of the conversation extend beyond the two directly concerned, that they affect the welfare of many others, the act acquires a public capacity, whether the conversation be carried on by a king and his prime minister . . . or by merchants planning to monopolize a market" (p. 13). The distinction between public and private, Dewey concludes, is quite distinct from that between the individual and the social. What makes an act public is that it has consequences "which are so important as to need control, whether by inhibition or by promotion" (p. 15).

Dewey's approach to the problem may be contrasted to the more conventional approach presented by Levitt (1973). If we follow Dewey, we may conclude that, while it is acceptable to speak of corporations or voluntary associations as "private" (i.e., not governmentally owned), it would be misleading to conclude that all acts of such private bodies are themselves private in their consequences. Such private sector activity may involve, as William Goldsmith and Harvey Jacobs have noted (1982), such questions as: "What shall be produced, and where? What shall be invested, and where? How shall work places be organized? How much shall workers be paid? Who shall get to work?" (p. 64).

Such questions have obviously become public issues in this age of economic anxiety; presidential campaigns are run on them, they are the stuff of our daily headlines, and they are left by almost no political grouping to the untrammeled workings of what economists formerly called, with a certain quaintness, "the private marketplace."

Relationships between governmental, corporate, and voluntary structures come to take a lively and dynamic appearance if the Deweyan view is accepted, and we begin to look at not only the public consequences of economic behavior but also at the social context of economic and political organization. Bruce Smith (1975) has referred to this welter of interrelations as the "new political economy," intending thereby to "convey the meaning of the large, and growing, share of the public's business that is conducted outside of the regular departments and ministries of government" (p. ix).

"So great is the interpenetration between the 'public' and 'private' sectors," Smith continues, "that this basic distinction—on which the political rhetoric and dialogue of modern times has rested—has ceased to be an operational way of understanding reality."

Applying the same line of argument to the relationship between voluntary organizations and government, Stuart Langton (1983) describes the closeness of this relationship: "In reality, the voluntary sector is not an independent sector, but an interdependent sector. Its fortunes are very much caught up in decisions made in Washington and in state capitols, as well as in corporate board rooms" (p. 19). Writing along similar lines, Waldemar Nielsen (1979) notes in chapter after chapter of his major policy study of American voluntarism, *The Endangered Sector,* how state and voluntary institutions have worked in tandem to meet societal needs for education, health care, science, and culture.

Notre Dame economists Charles Wilber and Kenneth Jameson (1981) apply the concept of "mediating institutions," as developed by a study group at the American Enterprise Institute (cf. Berger and Neuhaus, 1977), to the development of a theory of the new societal realities:

> Our modern political philosophies—liberalism, conservatism, socialism—have failed precisely because they have not understood the importance of mediating institutions. Liberalism has constantly turned to the state for solutions to social problems while conservatism sought the same in the corporate sector. Neither recognized the destructiveness to the social fabric caused by reliance on mega-institutions. Socialism suffers from this same myopia. Even though it places its faith in renewed community, it fails to see that socialist mega-institutions are just as destructive as capitalist ones (p. 28).

A central proposition regarding societal change is then developed by Wilber and Jameson (1981): "Choices made at the national level cannot be relied upon as the most effective manner of working toward revitalization of the U.S. economy. They will [only] create more mega-institutions" (p. 28).

There are several important implications in the Dewey–Wilber–Jameson position. First, the distinction between the public and the private sectors becomes far more complex than it initially seems. As the line between public and private blurs, the voluntary sector takes on startlingly new roles and responsibilities. Viewed as the locus of mediating structures, the voluntary expands to the very heart of governmental and corporate systems, to the core of the political economy. No longer simply the residual sector, voluntary action as mediating structure is a central focus in the life of society. The sector is no longer defined simply as residual, in negatives such as nongovernmental or not-for-profit.

Bellah and Sullivan (1981) have developed this argument by pointing to the need to develop mediating institutions within state and corporation, as well as in the voluntary sector itself:

> To view economic institutions as "private" made sense when most Americans spent their lives on family farms or in family firms. But today, when most American men and a rapidly increasing proportion of American women spend much of their lives in large economic structures that are for most purposes "public" except that the profits they make go to an impersonal collection of institutional and individual "private" stockholders, it becomes imperative to bring the forms of citizenship and of civic association more centrally into the economic sphere (p. 46).

Bellah and Sullivan link in their assertion three concepts that are central to the argument of this chapter: the public, the private, and mediating institutions. Their contention that mediating structures are important in the corporation and the state, as well as in the voluntary sector, echoes an approach to the study of voluntarism that can issue only from a consideration of its role in a broader political economy.

VOLUNTARY ASSOCIATIONS IN THE POLITICAL ECONOMY

A group of distinguished political theorists, writing in the NOMOS XI yearbook of the American Society for Political and Legal Philosophy (Pennock and Chapman, 1969), directly address how voluntary associations relate to other institutional structures in the contemporary political economy. From this work, I have identified seven major propositions that are useful in developing the perspective of voluntary sector relations as spanning and mediating all three major institutional sectors in modern society:

1. *All associations are in part voluntary in aim and principle.* This point is clearly established by Robert MacIver in his classic work, *Society* (1937), with its consideration of governments and corporations as associations. More recently, Fuller (1969) has argued that nearly all human associations contain within themselves two polar principles—that of "shared commitment" and that of "legal principle" (p. 12). It is the idea of shared commitment, freely given, that is central to the concept of voluntarism. And it is Fuller's point that such commitment is often found to some degree in both governmental and business activity, and not just in its most prevalent locus, the voluntary sector.

2. *Voluntary associations (those in which the principle of shared commitment predominates) may be either productive or destructive of democratic values and societal stability.* Rousseau warned of the dangers of "party, faction, and cabal" (quoted in Goldschmidt,

1969, p. 122). James Madison wrote of the "dangerous vice" of "faction"; the U.S. Constitution "contains no explicit guarantee of the right to form associations" (Fuller, 1969, pp. 12–13). Jouvenal argues (in Chapman's words [1969]) that "voluntary associations are not only agencies of defense and integration but also, and perhaps more importantly, demolition teams wreaking revolutionary reorganizations" (p. 102).

3. *Associational development involves a process of change, typically in the direction of Michels's "iron law of oligarchy."* As Fuller (1969) puts it: "When an association is first brought into being the principle of shared commitment will tend to be explicit and dominant. . . . In the normal course of its development an association tends to move toward dominance by the legal principle" (pp. 12, 13). Thus is seen a trend toward formalization and bureaucratization.

4. *Evaluation of voluntary associations is importantly affected by methodological proclivities, particularly the selection of either an individualistic or a holistic orientation.* McBride (1969) argues that the most fundamental reason to regard "voluntary association as so worthwhile . . . depends on a view of the individual as the focal-point of social values" (p. 229). And Boonin (1969) urges a middle position, which he calls "persons-in-relation," as best suited to the values of voluntarism (p. 82).

5. *The roles of voluntary associations become complex and labyrinthine as a society moves toward a "managed" or "managerial" form.* Lakoff (1969) and McBride (1969) note the increasing prevalence of executive domination in political and executive life. McBride "sees on many sides a growing advocacy of the principles of elitism and bureaucracy, together with growing resignation, willingly abetted by the elites, to this tendency on the part of large segments of the population" (p. 226).

6. *Careful attention needs to be paid to the role of the corporation as it relates to voluntary action.* As Miller notes (1969), not only did the corporation historically emerge defined as a voluntary association, but it still retains the constitutional status of a voluntary association (or "social group") (pp. 234–238). Miller's reasoning merits careful attention:

> There is no such thing as *the* corporation or *the* voluntary association. The convenient fiction of calling corporations persons in law should not be taken to hide the reality that they are collectives, federations of interest grouped together under a concept of cooperation, albeit often antagonistic cooperation (p. 241).

The corporation (is) perhaps the most important of the "voluntary," "private" associations within the American polity. That they are neither voluntary nor private is a second conclusion that emerges from this preliminary excursion into the constitutional position of the corporation (p. 258).

7. *U.S. society is well on its way to a corporative form.* As Miller (1969) puts it: "The corporate state, American style, is in process of being created. Best seen in these corporations that make up the 'military-industrial-scientific complex' (the power of which worried President Eisenhower) but also exemplified in the other super-corporations within the government–business 'partnership,' this is a new form of social order that demands systematic and comprehensive analysis. It has the most portentous (*and* actual) consequences for Americans and the nature of American constitutionalism" (p. 258).

These propositions are far-reaching. They suggest a close interpenetration of the voluntary sector with both government and corporations—that is, they portend a view of the voluntary sector as existing in the political economy of society. They challenge practitioners of voluntary action to accept a "pro-active" rather than a residual societal role. And they suggest that the building of effective interinstitutional partnerships will not be a simple or painless task.

The propositions are also controversial. Not everyone would agree with either the statements or the uses to which they might be put. The failure of consensus, or to put it more positively, the presence of pluralism, suggests that we need to pursue vigorously the search for theoretical positions from which to analyze and evaluate the role of the third sector in society. The next section considers a set of important social science theories that have emerged in recent years, centered on the interrelationships of society, polity, and economy.

VOLUNTARISM AND THE SOCIAL ECONOMY

The generation of theories of voluntary action has been most lively and productive in recent years in the "policy sciences," including the multidisciplinary fields of public policy, nonprofit law, and public economics. Researchers in these fields are tempted to stray from the comfortable systems of their particular disciplines into the real world of multifold problems and interdisciplinary solutions. And some interesting answers to long-stated questions are beginning to emerge from their work.

Since the student of public policy seeks to comprehend the full process by which policy is conceived, developed, and implemented, it is not surprising that voluntary activities figure in the major theories in the field. In this section, leading statements of such scholars are reviewed. These individuals come from a variety of disciplines of origin: Kenneth Boulding, Mancur Olson, and Burton Weisbrod from Economics, Amitai Etzioni and Severyn Bruyn from Sociology, Henry Hansmann from Law, and Lester Salamon from Political Science. But their work is unified by a concern to examine the joint workings of the three sectors in the generation and sustenance of policy and practice.

Kenneth Boulding and Amitai Etzioni are the dominant figures in the development of multisectorial policy study. Both base their work on a recognition that all societal organizations rest on a basis variously composed of three primordial forces. Etzioni (1968) speaks of these forces in terms of "compliance structures," or patterns of relations between leaders and followers. They are identified as normative (or consensual), coercive, and utilitarian (p. 364). Boulding (1973) is more graphic in his portrayal, imaging the forces as a "social triangle" whose points are love, threat, and exchange (p. 107). Both theorists agree that these forces roughly correspond to the bases for major societal institutions, government monopolizing (but not entirely) threat and coercion, the economy centrally involving utilitarian exchange, and the voluntary sector (along with the family, church, and school) involving normative relations and love as basic forces.

Boulding sets his analysis in the context of developing the concept of the "grants economy," an idea he suggests as novel to those economists inclined to view the whole world solely in terms of utilitarian exchange. He reminds his colleagues that between one-fifth and one-half of the U.S. economy is organized in terms of "one-way transfers" (p. 1). These gifts and tributes, or grants, do not involve the purchase of a product or service, and thus they confound the economists' world view that everything of value is bought and sold.

In the grants economy, voluntary service is a prominent form of "labor grant." Boulding notes that such activity borders on the realm of leisure, and often overlaps it. Three principal motivations are identified: personal satisfaction in performing the activity, benevolence toward the recipient of the service, and the perceived utility (or importance) of the activity. "There will be more volunteer labor, therefore, the more pleasurable the activity is in itself, the more it is perceived as being effective in increasing the welfare of others, the greater the rate of benevolence, and the less the value of the alternative uses of time" (Boulding, 1973, p. 31).

Etzioni's major theoretical statement is his massive *The Active Society* (1968), which seeks to present an integrated social and political theory. Interestingly, Etzioni has turned his prolific career toward more sharply policy-related work since this volume, but the base he developed in his early work clearly shows the central role voluntary action can be seen to play in modern society.

Etzioni struggles with the role of voluntary (as free-willed) activity in society, and like many sociologists before him, concludes that the concept can be accepted in a limited form. Developing a theory of action that involves both voluntarism and collectivism, he concludes his book with an examination of personal, group, and societal strategies that might create the desired end of the "active society."

Crucial to this process is the development of "projects," or worthy and concentrated programs of action.* Such projects allow persons to join together to transcend the limits of simply accepting things and institutions as they are. As Etzioni (1968) puts it, pithily: "Man is, thus, not a thing but an action" (p. 648). And joined together with others, men and women may build collective projects that transcend their individual creations:

> Collectivization provides a basis for mobilization because it frees the participants from at least part of the guilt they experience in taking an "anti-social" step, releases energies spent in self-defense, allows for more rational conduct, and serves as a basis for building counter-symbols and ideals as well as primary relations to satisfy the members' needs for recognition and affection—without their having to conform to the societal norms (Etzioni, 1968, p. 649).

To Etzioni, then, the crucial contribution of voluntary activity to public policy involves its mobilization of individuals to creative acts of societal reconstruction. Such creativity can only occur on the margins of the utilitarian and coercive institutions of society; it is centrally the province of normative activities and organizations. Ultimately, it involves the destruction of the "inauthentic society" and the creation of an active one (Etzioni, 1968, p. 645).

Severyn Bruyn (1977) presents a theory of the "social economy" that suggests that the basis exists to "activate" both economy and government (p. xii). In Bruyn's view, the economy consists of "associations and values created by people. . . . The modern economy is then seen to be socially designed." Bruyn (1977) distinguishes between two forms of economic organization, the manifest economy and the latent economy. The former refers to conventional economic structures; the latter pertains "to those forms of social organization that are ancillary to this manifest economic system and yet where economic activity remains significant and essential for survival. This includes churches, schools, voluntary associations, and the government" (p. 232). Use of this distinction leads him to reject the "three-sector" model because of the blurring of so many lines between business,

---

*On projects, see also Chapter 3, and Raskin (1971).

government, and voluntary organizations. Many voluntary organizations, he argues, such as trade unions, cooperative federations, and business associations, cannot be distinguished from the business sector. Business itself adopts social purposes as part of its agenda. And national associations take on a public character "because of their impact on so many people outside their own membership" (Bruyn, 1977, p. 232).

The term "social economy," while still an unusual one in U.S. scholarship, entered the French social science lexicon with increased frequency in the 1980s. Its prominence was highlighted by the appearance of a journal (*Revue de l'Economie Sociale*), published by a major mutual-benefit association, and the publication in 1986 of a major study by economist Thierry Jeantet translatable as *The Modernization of France by the Social Economy*. Jeantet's work expanded upon themes developed a decade earlier in the United States by Bruyn, and mapped a social economy closely linked to four other major sectors of French society. These sectors, 1) the public, 2) the private, 3) the community-based, and 4) the trade-union, are seen to be closely linked by four major institutional components of the social economy: 1) associations, 2) mutual-aid societies, 3) cooperatives, and 4) informal groups.

Six major principles of action are seen by Jeantet to characterize the social economy: 1) their associations are freely formed and entered into, 2) their administration is democratic in structure and process, 3) they do not allow their members to accumulate individual profits, 4) they maintain both internal and external solidarity, 5) they provide services and products of high quality, and 6) they contribute to the enhancement of the individual through participation in their activities.

Like Bruyn, Jeantet (1986) sees the social economy as an embodiment of principles as well as a set of societal institutions: "The Social Economy should not be envisaged as a separate sector or as a result of a process of subtraction from the two other sectors" (p. 99). Further, "It doesn't obey the rules set by the other sectors, but it is obliged to live in close relation to them. The Social Economy should not be seen as the Economy plus the Social, but rather as the Economy with the Social, the one combining reciprocally with the other. . . . It isn't properly measured the way one measures capitalism, in terms of salaries, revenues, etc., but its outputs integrate social results with indirect economic gains, for example the number of handicapped persons cared for well at home and not in hospitals, the degree of solidarity between persons of different age groups in a neighborhood. . . . The Social Economy is best understood in terms of results that add considerably to what traditional economics does not know how to or want to measure" (Jeantet, 1986, p. 78, translated by author).

The work of Boulding, Etzioni, Bruyn, and Jeantet shares a common perspective with the central issue of this book: it suggests that the distinctions between the three major sectors of society are sufficiently blurred that we need new ways of conceiving of these sectors and their interrelations. The prominent theories of three other policy scientists, on the other hand, tend to remain more conventionally within the bounds of disciplinary and sectoral structure.

Economists Mancur Olson and Burton Weisbrod and lawyer Henry Hansmann each present perspectives on the voluntary sector that tend to emphasize the limitations of that sector. Olson, in developing *The Logic of Collective Action* (1965), essentially seeks to explain the impossibility of voluntary action from an economist's point of view. The problem that concerns him most centrally in this work is that of the "free rider," the individual member of a large organization working for a common set of goals. The individual can drop out of such an organization and never be missed: therefore it is not economically "rational" for him or her to retain membership in the organization. By the terms of economic theory, if each member were to behave according to this rational calculus, then there would be nothing in society but small groups in which the effect of each member would be perceived. Imagine—no organizations sustained by direct mail support, no great foundations, no United Way organizations!

Olson confronts the age-old dilemma of economists: how to deal with a world in which the motives of people far transcend their own calculations of self-interest? Choosing between his own discipline and the development of a multidisciplinary approach, Olson (1965) chooses economics, admitting that such phenomena as philanthropy, religion, and a wide range of purpose- and solidary-based organizations exist, and are the proper study of other disciplines (pp. 160–161). In a later study, Olson (1982) confines himself to the examination of implications of the activity of the more economic-like voluntaries, and he develops a useful perspective on the power of cartels in modern society.

Another economist, Burton Weisbrod (1977), addresses the structure of the voluntary nonprofit sector in two essays published in his book by that title. Weisbrod's theory resembles Olson's in three main respects: first, it is centered on the provision of collective goods (desired products that all need or want, but would not or cannot purchase each time that they are needed —such as clear air or pleasant highway vistas); second, it deals only with a limited range of voluntary organizations; and third, it takes as a central concern the delimitation of the role of the voluntary sector.

In Weisbrod's view, what most centrally distinguishes these voluntary service-providing organizations from governmental organizations is their ability to provide collective goods for segments of the population. Voluntary organizations are seen as mini-governments possessed of "coercive and compulsive powers" (Weisbrod, 1977, p. 65). The penalties they apply are not the coercive ones of fines and imprisonment, but the social sanctions of pressure and opinion. The difference in this pressure is seen to be one of "degree, not of kind." Added to these quasi-coercive forces are other motives, which approximate economic gains: the satisfaction of giving to a good cause, the receipt of a tangible gift in return for a contribution, and (although Weisbrod does not mention it) the provision of a tax refund of a significant proportion of the donation.

As Weisbrod's theory develops, it increasingly comes to resemble the broader efforts of Boulding and Bruyn rather than the narrower discipline-based hypotheses of Olson. But it remains applicable to only one form of voluntary organization: the nonprofit corporation that provides goods desired by a segment of the population that each does not wish to, or cannot, purchase individually.

Law professor Henry Hansmann (1980) focuses on his own discipline in essaying another theoretical effort to comprehend the essence of the voluntary sector. To Hansmann, the crucial concept is "contract failure," and the crucial role of the voluntary organization is the assurance to the consumer of its services that the services meet quality standards. From this "consumer protection" view, the voluntary organization provides a mediating service between the buyer (the client) and the seller (the philanthropist, individual donor, or contracting government).

Political scientist Lester Salamon (1987) sees the work of Olson, Weisbrod, and Hansmann all involving a focus on institutional failure, whether governmental (Olson and Weisbrod) or contract (Hansmann). In response to these views, Salamon has begun to develop a theory of "voluntary failure," which sees governmental involvement as a response to inadequate voluntary sector organization. Essentially a Tocquevillian argument, Salamon (1987) roots his argument in the American experience with voluntarism:

> The central argument for this reformulation is that the "transaction costs" involved in mobilizing governmental responses to shortages of collective goods tend to be much higher than the costs of mobilizing voluntary action. For government to act, substantial segments of the public must be aroused, public officials must be informed, laws must be written, majorities must be assembled, and programs must be put into operation. By contrast, to generate a voluntary sector response, a handful of individuals acting on their own or with outside contributed support can suffice. It is reasonable to expect, therefore, that the private nonprofit sector will typically provide the first line of response to perceived "market failures," and that government will be called on only as the voluntary response proves insufficient. So conceived, it becomes clear that government involvement is less a substitute for, than a supplement to, private nonprofit action (p. 39).

Salamon describes four major forms of "voluntary failures," and identifies them as "philanthropic insufficiency," "philanthropic particularism," "philanthropic paternalism," and "philanthropic amateurism." The indicated role for government in his view is to support and enhance the quality of philanthropy and voluntarism: "government support to voluntary organizations, and government–nonprofit partnerships, emerge as the ideologically most palatable form that the government response to 'voluntary failure' can take" (p. 47).

Salamon's emerging theory clearly identifies a role and a structure to the voluntary sector. It does not seek to subsume the voluntary sector to government or economy, as do the theories of Hansmann, Olson, and Weisbrod. Nor does it seek to provide a single organizational theory of society, as do Boulding, Etzioni, and Bruyn. To be sure, the role posited for the voluntary sector by Salamon may be vastly overblown*: the welfare state may have long since consigned voluntary action to an ancillary role in societal affairs. But his theory does provide a clear focus on a voluntary sector, and it certainly seeks its roots in the American past, suggesting that we look carefully at the forces that have made voluntarism an important area of public concern in contemporary society.

ALBERT MEISTER AND THE TECTONICS OF VOLUNTARY ACTION

Perhaps the leading contemporary student of voluntary action to essay a tectonic analysis of points of perspective and departure is the late Swiss–French sociologist, Albert Meister. A review of his work will help clarify the meanings of voluntarism in our own, as well as the French society in which he lived, and which he analyzed in such splendid detail.

To Meister (1984), the forms and meanings of voluntary action are seen to vary directly with their societal and historical contexts. In preindustrial society, he notes, "The voluntary group does not exist, only the primary group." With modernization, voluntarism blooms in two variant forms— the liberal and the socialist. Finally, when industrialization is mature, a set of common problems develops in both capitalist and socialist societies. A similar response develops in both social forms, and individuals disengage from associations and withdraw into small groups (the family and various "nonrational" groups—religious and occult).

To Meister (1984, p. 12), effective voluntary action is a possible form of societal action that always fails to achieve its full potential. In capitalist societies (which he sees as "hard, pitiless, as much for the weak as for the unfortunate strong"), a brief period of associationism is followed by the rise of the mega-organizations. The association takes the form of a variety of immigrant and cooperative associations, but they go the way of all small organizations and come to be replaced by "giant political associations,

---

* For a dissenting position, see Gilbert (1983).

unions, social organizations, and the very large capitalist enterprises [which] set the tone everywhere." Associations find that "most of their demands are translated into law and regulations" and "find themselves less able to arouse popular participation."

Meister continues his analysis by noting that liberal capitalism increasingly "realizes, by connivance [between large enterprises] and the state, a sort of unofficial planning of economic activities" (1984, p. 18), and this informal planning process receives the approval of parties on both the left and the right. The lead agency in the process in the United States is the Department of Defense, under whose control "a sector of state capitalism has developed, controlling increasing numbers of industrial firms whose management subsidizes its most important functions."

Liberal capitalism thus becomes transformed, Meister contends, into a quasi-planned and partly state-capitalized political economy, whose "implicit value" is "social peace, channeling conflicts through institutions of dialogue and more or less imperative behavioral orientation of economic agents" (1984, p. 19). Myths of "free enterprise" or "worker's socialism" continue to be articulated, but "have lost much of their force." Societal life takes on the form of a giant and manipulative game in which the old values have withered, and no new ones save success and survival emerge to replace them: "This absence of values accounts for the extreme facility in social contacts, the growing informality of interindividual relations, and also for the cold instrumentalism of contacts (the tendencies are not contradictory). The modern individual feels at ease everywhere. Each one realizes that he is an element of the game played by others and his own game is to utilize the others for his own goals" (1984, p. 22).

A nearly identical process of state-enterprise planning, associational emasculation, and interpersonal game-playing is seen to characterize contemporary socialist societies. The modern political economy, Meister seems to be saying, comes to be characterized by the "withering away" of the association, and of associational life. Those associations that are seen to survive are those that can rally the largest number of adherents; people come to join associations not "for ideological motives but for instrumental goals." What Meister calls the "animator" (the facilitator, or even manipulator) becomes the prevailing leadership style of associations, while the "militant" (or organizer) is rendered redundant. "Animation has then largely extended its field of action. It has assumed a function of preparation for change in the service of those who orient it and plan it. The weakness of the militant movements has singularly facilitated this new role of animation and it can be asked if our epoch is not one of the beginning of the reign of the animators" (1984, p. 137).

Within associations, then, the "weak hold of ideologies tends to reduce the number of militants and responsible volunteers: the number of permanent functionaries paid by the association increases and communication between directors and members no longer rests on personal contacts" (1984, p. 23). Voluntary organizations become transformed into nonprofit corporations, and they become fully bureaucratized. To be sure, the "propaganda the association very often continues to employ" is that of the earlier era, but associations that take too seriously this rhetoric "regroup no more than the aged militants and have no hold on the young who understand neither the problems nor the vocabulary of an epoch gone by" (1984, p. 23).

Meister's analysis of the role of the voluntary association in the emerging political economy rests squarely on his belief in the intractability of the Weber problem, as described in Chapter 4. The predominance of the bureaucratic principle is compounded in his view by the failure of new values to take hold (the Tocqueville problem), the power of organizational elites to win their own games (the Michels problem), and the failure of Marxism to give birth to societies in any way superior to capitalist forms. The end result is thus neo-corporatism, with its accompanying institutionalization of stability, inequality, and societal mediocrity, in all the developed nations of the world.

The radical pessimism of Albert Meister's theory of voluntary action is not entire, as may be seen in his analysis of "new forms of association" in postindustrial society. Here Meister sketches his map of the voluntary sector, and it is a rich and useful one. First, he identifies four major categories of associations: 1) contributory participation, which consists of the participation of technocrats in the governance of the postindustrial society; 2) dependent participation, which consists of the adaptations of the members of the "zerostructure" to the limits and frustrations of their lives (under the tutelage and orchestration of trained "animators"; 3) survival participation, which consists of the segregation and benign neglect of the forgotten and the superfluous—those not even assigned the menial tasks and humble salaries of the zerostructure; and 4) contestation–participation, which includes all the options remaining for voluntary participation in society.

Meister's category of contestation–participation is diverse and multiple, including apathy (the sullen nonparticipation of the "silent" majority), violence for violence's sake (including certain forms of exercise and much of the mass media), partial contestation (like the limited dissent of the consumer movement), stoic refusal (as in the rejection of elements of the consumer society involved in the life-styles of "voluntary simplicity"), sectorial contestation (such as the civil rights movement, the women's movement, and the struggle for sexual liberation), contestation of the quality of life (as embodied in much of the environmental movement), initiation–contestation (as in the varieties of the youth movement), and communal contestation (as in the varieties of communal experimentation and living).

Meister's master map (Table 1) may be seen to encompass all the terrain surveyed by the maps presented in Chapter 5. Contributory participation includes the realms of government, corporation, and voluntary organizations aimed at professional and trade assertion. Dependent participation includes most social service associations and the realm of group life for its own enjoyment (the sector so central to Tocqueville and Kramer). And survival participation involves the regulation of disorderly behavior most generally thought to be the realm of governmental authority.

The limited realm of voluntary participation involves a broader image of the action than that provided by Gamwell's "public-regarding associations." Here the common theme is disaffection from the dominant order, and the options for expression of this disaffection are seen as wide-ranging. Clearly, Meister does not view each of these forms of action as of equal desirability or common consequence. The question he poses becomes one of "assimilation, repression, or surpassing."

TABLE 1. MEISTER'S TECTONIC MAP OF THE MODES OF PARTICIPATION

Official Participation (most of what goes on within the organizational bounds of the three sectors)	Voluntary Participation (the limited realm of human freedom and autonomy)

Contributory participation
Dependent participation
Survival participation
	Contestation–participation
	  Apathy
	  Violence for its own sake
	  Partial contestation
	  Stoic refusal
	  Sectorial contestation
	  Quality of life contestation
	  Initiation contestation
	  Communal contestation

There is a way out of the morass of technocratic gaming, Meister asserts, with all its destructiveness of human values and individual concerns. This way involves the infiltration of the technostructure by voluntary sector-led forces informed by values and committed to goals of social development. This, Meister pronounces, is the dream of "self-management" built on the "celebrated aphorism of Lenin: 'democratic socialism = information + self-management' " (1984, p. 241). The implication of this equation is that "participation in power occurs by taking power. For it is necessary to understand that there is no programmed society, but only ruling classes, programmed and programming their domination. The new character of our postindustrial societies resides in new forms, still more alienating than domination, so subtle that participation in them is already occurring and risks finding itself more and more ensnared there" (1984, p. 241).

Meister, like Gamwell, thus sees in the nurturance of voluntary action the best path toward the preservation of values and the development of meaning in modern society. It is clear in Meister's conception that the primary value of voluntarism lies in its contribution to human freedom. Indeed, the various forms of contestation–participation he identifies are seen as the only major way in which individuals can freely act, locked as they are in the confines of a bureaucratic postindustrial society. In such a dilemma, it is not the presence of a set of institutions identified as "voluntary" or "nonprofit" or belonging to the "third sector" that is crucially important; rather it is the willingness of individuals to act together, whatever their institutional setting, to assert their sense of how society should be made right. In Meister's view, the hour is late, and the prospects for positive societal development are slim. The animators and their masters are firmly established; the games they play are widely accepted; and the role of voluntary action is hedged in on every side by apathy, power, and despair.

THE ROLE OF VALUES IN VOLUNTARY ACTION

Meister's view of the contemporary social economy and the role of voluntarism within it may usefully be contrasted with those of a number of other contemporary observers, including the futurist John Naisbitt, the economist Dennis R. Young, and the sociologists of religion James R. Wood and Robert Bellah. Each seeks to comprehend the role of the voluntary in contemporary society. Each assesses the primacy of voluntarism as a principle of action against voluntarism as an institution. And each highlights aspects of the societal map drawn by Meister.

Naisbitt's work is significant in large part as a result of its extraordinary circulation and influence. A confidant of many world leaders, his phrases have appeared in Ronald Reagan's State of the Union addresses. And the sales of his 1982 effort, *Megatrends,* amount to a significant multiple of the combined figures of all others who have addressed the role of voluntarism in society. In many respects the Mr. Pangloss of his age, Naisbitt's radical optimism contrasts sharply with the generally pessimistic orientation of Albert Meister.

On one fundamental point, however, Meister and Naisbitt are in agreement. And that point involves the potential power of the voluntary principle of action to pervade all aspects of the human experience. To Naisbitt, we live on the cusp of an exciting new era of personal and societal creativity and development. In this era, individual enterprise will be liberated from the constraints of outmoded bureaucratic control. It is a time in which the megatrends of participatory democracy, decentralization, networking, and self-help will flourish—a time in which centralized hierarchial organizations and institutions will become outmoded and eventually extinct. Sleek transnational corporations and purposive local organizations will flourish; national governments, labor unions, and conventionally organized corporations will go the way of the dinosaur.

Naisbitt's catechism, drawn from the pages of local newspapers in California, Washington, Colorado, Connecticut, and Florida, may not receive high grades from social scientists for either its theory or its methodology. But his ability to turn the news of the day into a vision of a glowing future accounts for Naisbitt's success, and his identification of themes that essentially pertain to voluntary action (self-help, participation, networking) place him squarely on the side of those who see the primary importance of voluntary action in its ability to pervade all aspects of human life, whether it be the family, the state, the corporation, or the nonprofit organization itself. Naisbitt's map of the role of voluntary action in society, like those of Gamwell and Meister, places central importance on the voluntary principle, and not on the contributions of an institutionalized voluntary sector.

The focus of the studies of economist Dennis R. Young (1983) is on the qualities of leadership in contemporary institutional life. Like Meister, Young finds voluntary leadership under seige, viewing the typical nonprofit organizational leader as a beleaguered entrepreneur (an image that would please John Naisbitt). Using a case method for his study, Young identifies a range of entrepreneurial styles for organizational leadership. "Income seekers," "independents," and "architects" are most characteristic of the for-profit sector; "players" and "controllers" are best suited to the public sector. Leaders in the nonprofit arena characteristically take the forms of "believers" (Wood's ministers and Meister's militants), "conservers," "poets," "searchers," and "professionals."

Young elaborates this typology in relation to such factors as "industry screening," constituents, "venture outcomes," time constraints, and managerial behavior. Young concludes with a set of intriguing observations regarding the impact of increasing funding to nonprofit organizations, whether by a strategy of "nonprofitization" or by one of enhanced targeted funding to nonprofit organizations. Writing of the second policy, he notes: "As a consequence, the nonprofit sector will become more heterogeneous in its mix of entrepreneurial motivations. More specifically, such a policy will, like nonprofitization, induce a shift of income seekers and, perhaps, independents from the proprietary sector and a shift of power seekers from the public sector to the nonprofit sector of the industry. Unlike nonprofitization, however, a policy that targets resources to the nonprofit sector will encourage rather than discourage an influx of such types from outside the industry as well. Thus the nonprofit sector will become more heterogeneous, more responsive, and less trustworthy than it would be without such a policy, as will the industry as a whole" (1983, p. 152). Young thereby suggests that the power-seeker and the bureaucrat may come to be the dominant voluntary leader, thereby assuring the reign of the animator in the not-for-profit sector for years to come.

Young's work suggests that as "industries," the three sectors are developing organizational forms that increasingly come to resemble each other. Should power-seeking and bureaucratization prevail as styles of leadership in nonprofit organizations, as they do in so much of corporate and governmental life? Young, in a theme echoed by Ralph Kramer (1985), suggests that the fundamental contribution of voluntary action will be greatly reduced.

The work reviewed thus far in this chapter appears to suggest that the organizational context of voluntary action is of less significance than the principle of voluntary participation itself. That is, a voluntary organization may be highly bureaucratized and centrally driven by the desire to increase its ability to control resources and add to its "retained earnings" (the euphemism for "profit" in the tax-free world). In such a situation, little of any purpose or commitment to serve a charitable purpose may be evident. Are we then to conclude that the organizational form of the nonprofit organization often becomes shed, and that all organizations may at heart be fundamentally alike?

This question has been addressed by James R. Wood (1981), who seeks to discover in *Leadership in Voluntary Organizations* if the deviation of leaders from members' majority opinion always consists of the betrayal of legitimacy so vividly described in Michels's "iron law of oligarchy." Studying 58 Protestant churches and their members in Indianapolis in 1973, he analyzes the clear tendency of the ministers to take social action positions of a more liberal-activist cast than membership preferences would have dictated. Such "organizational transcendence," as Wood identifies it, is analyzed in terms of its degree of legitimacy or illegitimacy.

Wood details the ways in which ministers moved their unwilling congregations to support actions they initially found undesirable. He finds that "leaders seemed to claim legitimacy for their policies on the grounds that these actions were derived from the core values of the church." This leads him to an overarching (and Durkheimian) conclusion about leadership in voluntary organizations: such organizations in a very real sense transcend their members and their particular interests; they have a "sociological reality" of their own; and leaders, more deeply rooted in such organizations than members, can and do use that reality to effect change.

The ministers Wood studied were not pure "militants," as Meister describes them, but neither were they merely "animators" following Meister's image of the *curé* preparing "the cage in which the people live." Meister's world has no place for religions that embody Wood's "core values" of equality and justice; his view of Protestant liberalism is one of a "hard" and "pitiless" austerity. Further, Wood's image of societal fragmentation counters Meister's view of relentless centralization and bureaucratization. Thereby, Wood moves with consistency to the guarded optimism of his own conclusion: "If a society is too diverse to have a widely agreed upon set of core values, then it appears that national leaders must forge policy in cooperation with leaders of those organizations that are the repositories of the various values within the nation" (1981, p. 100).

The ability of voluntary organizations to articulate the core values of human meaning and concern is seen by Robert Bellah and his associates (1985), in their influential volume *Habits of the Heart,* as the greatest value of voluntarism. Bellah writes of the importance of the ability to articulate a "second language" that "organizes life by reference to certain ideals of character" and "commitments to institutions that are seen as embodiments of those values" (Bellah et al., 1985, p. 160). Among these ideals are courage, honor, justice, community, and human dignity.

The core problem of contemporary urban postindustrial society is found in severing the link between the articulation of the second language and the structure and actions of voluntary associations. Bellah and associates write: "Though urban Americans still get involved in an astounding variety of voluntary associations, the associational life of the modern metropolis does not generate the kinds of second languages of social responsibility and practices of commitment to the public good that we saw in the associational life of the 'strong and independent township' " (1985, p. 177). Their resolution of this dilemma lies not in recreating the voluntary sector but rather in creating a second language that can pervade all major institutions: work, family, church, government, and nonprofit alike. The hope Bellah offers resembles the concluding message of Meister, in tone if not in full content: "Perhaps the truth lies in what most of the world outside the modern West has always believed, namely that there are practices of life, good in themselves, that are inherently fulfilling" (1985, p. 295).

In short, we need to develop a society pervaded by "social economics," and such a society may well be one in which principles of voluntarism are widely practiced and voluntary associations are strong. The next chapter explores in further detail how progress toward developing that kind of social economy is faring in the prominent Western societies of the United States, Britain, and France.

7

Third Sector or Voluntary Action: The Social Economy

It begins among friends, to defend an idea, or to combat an injustice; a group of volunteers meets to prohibit a nuisance in their neighborhood or to promote a regional product.

—Bernard Kouchner, *Charité Business* (1986, p. 99)

INTRODUCTION

Voluntary action has emerged in recent years in the United States as an arena of considerable national attention. President Carter, a committed volunteer, sought to revitalize the governmental commitment to neighborhood and community volunteerism during his term in office. President Reagan attributed an even more central role to voluntarism in his statements on national redirection, establishing a prestigious Task Force on Private Sector Initiatives. No less a policy research body than the Urban Institute gives voluntarism one full chapter (out of ten) in its recent review, titled *The Reagan Record* (Palmer and Sawhill, eds., 1984).

Despite this presidential attention, the voluntary sector has experienced a dual attack on its resources in recent years. Federal dollars, which amount to some 40% of the income of nonprofit organizations, have been greatly cut since 1982, and charitable contributions have stayed below 2% of total income as a series of tax changes have reduced philanthropic incentives, particularly for persons in the highest income brackets.

Yet, as Lester Salamon (1984, p. 264) notes, "voluntary organizations continue to play a vital role in American society: they account for about five percent of the gross domestic product and about a quarter of the service employment in the nation." Virginia Hodgkinson and Murray S. Weitzman (1984, p. 1) note that when volunteer time is counted, over nine percent of the nation's employees are to be found in not-for-profit work. In economic bulk, the third sector is one-half the size of government in total employment, one-fourth its size in salaries paid, and one-half its size in earnings (when the value of volunteer time is added in).

In a policy context, Salamon (1984) has focused on the Reagan administration's initiatives to revitalize the voluntary sector while simultaneously reducing its share of federal funding. By relying "mostly on rhetoric," he asserts, the administration has put the nonprofit sector under "considerable financial strain." Salamon (1984, p. 285) concludes that the administration "may have set back its own private-sector agenda for some time to come and discredited voluntarism further as a serious policy alternative."

The potential of voluntarism has become a central focus of recent administrations. Achieving more of that potential and learning from past mistakes thus become important policy considerations. The breather offered by the "missed opportunity" (as Salamon puts it) of the Reagan voluntarism initiatives gives the chance to develop perspectives and approaches for the next time around.

High among the reasons that Reagan failed to create a successful voluntarism initiative stands his failure to comprehend the nature of what we have earlier identified as the Parsons problem (Chapter 4). More specifically, he did not perceive the implications of the interconnections between the voluntary sector and government. As the most determined antigovernment president in U.S. history, in both rhetoric and domestic practice, Reagan failed to understand the reality of what Bruce Smith (1975) has called the "new political economy," and Salamon named "third party government." As Smith puts it, "So great is the interpenetration between the 'public' and 'private' sectors, that this basic distinction—on which the political rhetoric and dialogue of modern times has rested—has ceased to be an operational way of understanding reality."

Reagan also failed to establish the connection between the individual act of the volunteer and the larger context within which political, economic, and social institutions of modern society relate to voluntary action. Thus he preached about dated conceptions of voluntarism, wholly unrelated to the workings of the contemporary society. And so his errors require both correction and redress: a major challenge to those who seek to create a humane and just social economy for the remaining years of this century and beyond.

As Reagan and his fellow Americans faced their opportunity, so did the leaders and citizens of other Western democracies. In this chapter, examination is provided of recent American, British, and French efforts to grapple with the role of voluntarism and voluntary associations. In the experimentation and travail of these three experiences may be found some clues to the eventual integration of productive voluntarism into the fabric of contemporary society.

VOLUNTARISM POLICY IN THE UNITED STATES: THE WAR BETWEEN THE SECTORS

Voluntarism and public policy have developed in a complex interdependence throughout American history, and the closeness of their connections has steadily increased over time. Nevertheless, the consequences of these closer interactions have tended toward increasing inter-sectoral conflict, and a continuing national confusion about the potential role of voluntary action in resolving social problems.

Four major areas of voluntarism policy are examined in the sections that follow: 1) the shifting of functions between government and voluntary sector, 2) tax policy, 3) other privileges of nonprofit organizations, and 4) regulation and reform.

The Shifting of Functions between Government and Voluntary Sector

A conventional hypothesis in the celebratory literature on voluntarism reviewed in Chapter 1 is that government has assumed more and more responsibility for initiatives developed in the voluntary sector, and that this relationship has been a one-way affair. Susan Greene's statement (1977) of this view is eloquent and exemplary:

> Without groups of people voluntarily banding together over principles and philosophy, our country would not have been born. Without concerned people voluntarily addressing political, social, and economic inequities, women would not have the vote, nor would orphanages, settlement houses, hospitals, fire departments, and museums have been established. The Abolition Movement was a voluntary movement. The Civil Rights Movement was born in the private sector. From the voluntary sector comes the initiative, experimentation, implementation, and proof of a concept's worth. It is then at this point that the governmental sector, and sometimes the corporate or profit-making sector, can begin to support the proven service, concept, or principle and voluntarism moves on to find other methods, in a million different areas, to improve our civilized society (p. 2).

The whole structure of the contemporary welfare state, tenuous as it often seems to be, emerged from voluntary roots. Its linchpin in the United States, the Social Security Act of 1935, established governmental programs to provide services formerly provided only by voluntary organizations. Its steady expansion through other New Deal programs, and through the Great Society programs of the 1960s and the New Federalism programs of the 1970s, moved government into greater prominence as both a developer and funder of formerly voluntary activities.

Despite this increasing governmental presence in the provision of social services, the actual relationship between government and the voluntaries had been far more complex than suggested by the "one-way" hypothesis. Voluntary organizations have frequently been identified by governmental programs to serve as the service conduits for delivery, and they have increased their size and scale in light of these funding possibilities far beyond what they might have achieved without policy support. Moreover,

the contemporary thrust to "privatize" governmental activities gives promise of reversing the tendency to move functions toward governmental
provision.

It is clear that, throughout the 1960s and 1970s, "third-party" government became a dominant principle for social service delivery. Revenue-
sharing programs expanded greatly, and the federal government assumed
the role of grants provider to many thousands of voluntary associations. As
the Filer Commission put it, government had become a "major philanthropist" (Commission on Private Philanthropy and Public Needs, 1975, ch. IV).
Nelson Rosenbaum (1981, p. 82) has described this period as one of
"increasing dependence of voluntary sector institutions upon government
financial support." Rosenbaum sees two major problems associated with
this dependence: management of associations becomes more bureaucratized in light of governmental funding requirements, and the governance of
associations becomes more distant from grass-roots sources of control and
influence.

In the 1980s, the assumption of power by a conservative Republican
administration that aimed to reduce the domestic scope of the federal government has given powerful force to the privatization tendency. Not only
did government support of nonprofits fall precipitously, but the effort to
convert "collective" goods to "toll" or "private" status proceeded at an
unprecedented pace. Proposals were made to privatize the Federal Housing
Administration, to defund Amtrak, and to move a variety of social services,
including corrections and family planning, into the hands of private agencies, federally funded or not.

Competition for the control of service areas between proprietary, governmental, and nonprofit organizations is nothing new in American life. In the
1930s, as David Morris (1982) has shown, the General Motors Corporation
succeeded in a determined campaign to replace the government provision of
rail commuter transit by systems, public and private, of bus service (which
would employ vehicles manufactured by General Motors). In our own time,
the health field has seen the precipitous demise of public hospitals, a weakening of the role of nonprofit hospitals, and the steady replacement of both
by proprietary institutions (cf. Clark, 1980 [cited in Hansmann, 1983]; Gray,
1986). We have also observed the claim by the Small Business Administration that a bias exists in public policy, such that nonprofits are favored over
proprietary enterprises.

The competition among the three sectors for control of turf, resources,
and the right to provide service may also be traced in such arenas as education (where the publics have been growing), private security (where proprietary services have been the biggest winners), waste collection and disposal
(always a multi-sectoral battleground), and the arts (where public support
has traditionally been problematic). Such competition seems endemic in our

reluctant welfare state, and there is no sign that it will abate in the years ahead. Whether the commodity is blood, low-income housing, opera, or food—there is money to be made, a public interest to be weighed, and a voluntary tradition to be assessed. There will be multiple claims, and there always have been. What is most important is that no immutable natural law is at work, and no one-way developmental processes. The policy arena is nowhere so neat— it is an endless struggle between contending concepts, claims, interests, and programs.

Tax Policy

In the persistently capitalist U.S. society, the fundamental "bottom-line" difference between nonprofit and proprietary organizations is that the former are tax-exempt, while the latter must seek to limit their tax liabilities through the policy arena. Those nonprofit organizations deemed by governmental review to serve a worthy charitable or educational purpose are excused from all taxation, whether local property taxes, state sales taxes, or federal income or excise taxes. Moreover, people who donate to the support of such tax-exempt organizations receive a "charitable deduction" for their contributions. That is, they are excused from including their donated income from the total subject to proportioned taxation.

The charitable deduction has the effect of "socializing" personal philanthropy in the United States. That is, all taxpayers provide a portion of the contribution made by any one taxpayer. An example makes this clear: under The 1986 Tax Reform Act, a family whose taxable income amounts to $100,000 per year will effectively find itself in a "33 percent " tax bracket. That is one of each three dollars earned by this family will be taken in the form of income taxes. If the family should make a donation of $1000 to any certified charitable organization, its tax liability will be reduced by $333. In other words, the family donates $1000 to the charitable organization, and its fellow citizens, through their taxes, return them $333 to use for the family's own purposes, a partial reward for its benevolence.

An alternative way of viewing the charitable transaction is to see the family's donation as being in two parts: one of $667 provided by it from its own resources, and the second of $333 provided by fellow citizens to the charity of the family's choice. Either way the outcome is the same: the philanthropists's gift has been matched, unwittingly but as a consequence of public policy and tax law, by every other taxpaying citizen.

The same process accompanies any other tax-deductible contribution of any other citizen. But the magnifying effect is less as one descends the income ladder. For the citizen in the 15% bracket, a contribution, say to the United Way, reduces tax liability by only 15 cents for each dollar contributed. Thus persons of lower means find their contributions matched to a far lesser extent than those of higher means. The contribution of the person in the 15% bracket requires fellow citizens to provide less than one-sixth of the total contribution, compared to the one-third they offer to the wealthy philanthropist.

The value of the charitable contribution is directly linked to the progressivity of the income tax system. When the marginal tax rate was pegged at its pre-1981 level of 70%, 70% of the contribution of those in that tax bracket was socialized, or paid by fellow citizens. As the marginal tax rate was reduced in the Reagan years, the direct cost of contributing rose for the contributor. In that fashion, recent tax reform may be seen to have lessened the incentive for individuals to contribute.

Considerations regarding the equity of the charitable deduction have been debated in a long and heated fashion. The Filer Commission identified two sets of challenges, "philosophical" and "pragmatic," and concluded that such challenges could be expected to be more frequent in the years ahead. And the discussions surrounding the tax law of 1986 suggest that a consensus no longer surrounds the view that charitable contributions should always be exempt from taxation. Protection of the charitable deduction itself, and assurance that it can continue to be employed by all taxpayers, regardless of income (that is, including those covered by the "standard deduction") became issues of contention during the tax bill's consideration, and non-itemizers eventually lost the deductibility of their contributions. Under the 1986 Tax Law, persons of modest means have no power to leverage the contributions of fellow citizens to the charities they choose.

Regulation and Reform; Other Privileges

A variety of policy concerns involve issues of regulation and reform, and these are directed by both voluntary and government agencies toward each other. Government agencies have as a part of their mandate the certification of nonprofit organizations as appropriate for tax deductibility, and many voluntary organizations reciprocate by playing a watchdog role toward governmental agencies.

Government oversight of voluntary organizations is a responsibility of the Internal Revenue Service on the federal level and of various law enforcement agencies on the state level. In recent years, these agencies have concerned themselves with the closer auditing of foundations (a controversial 4% "auditing tax" was applied to foundations in 1969, and later reduced to 2%), the restriction on the amount of effort a nonprofit may address to purposes of lobbying, and the assurance that foundations pay out at least 5% of their assets in donations each year.

A variety of judical decisions have also had an impact on the voluntary sector. For example, in the *Schaumburg* case, the Supreme Court ruled unconstitutional a local ordinance that limited fund-raising costs of an approved charity to 25% of total solicitations. In the *Greenburgh* case, the same court ruled that a civic association could not place unstamped communications in private postal boxes. The tax exemption of schools engaged in racial discrimination and the rights of public charities to the same lobbying privileges as business and trade associations are other issues that have concerned the Supreme Court in the 1980s.*

Within the voluntary sector itself, a wide range of self-regulatory efforts is carried out (Suhrke, 1983). Various self-study and standard-setting activities have been completed in the sector: a uniform annual reporting form, the "990," was developed jointly with the IRS and state governments; a puissant national organization, INDEPENDENT SECTOR, was developed to represent the sector; certification programs have been developed for fundraising executives; and a variety of donor and donee organizations have developed to represent their particular perspectives and needs.

From the voluntary sector side, the influencing of public policy is often a major goal. Sometimes the aim is a new piece of legislation or a redirected program; sometimes it is a judicial reinterpretation. Whatever the objective, government programs are frequently a major concern of a voluntary organization. Henton and Waldhorn (1983) identify six ways in which voluntary organizations seek to affect public policy: by influencing regulation and deregulation; by advocating tax policy changes; by seeking administrative reform; by developing collaboration with the private sector; by promoting self-help; and by engaging in public sector advocacy (pp. 167–168). These functions exist beyond the simple search for more money to provide more services. Henton and Waldhorn (1983, p. 176) contend that the search for such "basic governance reform" will advance the goals articulated by the Filer Commission of enhancing citizenship, "initiating new ideas and processes, developing public policy, overseeing government and the marketplace and bringing sectors together."

The methods used by voluntary associations to affect public policy are as diverse as the realm of voluntary organizations itself. Some organizations choose methods of direct action and citizen protest. Others prefer "suit and tie" lobbying and the activation of networks of personal influence. Choices are made of a structural focus: legislative, executive, administrative, or judicial. Over the years, a different balance is struck between service, advocacy, and facilitative roles. But the constancy of focus on public policy outcomes and processes remains a characteristic of third sector activity.

However the advocacy of particular policies or causes may be assessed, it is apparent that it forms a major portion of what remains in the American policy of effective citizen participation. Organized lobbying and advocacy is a central focus of third sector organizations, a mediating force of consider-

---

* For a fuller discussion of these issues, see Fremont-Smith (1983).

able importance in the sustenance of American democracy in an era of dwindling voting rates and a pervasive arrogance of governmental power.

A substantial focus of third sector lobbying, however, must be directed toward the protection of those limited privileges already accorded to voluntary organizations. We have already discussed the impacts of fiscal and tax policies; mention should also be made of a variety of other sectoral interests that require constant protection. The U.S. Postal Service, for example, offers reduced rates for the franking of its mail, telephone taxes are excused in nonprofit hospitals and some nonprofit educational institutions; and charitable "drawings" are exempt from the 10% federal tax on wagers (Commission on Private Philanthropy and Public Needs, 1975, p. 104). Each of these privileges is challenged from time to time, and each challenge is answered by sector-serving organizations with a wave of lobbying and the mobilization of constituents.

The various public and legislative discussions of the role of voluntary associations in public policy often evince a diversity of perspectives on voluntarism in American society. They are part of a seemingly endless set of skirmishes that characterize the boundary wars regarding American voluntarism that are the central focus of the next chapter. In a search for societal practices that might offer a way out of the morass of inter-sectoral warfare, an examination of recent events in Britain and France is offered as a source of new ideas.

VOLUNTARISM IN BRITAIN: BEYOND THE WELFARE STATE

The British experience, mother to the American, presents a case with many parallels to it. To be sure, the experience of the new American nation offered greater opportunities for a variety of post-colonial experiments in voluntarism, but the fundamental traditions of charity and poor law moved along similar lines (cf. Feagin, 1975). Images of distinctiveness between the two experiences center on the greater salience of social class in the British experience, first, and on the more extensive development of its welfare state through 1960, second. The factor of class explains the formidable British charity tradition and the relative weakness of its traditions of radical opposition; its 20th century history of welfare state development suggests a replacement of voluntary functions by a puissant state. Both factors may easily be overestimated in their differences from the American experience.

Strickler (1986) notes that: "Historically, Great Britain has exhibited a strong belief in the principles of both mutual aid and the right of association" (p. 5). Through the 19th century it was "taken for granted" by Britons that "social welfare . . . was the proper field for philanthropy and not for the State, which would intervene only where the crisis lay plainly beyond the capacity of private agencies" (Owen, 1964, p. 596). The public obligation to care for the unfortunate and needy resulted in a vast array of organizations and associations devoted to the provision of social services. Strickler (1986) cites the founding charter of the Sociable Society in 1912 as an example: "We, the members of this society, taking it into our serious consideration, that man is favored a social being . . . in continual need of mutual assistance and support; and having interwoven in our constitutions those human and sympathetic affections which we always feel at the distress of our fellow creatures . . ." (p. 5).

The vital social role of volunteer societies was manifested in the creation of the National Council of Social Service in 1919 and clearly articulated by such leading social thinkers as A.D. Lindsay and G.D.H. Cole. In 1945, four decades after the rapid development of the British welfare state, Cole introduced a volume of essays on *Voluntary Social Services*:

> It is a great mistake to suppose that as the scope of State action expands, the scope of voluntary social service necessarily contracts. Its character changes, in conformity both with changing views of the province of State action and with the growth of the spirit and substance of democracy. It transforms itself gradually from benevolence *de haut en bas* . . . into communal service, designed to widen and deepen the expression of the spirit of democratic co-operation. As long as there are rich and poor, the social services will necessarily continue in some degree to reflect inequalities of class and income. But under modern conditions there can and does enter into them much of a different and more equalitarian spirit (p. 29).

Cole believed that the interaction of the paid professional and the volunteer would have a salutary effect on the volunteer, leaving the latter "much less open to suspicion of condescendingness or patronizing than the voluntary 'lady helper.' " Indeed, the interdependence of the voluntary and public sectors had long been quietly recognized in Britain, and was clearly articulated in the celebrated Beveridge Report of 1948 and ensuing Parliamentary debate (cf. Owen, 1964, pp. 574–575). Beveridge called for the development of "fruitful cooperation between the two sectors" and he urged the State to "use where it can, without destroying their freedom and spirit, the voluntary agencies for social advance, born of social conscience and of philanthropy" (Owen, 1964, p. 574).

The British tradition of voluntarism, then, brought to the postwar years an appreciation of the role of voluntary social service and the need to protect the right of association. Voluntary agencies were seen to play an even more important role in the assurance of care to those in need.

Contemporary British Voluntarism

The driving forces behind Britain's experience with voluntarism in this century are well described by Owen (1964):

It became increasingly obvious that private charity had left the essential problems of urban-industrial life only slightly altered. Housing congestion, ignorance, unemployment, and poverty remained about what they had been. Both by its successes and its abysmal failures, philanthropy helped to reveal the outlines of the problem. . . .

The intervention of the State extended rather than reversed the long tradition of voluntary effort. In no sense a monolithic structure, the Welfare State of the 1960s depends, in an extraordinary degree, on voluntary resources, human and financial. . . . Ancient donors and pious founders, devoted evangelicals, humanitarian promoters of organizations, and the rest of the charitable host would, no doubt, be mystified by the welfare world of modern Britain. But they could hardly miss the ineffaceable stamp left on the British community by their own labors and gifts.

As the welfare state continued to grow through the 1960s and into the 1970s, new forms of voluntary action arose, among them groups perceived as the "bad and ugly" (Sills, 1980), which addressed public policy issues in a more strident and critical manner than before. Nonetheless, the Seabohm Report of 1968 recommended the use of volunteers by local governments, and the Aves Report of 1969 called for government funding of voluntary initiatives (Strickler, 1986, p. 7). The formation of the Volunteer Centre in 1974 added a second national voice for sectoral organizations to that of the National Council of Voluntary Organisations (NCVO).

The Search for Welfare Pluralism

A lively debate has been joined over the past decade in British social administration on the question of "welfare pluralism," or the proper mix of public, voluntary, informal, and proprietary provision of social services. Theoretical studies by Stephen Hatch and Roger Hadley (Hatch, 1980; Hadley and Hatch, 1981) advocated a more prominent role for voluntarism in the welfare mix, celebrating values of decentralization and local control while criticizing the bureaucratic sterility of the contemporary welfare state. Governmental reforms in social service provision were introduced pursuant to these ideas in the form of the "patch" model, involving "the deconcentration of local authority social services from their large area offices to smaller administrative areas and even neighborhoods" (Brenton, 1985, p. 119). Later studies by Hadley, Hatch and associates (cf., for example, Hadley and McGrath, 1980) examined a number of these patch reforms in detail, as did the more critical research of Beresford and Croft (1986).

Together with these forays into policy discussion and the evaluation of innovations in service delivery involving voluntary sector organizations, recent British social researchers have paid careful attention to the role of informal social activity and care-provision (cf. the work of Abrams cited by

Bulmer [1987]; the ongoing work on domestic care provision by Claire Ungerson of the University of Kent; and the detailed research on community care by Davies and Challis [1986]). A recent and careful summary of much of this experience is provided by Brenton (1985, p. 220), who concludes that the most productive voluntary sector role is a dual one, involving on the one hand the provision of services complementary to those of the state (mutual aid, self-help, community and neighborhood action, information services) and on the other the "mounting of a watchdog role over the main-line provisions of the welfare state." Brenton is dubious of "partnership" arrangements that are undertaken in times of welfare-state retrenchment. As Beresford and Croft (1986) put it from their action-research perspective:

> The irony is that while patch and welfare pluralist philosophies are framed in terms of giving a greater role to voluntary organisations and informal effort in place of statutory provision, it is the *state* which is seeking to mobilise such non-statutory and unpaid caring. Thus they can be seen as concerned not so much with a reduced role for the state, as a different kind of intervention. Instead of primarily providing services to meet our needs, the state will be involved in organising, supervising, extending and even reinterpreting our own self-help (p. 149).

The welfare pluralism debate had by the mid-1980s reached an impasse as political philosophy, but the proponents of the concept had been influential in introducing the policy innovation of the patch reforms. Many British social administration researchers who specialize in the study of voluntarism began to articulate support for limited sectoral autonomy and a clearer distinction from governmental control (particularly Brenton, and Beresford and Croft), while others observed a softening of the "ideological edge" of the debate and a blurring of institutional lines between organizations in the three sectors (particularly Davies and his associates).

The question remains of the next step in the recognition and definition of a role for voluntarism in the British political economy. The direction of the accommodation between the voluntary sector and government had been rendered considerably more complex by the resurgence of conservative ideology in the mid-1970s and by the election of Margaret Thatcher as Prime Minister in 1979. Mrs. Thatcher moved to centralize control of the central British government, taking a series of steps to restrain and weaken local councils. And, although voluntary associations receive twice as much funding from local councils as from central government (Strickler, 1986, p. 9), associations have been both reluctant and weak in expressing their opposition to the restriction of local government (Pickvance, 1987).

Thatcherism in practice confronts the voluntary sector with the same set of contradictory themes as Reaganism in practice. Rhetoric is profusely provided to assert the virtues of local self-reliance and problem-solving while funding is drastically cut for social spending by a growing centralized government. Furthermore, voluntary organizations are subject to increasing restriction of their political advocacy of causes that are unacceptable to the conservative government. Thus in Britain the elimination of the London County Council led to the closing of voluntary organizations at the rate of two a week (*New Society,* 6 June 1986), while passage of the 1986 Local Government Act prohibited local governments from funding voluntary organizations to issue publicity on political matters or issues not "the proper concern of local government" (*New Society,* 30 May 1986).

Although she was not able, in her first turn as Prime Minister, to mount a significant assault against the broad consensus in Britain that surrounds the welfare state, Mrs. Thatcher's government nonetheless picked away, through administrative reforms, at the putative excesses of that state. But as the unemployment rate ranged well above 10%, the Prime Minister was forced to rely on the voluntary sector to serve as the conduit for a massive program of low-wage, publicly funded employment. Analogous to the CETA programs of the 1970s in the United States, the complex employment programs of the Manpower Services Commission in Britain served to link the state and voluntary organizations in a set of political and contractual arrangements that recalled another dilemma of American voluntarism in the 1970s—the concern with overregulation by government (cf. Rosenbaum, 1981). In contrast to the fate of voluntary organizations in the United States under Reagan, where governmental funding levels were significantly reduced, Thatcher's Britain increased the funding of nonprofit organizations in an effort to control the ravages of unemployment.

Studying the responses of voluntary organizations' senior staff to the new expectations for their roles, Billis and Harris (1986) find that "the single most mentioned general concern was the conflict between agencies' own *priorities as regards expansion* and those of central Government and other large funders" (p. 4). Voluntary organization leaders were found to perceive their "advocacy role" at risk, "not only because funding for service-provision can divert efforts away from campaigning, but also because the fear of jeopardizing funding for service provision tends to inhibit open discussion and make agencies 'docile' " (Billis and Harris, 1986, p. 11). In the United States, such themes emerged early in the 1980s, when such moderate Republicans as Senator Dave Durenberger of Minnesota sought to articulate an ideology of voluntarism consistent with the strong preference expressed by conservatives for services as against advocacy and protest. In the British literature, as discussed above, these themes have been identified by Brenton as themselves threatening the autonomy and contribution of many voluntary organizations, deflecting such organizations from their most appropriate focus on self-help and advocacy/protest.

The Search for a Third Way

Clearly, the attempt by British intellectuals to define a welfare pluralist approach in a time of fiscal retrenchment and Conservative ascendancy in government was fraught with difficulty. While the work of Hatch and Hadley gave rise to considerable interest on the part of leaders of all three major British parties and ushered in a not inconsequential policy change, it did not result in a fully articulated political theory. The quest for a new theory of voluntarism in the modern political economy was stalled by the stark political difficulties of urging the replacement of mandated governmental service by decentralized voluntary response.

As Brenton observed, the welfare pluralists had married the theory of political pluralism to the assumption that "society's welfare is the natural product of voluntary enterprise manifested by a multiplicity of groups and organisations outside the formal political system." In such a view, there is no space "for a structural view of society as the arena of conflicts between the interest of institutionalised and concentrated power and the powerless" (Brenton, 1985, p. 172). Welfare pluralism comes to be seen as a game played within the context of existing class relations, in which the poor remain poor but are granted a somewhat larger voice in their poverty. The distance between dictates of participatory democracy—in the absence of a vigorous policy redistributing power and income —and Conservative privatization policies proved rather short. And the voluntary sector can easily be identified as the pacifier on this turf, however inappropriate this vision of its role may be seen by those attentive to its historic calls for justice and empowerment.

Several voices in contemporary Britain seem to offer alternative visions to what economist David Donnison (1984, p. 55) has called the "more brutal forms of 'privatisation' now being imposed" and the policies of the pre-existing welfare state. Such a third way might involve a critical appreciation of several important kinds of organizations largely ignored by the welfare pluralists. Beresford and Croft (1984, p. 24) identify two of these types: collective and cooperative voluntary organizations aimed at the organization of persons in racial and class minorities, and "commercial organizations." Both the potential of autonomous voluntarism, directed at both resistance and coproduction, and of privatization, with its acceptance of the outcomes of markets, need to be part of any understanding of the role of voluntarism in contemporary society. As Donnison observes: "Equity and efficiency should still be our combined aims; but those words are far too brief to offer sufficient guidance. Community, democracy, enterprise, self-management, open government—these are some of the key concepts inspiring the new trends." In such a vision of voluntarism, Donnison concludes, "Government's most important role is to help in creating the culture and the material environment in which progress to a more humane and rational society, built on an evolving consensus, comes about."

On a more practical level, the new director of the National Council of Voluntary Organisations, Usha Prashar, comes from a background of community organizing in the minority communities of Britain. She has identified an agenda for NCVO that will focus on three major goals: first, to develop research on the impact of governmental budget-cutting on support levels for voluntary organizations; second, to counter the prevailing "management ethos" in society by identifying and focusing on the particular strengths and capacities of voluntary organizations; and, third, to develop a "fiscal policy" for the sector that will assure sufficient funding from both public and private sources, including corporate and business support.

Such a strategy focuses on the particular strengths of voluntary organizations and takes careful note of their setting in a complex context of political economy. It recognizes that voluntary organizations play a role that is crucial and yet limited in society, and that they thereby require a strong governmental, and possibly even corporate, commitment to social goals of justice and progress if they are to contribute to the development of a humane society. It is a strategy, as defined by Brenton, that sees voluntarism as impoverished when it becomes, in large part, a vehicle for the disposition of state-funded services, or the provider of services divested by government in a contemporary infatuation with privatization. The core of such voluntarism is found in the twin themes of self-help organization and advocacy/protest assertion. Its role is to assure that the state and the corporation do indeed work for the common good, do indeed serve the interests of more than the rich and powerful. It is an approach to voluntary action that strikes a chord that may be new to Britain but that resonates throughout a rather different tradition in France.

VOLUNTARISM IN FRANCE: A SUBVERSIVE TRADITION

France is described in the literature on voluntary action research as being most removed from the American situation, with Britain in a more intermediate position. The work of Arnold Rose (1954) has been influential in drawing the image of a French society in which associations are infrequent and associational life is of limited social and political relevance. Rose's hypothesis has been modified by Gallagher (1957), who found that many French associations that appear on the surface to be oriented toward "expressive" rather than "social influence" goals do orient themselves toward the provision of charity as well. Further, Gallagher identified the working class as the segment of French society most devoid of associations: only the café is seen as replacing weakened ties of community, church, and family among this group.

In a recent review essay, Strickler (1986) notes the paucity of research on volunteerism in France and explains this fact in terms of the weakness of the

French tradition of volunteering. She reiterates the theme of distrust and unwillingness to cooperate and adds to her analysis a discussion of the relatively recent acceptance of associations by French law. The celebrated Law of 1901 did assure the right to association, but it also specified a number of onerous regulations that associations must follow. The tendency to rely on the state for social services further contributes to the weakness of volunteering in France, as does the conception of democracy as embodied in the actions of elected officials, Strickler continues.

Even Meister's own historical analyses (1984) strike the dominant theme of difference rather than convergence. French associations are seen to be "slowly ridding themselves of their medieval elements" while in the United States "mass immigration and the break with European traditions give different characteristics to associations" (p. 27). Meister specifies the American conditions that differed from the French in a long list, including the magnitude and diversity of the American experience with immigration; the absence of putatively "natural" hierarchies in the New World; the organizational requirements necessitated by frontier living; the diverse ethnicities of new industrial workers; the individualizing impact of Protestantism; the social isolation of the immigrant experience; the suspicion of established social and political structures in postcolonial America; and the absence of restraining legislation. Of these factors, liberalism and the lack of a strong state join with the diversity of population as most important in explaining the differences between the American and French traditions, Meister (1984, p. 54) asserts.

Corporations, religious fraternities, and mutual associations are identified by Meister as the "three strands of modern French associationism." Among these, what centrally concerns Meister are those that address the rights of workers and classes to organize. His full discussion (p. 39) of the 1848 uprisings in France shows clearly the way in which varieties of voluntarism have been regarded by authoritarian rulers:

> Once the red specter was evoked, repression was extended to the Republican groups also. Hence the decree of July 28, 1848 on clubs, distinguishing four categories: (1) clubs whose formation was free under the condition that they be open to nonmembers, that their minutes be drafted, that no one discuss therein "any proposition contrary to public order and to good morality, or tending to provoke . . . denunciations against persons, or individual attacks." "Public order" meant "social property," for as the report declared, "public order means family and property"; (2) secret societies, which were forbidden; (3) circles which had no political goal and which could be created freely; (4) nonpublic political meetings which required permission from the municipal authority.

The distrust of associations by citizen and authority alike remains an important restraining force in French society, Meister asserts. In this regard, any convergence must surmount strong historical, structural, and cultural obstacles.

The Contemporary Discovery of Voluntarism in France

If recent British experience suggest a *re*discovery of the voluntary sector, despite an inability to find a satisfactory resolution of the relationships between the three sectors, recent French experience indicates the beginnings of a process of an initial discovery of the role of the third sector in modern society, and an emerging effort to think through the most productive relationships between the sectors.

Numerous associations are created each year in France (43,000 in 1983 alone), in such areas as social welfare, popular education, labor, environmental action, adult education, and (most recently) municipal action. Many of these groups continue to exhibit organizational fragility: the mortality rate of associations is high, membership rates and public contributions do not always show increases, and the overall societal impact of associations remains limited.

Voluntary associations are not yet accepted as a "normal" part of the French political economy, nor have they achieved a puissant institutional position in society. The legitimacy of associations has always been derived from the French political structure, and it has always been questioned. The administration of voluntary activities has typically given rise to strong demands for the regulation and assurance of the probity of such expenditures. Neither philanthropy nor volunteerism has a strong tradition in France. Moreover, critiques within the world of French voluntarism have raised serious questions regarding the quality of participation in associations, the role of patronage, tension between paid staff and volunteers, control, and administrative effectiveness. The conversion to the status of political party by the ecological movement of the late 1970s indicates the tenuousness of the standing of voluntary associations. In political thought, the rise of the concept of the "independent citizen" has not been coupled with an associational embodiment of this figure.

The ambiguous legacy of voluntary action in France is well depicted in a recent essay by Bernard Kouchner, a medical doctor reknowned in France for his work on international health and hunger. Kouchner titles his book *Charité Business* (1986), and in one paragraph he graphically depicts the French conception of associations:

> It begins among friends, to defend an idea, or to combat an injustice; a group of volunteers meet to prohibit a nuisance in their neighborhood or to promote a regional product. They meet in the living room in someone's apartment or in an empty back shop and decide to found an association.

It's a time of gearing up, of launching some tasks such that several years later, if the project has survived its adolescent crises, it finds itself perhaps engaged as a multinational organization. Such is the poetry of associational risks. . . . With success comes the risk of the inevitable jealousies, the weight of bureaucratization, the deflection of purpose, the loss of soul, financial manipulations, and various organizational maneuvers. The beautiful word is fraught with perils: to associate (p. 99, translated by author).

Despite these limitations, however, a gulf has widened in French life between the realities of a limited public fisc and the societal needs of the citizenry. Even the election of a socialist government in France in 1981 failed to blunt the necessity of reducing domestic expenditures. The process of socialist *rigueur* proved as painful as that of capitalist "austerity," as Kesselman (1983) has shown. The existence of the gulf between public expenditure and social need provided an opportunity for the development of a new relationship between the three sectors in France. Strickler sees in the strengthening of local government by the Deferre Act of 1982 and following legislation, and an increasing concern with the welfare of the aged, the opening of opportunities for voluntary action. Strickler (1986) quotes a recent governmental report which observes that the "morale and human problems" of the elderly "cannot be solved by statutory services. Loneliness, inactivity and lack of personal relations are mainly human problems, and in this sphere of life there is a clear place for voluntary services which are complementary with material paid services." Perhaps, Strickler observes, voluntarism in France will increasingly come to resemble the British model of complementary rather than competitive social services between government and association.

Perhaps the most significant voice describing a reoriented voluntary contribution to French society is that of the "FONDA" organization *(fondation pour la vie associative)*, formed in 1981 as an analog to the U.S. organization INDEPENDENT SECTOR. Noting that 700,000 employees are paid by voluntary sector organizations, FONDA leaders speak of a vibrant role for French voluntarism in society. Noting that associational power involves freedoms of speech and action distinct from the political power to vote, FONDA Vice-President Leon Dujardin adheres to the tenets of classic pluralistic theory, describing a process in which ideas emerge from the voluntary sector to affect political decisions. Voluntarism, Dujardin explains, provides for the "spontaneous expression of power directly" and also nurtures and develops those ideas of minority groups that form the seeds of future orthodoxy.

FONDA has focused its attention on several critical issues in French society, most notably youth unemployment and the development of local par-

ticipation. In 1984 it convened an assembly of representatives of 800 associations and appropriate elected officials to launch a joint voluntary sector-
sector-government effort to reduce the problem of youth unemployment.
The deliberations of this assembly are replete with the kinds of references
that one might find at a similar American gathering—references to the
magnitude of associational life and the contribution of associations to the
development of public–private partnerships for problem resolution in society. How, and if, this rhetoric will be transformed into effective action is to
be determined, but French voluntarism has clearly found its voice. A role
combining citizen action with organized service provision is now being
articulated as a vital part of that society. The concept of the voluntary
organization as impotent and yet potentially subversive is being revamped.
Surely that step is required if the French voluntary sector is to become as
active as its confreres in Britain and the United States.

A 1986 FONDA assembly focused on the role of associations in French
society. Guy Raffi, former Minister of Agriculture in the socialist government, provided the keynote address. Noting that associations have come to
be seen as more powerful and responsible by both themselves and government leaders over the past 30 years, Raffi (1986) observed that the modern
world sees as increasingly effective those organizations that are "supple,
autonomous, less hierarchical, and decentralized." Associations, standing in
a "social economy" between the world of pure voluntarism and that of capitalist enterprise, are seen to embody a pluralistic force intolerable to the
totalitarianism of East or West. Moreover, such organizations appear more
and more as a dynamic field of social force unto themselves, and as a primary engine of change in modern society.

The social economy concept opens to the French analyst of his or her
society a way of comprehending social forces long since ignored by the
intellectual and political establishments of that society. FONDA Vice-President (there are two) Jacqueline Mengin speaks (personal interview, 1986) of
the possibility of recognizing the cultural contribution of two groups in
France that have conventionally been ignored by mainstream French institutions: youth and immigrants. In each subgroup innovative and exciting
associational forms are evident. Indeed, as I interviewed her on December 3,
1986, a vast student movement was preparing to take to the streets for a
demonstration that shook the French government considerably. The student movement had been organized with great skill and detail, including
making provisions for the sharing of notes from missed lectures and the
preparation for examinations in informal study groups. Not conventionally
seen as part of the associational structure in France, such social movements
as those mobilized by the students retain much of their "mass society" quality, to use Kornhauser's (1959) terms. Thus, their actions tend to escalate
quickly, and often call forth the kind of official violence that surrounded

the student protests of 1968 and 1986. It is important to note that the mass characteristic of the movement is engendered in large part by the refusal of the French establishment to view as legitimate this thrust toward student organization. By restricting association, they limit pluralism. And thus results the cycle of mass behavior and official repression, so familiar in French political history.

Recognition of the dynamic forces contained within its immigrant communities might also allow for a greater integration of French society. Long content (some might even say smug) with their unitary culture (social, religious, and political), the French might benefit considerably if they recognized more clearly and positively the contributions of their newer neighbors. In any case, as Little's classic work (1965) presaged, the immigrant communities in France are developing associations at a rapid rate, and that process can be expected to affect powerfully the shape of the associational sector in France, as Meister's work, reviewed above, would suggest.

SUMMARY: THE SOCIAL ECONOMY
IN THE UNITED STATES, BRITAIN, AND FRANCE

That a reorientation of roles and relations between the three sectors was required in late 20th century life became increasingly apparent in the United States, Britain, and France. The transition in both thought and practice has been difficult in all three countries, despite the greater continuity in traditions of voluntarism in the United States and Britain. By no means has France converged with either the British or the American model, but a fundamental reorientation of thought and beginning changes in practice may be discerned there as well.

It seems apparent that each nation has lessons it could teach the others about the traditions and practices of voluntarism. Americans, for example, could learn from the long tradition in British social administration and the more recent French studies of social economy about the usefulness of conceptualizing a fourth major societal sector: the informal sector of neighborhood organization, extended family and kin relations, and intermittent associations. The addition of this fourth sector to our topographic map is certainly overdue in American studies, and its structure is examined in greater detail in the following chapter.

A second lesson Americans might profitably learn, from the British in particular, but also from the French, concerns the relationships between voluntary action and political ideology. Discussions of voluntarism in Britain and France consistently relate conceptions of voluntary action directly or indirectly to more overarching conceptions of political ideology, as indicated by the diverse conclusions regarding the validity of the concept of "welfare pluralism." To the British student of voluntarism, the first question to be answered is the degree to which an organized action will contribute to politically structured goals of progress and justice. Only then do topographic or climatic concepts have the context deemed necessary for the evaluation of social action. Americans might do well to examine such linkages between voluntary action and social progress in their own evaluation of different types of voluntary action: it is one thing to contribute to a fund distributing weapons to a foreign guerrilla army in violation of existing law; and another to support an organization aiming in part to alter that law. No cant regarding the values of voluntary action or an independent sector can cover and justify both forms of organized activity.

A third lesson for Americans is inherent in the efforts of contemporary French scholars to delineate the role of voluntarism in their society. The articulation of the theory of social economy in rather full dress shows the role of ideas in social action, and it suggests a voluntarism primarily characterized by emergent principles of democracy and social concern. Such principles, embodied in the actions of a social economy, may be highly useful in avoiding the ossification of the citizen role in late 20th century America, embodying as they do central principles in the democratic traditions of populism, idealism, pluralism, and social democracy.

Our brief journey to Britain and France also suggests that there is some evidence to assert a modest convergence of the French, British, and American experiences. To be sure, historical, cultural, and structural differences among the three countries make total convergence most unlikely. However, the review of this chapter does indicate the emergence of similar themes, among them the need for public–private partnerships, an expanding voluntary contribution to the provision of public services, and a broader societal response to a declining governmental effort in the provision of domestic assistance. These forces, clearly contradictory in their imbalance between the expectation for voluntary service and the decline in support—particularly public support—for such provision, have nowhere been organized to achieve the desired product. Rhetoric abounds, as does frenzied organizational response. As in the United States, voluntarism and the relationships between the three sectors in Britain and France remain in some disarray, awaiting clarification of their roles and support for their major functions.

8

Along Sectoral Boundaries: Interdependence and Permeability

Carl R. Channell, a professional fund-raiser, pleaded guilty in Federal court today to charges of conspiring to defraud the Government by raising tax-exempt funds to arm Nicaraguan rebels. He named Lieut. Col. Oliver L. North as a co-conspirator.

—*The New York Times*, April 30, 1987

Joe Coors also defended his $65,000 donation at the Congressional hearing, but he looked to me like someone who had bought tickets to send handicapped kids to the circus and then learned that the voice on the phone kept 97 percent of the money for "expenses."

—Glennys McPhilimy, *Daily Camera* (Boulder, CO), June 14, 1987

As a businessman I never pretended to undertake the tasks I was asked to perform for philanthropic purposes.

—Albert Hakim, Testimony to the Select Committee on the Iran-Contra Affair

Sometimes you have to go above the written law.

—Fawn Hall, Testimony to the Select Committee on the Iran-Contra Affair

INTRODUCTION

The topographic maps of the third sector are conventionally drawn on the reality of certain differences between major societal sectors. Corporate, governmental, voluntary, and household activities are seen as distinct in their purpose, activity, and implications. This view of sectoral distinctiveness presupposes the presence of boundaries between the sectors. The presence of boundaries, as we have seen, gives rise to both imprecision and conflict. The purposes of this chapter are to pose the issue of sectoral boundary definition and to explore relationships between major institutions in light of prevailing "tectonic" and "climatic" realities.

Discussion in the previous chapter identified a number of boundary issues. It was noted that governmental powers to tax (and to exempt from taxation) allow for the chartering and regulation of nonprofit corporations. This power adds fuel to a perennial conflict between business and nonprofit organizations. A second area of major conflict is located on the boundary between the governmental and voluntary sectors. Focusing on the appropriateness of images of social change, that conflict leads to assertive, often aggressive, attempts by actors in each sector to restrain others. A third example involves the role of philanthropy in the political economy and involves not only each of the three sectors but also the household sector. The analysis of such boundary issues is aided by setting a framework, and the work of Talcott Parsons provides an admirable one.

As noted in Chapter 4, Parsons identified four institutional sectors as central organizing structures of modern society. These institutions were seen to perform the four major tasks of societal development and maintenance, which Parsons identified as adaptation, goal-attainment, integration, and latent pattern-maintenance.

Parsons explained that the problem of adaptation, of securing the economic resources needed to establish the basis of societal existence, is assigned to the economy. The problem of goal-attainment, of achieving the ends deemed crucial for societal development, is the task of the polity. The third task, integration, involves linking disparate social groups and is the focus of the integrative sector. The final task, latent pattern-maintenance, is that of achieving meaning and coherence, and is the work of the cultural institutions of church, school, and family.

Parsons's four sectors translate roughly into the three sectors thus far discussed, with our third sector arrayed across his third and fourth. When Parsons (1966) elaborates on the structure of the integrative sector, he clearly notes the central role of voluntary associations therein: the "integrative system . . . involves the associational aspect of group structure and solidarity in relation to the system of norms (legal and informal)—as distinguished from values" (p. 262). In a figure on the same page, Parsons identifies the integrative system as existing where law (as norms) and social control intersect. The latent pattern-maintenance system, on the other hand, is viewed as the cradle of values, or, as Parsons puts it, "cultural and motivational commitments." Such associations as churches and cultural organizations fall into this sector, as well as such clearly non-third-sector organizations as households and schools (the "informal sector" we have been referred to by British social scientists).

It is apparent from this review of Parsons's model that the voluntary sector is centrally involved in two of the four major functions of society: integration and latent pattern-maintenance. Viewed as associations expressing influence, the third sector rests on the value-principle of solidarity and coordinates by means of consensus among individuals. Alternatively, viewed as associations expressing commitments, many third sector organizations build on the value-principle of integrity and coordinate their activity by means of the consistency of their patterns. The combination of the two basic forces, influence and commitment, would appear to identify precisely the special space of "teleological priority" identified by Gamwell (1984).

The Parsonian model suggests that the third sector is inhabited by organizations whose central focus is either influence or commitment, and perhaps by some organizations whose focus involves a blending of the two forces. Thus, pressure groups and lobbying organizations are quintessentially involved in influence. In contrast, churches and arts leagues are predominantly guardians of commitments to larger systems of meaning. Perhaps it is in the blending of the two principles, when the church group takes a stand for social justice, or the lobbying organization seeks to involve itself in the extension of social rights beyond the immediate interest of its members, that the true potential of the third sector is realized.

To be sure, there remain many influence associations that are essentially members of the first or second sectors, essentially appendages of business or governmental life (perhaps trade associations and political parties are the best examples). And just as certainly, many commitment-based associations should not be considered to be part of the third sector, such as households and schools. The boundaries between the sectors may not be precise lines, but rather may involve wide swaths of indeterminate territory, and considerable conceptual, as well as organizational, blurring. The role of organizations on the margins of the state has been studied by Sharkansky (1979), who finds "much proliferation of administrative bodies" on these margins. This organizational "blurring" solves some problems, he concludes, but it creates others—most notably increasing the "incoherence" of government and policy (p. 145).

Parsons approaches the question of sectoral boundaries by examining transactions between the major sectors. Each of these relationships is described by Parsons as involving a particular set of exchanges of both inputs and outputs. Six sets of relationships are identified between the four subsystems, taken two at a time. Thus, to take the one example not involving the third sector, government offers the economy resources and opportunities for effectiveness, and it receives in return services and control over productivity. This interchange is identified by Parsons as the "resource mobilization system." It is also the problem Lindblom (1977) identifies as "policies and markets"—the central focus of contemporary political economics.

Five other relationships potentially involve third sector organizations, arrayed as they are near the intersection of influence and commitment. Government offers the commitment system moral responsibility for the collective interest and operative responsibility, and it receives in return legality for its powers of office and legitimation of its authority. This is identified as the "legitimation system" by Parsons. The economy offers the commitment system wage income and receives in return labor capacity and commodity demand. This is what Parsons identifies as the "labor consumption market system."

Government offers the influence system leadership responsibility and policy decisions, and it receives in return political support and interest demands, forming the "political support system." The economy offers the influence system claims to resources and their justification, and it receives in return standards for the allocation of resources and their ranking, forming the "allocative standard system."

Finally, the two component parts of the third sector transact between themselves. The influence system offers the commitment system common values and justifications for the allocation of loyalties. In return, the influence system receives value-based claims to loyalties and commitment to valued association from the commitment system. This transaction is identified by Parsons as the "loyalty-solidarity-commitment" interchange.

Parsons's model of the social system provides a powerful way of perceiving the boundaries between institutional sectors in society. Using his approach as a point of departure, but not necessarily as a theoretical straitjacket, let us now proceed to examine the state of boundary relations between the voluntary sector and other institutions in contemporary society.

RELATIONS BETWEEN GOVERNMENT AND THE THIRD SECTOR

Some of the ground on the subject of government–third sector relations is covered in Chapter 7. As voluntarism has emerged as a policy issue, the formal relations between government and voluntary sector have received heightened attention.

Political scientist Jacqueline DeLaat (1987) notes that a substantial amount of volunteered activity takes place at all levels of government: many domestic federally funded programs came to require some citizen input in the 1970s (though this practice is far less common in the 1980s); volunteers play pivotal roles in political campaigns; and the coproduction of services by citizens and bureaucrats (about which more is said in Chapter 9) has come to be a routine practice in municipal administration. DeLaat also mentions the continuing presence of volunteer firefighting organizations, volunteer teachers' aides, and citizen advocates.

Relations between voluntary associations and government may be viewed as being of two major types—formal and policy-related. Key among the formal relations are questions of charter and tax exemption. Governmental agencies review the applications of third sector organizations to determine their eligibility under the tax code, and then proceed to review this eligibility on an ongoing basis. The income tax law determines which forms of charitable contributions may be properly deducted from their tax liability by individual givers. Foundations themselves are regulated by law as to their practices and income reporting. Additionally, certain voluntary associations are deemed appropriate, and others inappropriate, to be favored by governmental support through grants, contracts, or the use of publicly owned spaces and buildings for their meetings and activities, while others are denied access to these privileges. At times, approved associations are used by government to relieve the overcrowding of their facilities: many states allow convicted felons to "volunteer" to perform community service as an alternative to serving time in prison, in curious though largely unrecognized contradiction to the conventional motivation of volunteers (See Chapter 1).

As we have seen in considering the idea of "third-party government," the role of voluntary organizations in delivering social services is a large one. Sharkansky (1979) summarizes the bright and dark corners of that relationship:

> Some observers applaud the diversity in social service delivery achieved via contracting. Clients are freed from dependence on government agencies that monopolize service programs, and the clients may even benefit from competition between service providers. Other observers focus on the dilemmas created by extensive contracting with voluntary agencies:
>
> - Problems of coordination among separate agencies that deal in similar services in the same community
>
> - Challenges to the autonomy of voluntary agencies via mechanisms of governmental control
>
> - Lack of public control over the programs administered by voluntary agencies seeking to maximize their autonomy
>
> - Dilution of the benefits derived from voluntarism in social services, as agencies and their contributors come to rely on government contracts for the bulk of their funds
>
> - Problems of church-state separation, felt both by secular interests toward social service agencies having a religious sponsorship and by religious sponsors who feel the erosion of their traditional social service roles (pp. 116–117).

When a government is controlled by individuals possessed of a particular ideological bent, the voluntary sector may be the subject of considerable interest and scrutiny on the part of governmental leaders. Such policy-related activity characterized the administration of Ronald Reagan, which sought in a determined fashion to keep a number of politically active organizations off the list of eligible donees for government-based charitable drives. The notorious OMB Circular 122 was one of several "federal policy initiatives . . . designed to curb specific types of politically active voluntary associations" (Wolch, 1986, p. 479). As discussed in Chapter 7, governmental activity designed to repress voluntary associations deemed politically unacceptable has been more fully practiced in Great Britain than in the United States, but it seems a temptation to any ideologically driven governmental official.

The Reagan thrust to defund voluntary associations not deemed to act in accordance with its own conservative ideology was joined to its frontal assault on the welfare state. The effort to severely restrict the reach of public welfare led to the dual policy of governmental cutbacks and restriction of funding of nonprofit service providers. This history, amply recounted and documented by Lester Salamon (1983, 1987) and associates (1984), and briefly told in Chapter 6, finds positive form only in the theory of "privatization" (cf. Savas 1981). This theory, essentially one of private sector supremacy over both government and voluntary organization, fueled one of the more interesting boundary conflicts of the 1980s, that between small business and nonprofit corporations.

If it is true, as Ronald Reagan's favorite predecessor in the White House, Calvin Coolidge, contended, that "the business of America is business," then the effort of the Small Business Administration to discredit nonprofit activity will not appear surprising. Corresponding to Coolidge's dictum is the unspoken assumption that the business of government is to serve largely as a watchman, assuring domestic stability and international hegemony. The result for third sector organizations, as Ralph Kramer's "reprivatization" model implies, is to join the domestic functions of government in severe decline.

ON THE BOUNDARY BETWEEN BUSINESS
AND NONPROFIT CORPORATIONS

Classical political theory reminds us that the corporation is an invention of Western civilization, and its emergence in two fundamental forms (for-profit and not-for-profit) has been a significant aspect of contemporary institutional development.

The boundary between business and nonprofit activity is often crossed, and DeLaat (1987) identifies four major ways in which work and volunteering are commonly connected:

> 1) volunteering is supplemental to primary work roles, and often compensates for needs not met in the work role situation; 2) volunteering is *instrumental* to primary work roles, or helps in the achievement of

career objectives; 3) volunteering is a form of *expanding* the work role by doing additional, unpaid labor somehow related to the work role; or, 4) volunteering is, in itself, a conscious work activity (p. 103).

The nonprofit corporation is required by law to possess a charitable purpose, and to pursue that purpose in the larger portion of its activities. The intricacies of nonprofit law, however, serve as a constant temptation to nonprofits to develop money-making activities within their own structures, or through the creation of profit-making subsidiaries.

This thrust is commonly explained as a rational response by nonprofit managers to the financial crisis in their sector occasioned by cutbacks in funding. As Gregory Gray (1985) puts it, "Reagan's challenge to provide even more services made many nonprofit managers realize they could not survive in the '80s without aggressive, businesslike marketing of their services and products" (p. 13). Moreover, the development of a cadre of consultants and support organizations aimed to assist nonprofit organizations in the 1980s has given rise to a good deal of information and expertise on money-making within the third sector.

Business interests, led by the Small Business Administration (SBA), responded to this development of entrepreneurial spirit and capacity on the part of nonprofits with loud and influential objections. It was not difficult to identify a long list of questionable practices. Gregory Gray (1985: 12–13) gives a number of leading examples:

- The nonprofit Children's Television Workshop netted $8 million in 1983 by marketing miniature versions of Kermit the Frog, Big Bird, and other Sesame Street characters and products.
- Chicago's Lincoln Park Zoo earns up to $10 thousand per week on stuffed animals, jewelry, and souvenirs.
- Many YMCAs are operating membership-only health clubs which are subsidized at least in part by funds donated through United Way or local community chests.
- The New York Museum of Modern Art sold air rights above the Manhattan museum to a developer for $17 million. The developer erected a 44-story condominium tower and sold units to private individuals who pay no property taxes; instead, they pay fees to a tax-exempt trust which benefits the museum.
- A number of nonprofits, including the Bank Street College of Education, the Minnesota Educational Computing Consortium (MEEC), and two large American Red Cross blood centers are marketing software at bargain rates. The MEEC sells millions of dollars worth of microcomputer software to schools throughout the United States and commands about 35 to 40 percent of the educational software market.
- Colleges and universities actively sell microcomputer equipment, software, and computer use time to faculty, staff, and students, operate discount travel

agencies, and rent their dormitories, student unions, and auditoriums for convention purposes while simultaneously collecting revenue from government grants and contracts.

Gray (1985) notes that:

> As for-profits are quick to point out, all these nonprofit groups compete with small business enterprises while enjoying the benefits of reduced postal rates, free unemployment insurance in some instances, freedom from minimum wage rates, exemption from federal trade competition laws, and several other benefits. . . .The competition was keenly felt in a wide range of traditional for-profit industries, including computer services and software, research laboratories, health clubs, travel agencies, restaurants, parking garages, nursing homes, and day care centers, to mention a few (p. 13).

Among these enterprises, the sorest spots seemed to be in the areas of travel agency, university marketing of engineering products, and the selling of jewelry and gifts by museum stores.

The 1986 White House Conference on Small Business (1986) included high among its list of recommendations (third of sixty; and 800 were presented to the conference) the following:

> Because government at all levels has failed to protect small businesses from damaging levels of unfair competition, federal state and local laws, regulations and policies should:
> a. Prohibit unfair competition in which non-profit tax-exempt organizations use their tax-exempt status and other advantages in selling products and services also offered by small businesses.
> b. Prohibit direct, government-created competition in which government organizations perform commercial services.

As remedy, the conference called for a variety of steps, including new regulatory laws for nonprofits, "strict government reliance on the private sector for performance of commercial-type functions," and the creation of a Federal Private Enterprise Review Committee in the SBA.

The response of organizations serving the third sector has been to counter the claims of unfair competition made by the business-serving organizations, noting the many tax advantages such businesses receive under prevailing tax law. In New Jersey, the Center for Nonprofit Corporations has developed its own Committee on Business Ventures, designed in part to model the creation of profit-making centers within other nonprofit organizations.

The results of this lobbying and jousting have yet to be viewed, but the net effect of the process will surely call into further question the clarity of the boundary between the first and the third sectors. The pressures confronting nonprofits force them to rebound between the dual pressures occasioned by the withdrawal of government funds, on the one hand, and the privatization of much of the political economy, on the other. If nonprofits seek to counter the withdrawal of federal funding by establishing "new ventures," they are increasingly accused of competing with proprietary enterprises. And if they do not seek to cultivate new funding sources, they see their programs reduced and their organizational bases threatened.

Whatever the fate of the legislative initiatives taken by small business spokespersons to restrain nonprofit enterprise, there seems little question that in the 1980s a growing number of nonprofit organizations have come more and more to resemble "tax-exempt businesses." How much of their "teleological priority" has been compromised in this process is yet to be seen, but once again the drift of change seems to be away from a clear set of sectoral distinctions.

ON THE BOUNDARY BETWEEN
THE VOLUNTARY SECTOR AND THE INFORMAL SECTOR

Perhaps the blurriest of all the boundaries between major sectors involves that between the voluntary sector and the realm of informal social activity, such as the household and the neighborhood. Parsons's scheme, it will be recalled, places the voluntary sector squarely in the middle of the integrative and commitment sectors of society, including both influence groups and churches. The household itself, and the institutions that directly surround it and direct themselves to the task of sustaining families and nurturing individuals as they develop—the school, the church, and the community—are typically perceived as distinct from the voluntary sector, although voluntarism is seen to spring from these structures in the form of parent groups, church-related organizations, and neighborhood associations, respectively. The central point, though, is that the solidary organizations that are most basic to any society—family, church, and community—are linked to the larger society by the voluntary associations they generate, as well as by the economic organizations that provide their members employment; hence, their common identification as "mediating structures," institutions that link individuals in their solidary structures of family and community to the larger world.

The perceptive observer of neighborhood life, Hans Spiegel (1982), describes well the way voluntary organizations arise from the basic stuff of everyday life when he describes the rise of the neighborhoods movement in the 1970s:

> There were significant stirrings in urban back alleys. An unlikely coalition of housewives, parish priests, small shopkeepers, and life-long residents

decided to stand up for their neighborhoods. They took on overwhelming odds in the form of neighborhood deterioration surrounding them, failure of banks to lend them home-improvement funds, decreasing governmental services, and a hovering stigma of being left in the undesirable backwash of the rush to the fashionable sections of the city or the affluent suburbs. These neighbors organized themselves to challenge the conventional wisdom that you can't fight City Hall and the powerful economic institutions. "The backyard revolution," as Harry C. Boyte calls it, had begun (p. 7).

The voluntary associations that bloom from the rich soil of family need and aspiration, religious conviction, and neighborly interaction are overwhelmingly informal and even intermittent. Donald and Rachelle Warren (1985) have documented the significance and extent of "problem anchored helping networks" in American society. Their research shows how individuals seek help when problems arise in ever-widening circles that begin with spouse and immediate family, and them move toward friends, neighbors, co-workers. Less than ten percent of these problems are brought to the attention of governmental or private professional service-providers, or to clergy or co-members of a voluntary association.

Some of the problems that are dealt with through such networks are ongoing, such as the provision of child care by the sharing of parent time and home space, or the meeting of shopping needs of a home-based invalid by one or more friends and neighbors. On some occasions, though not all, these networks will be signified by a group name. Only rarely will the group move toward formal incorporation and join the ranks of certified nonprofit organizations within its state.

Elaine Lindgren (1987) has been following one such organization for the past 15 years, a group of volunteers that has, for over a quarter-century, maintained a focus on protecting a small city's neighborhood from the incursion of bridge and highway construction. She writes:

> Around the notion of upholding the public interest has emerged a group held together by a mutual grievance and strong bonds of comaraderie. These bonds have evolved, not from overlapping friendship networks or volunteer memberships, but rather have been forged over time through interaction resulting from members' participation in activities associated directly with the DACO protest. . . . An ad hoc group which is able to combine goal specificity with an informal-intermittent structure and inclusive membership can become an effective, resilient force.

The ability of voluntary organizations to form and reform, to hold constant and change, to stay informal and to move toward formalization, assures that the voluntary sector will remain a many-faceted and diverse one. In its flexibility of form and purpose lies an ability to meet many needs, old and new, large and small. It is in the ability to shape the cloth to genuine human needs that voluntarism particularly distinguishes itself.

AT THE FOUR CORNERS

An intersection not discussed by Parsons is formed at the common junction of his four sectors, a point of convergence at which philanthropic institutions, in particular, stand. At this boundary money may be simultaneously exchanged for power, influence, and the commitment of values. Saved from the earnings of "private" economic activity of individuals in first sector institutions, philanthropic contributions are removed from household expenditures to serve the purpose of advancing the common good. Sometimes directed to the funding of influence or advocacy organizations, and sometimes directed to the funding of social service or income transfer itself, the greatest portion of U.S. philanthropy sustains value-based organizations, particularly churches.

The boundary area between the four sectors that is philanthropy gives rise to a wide range of problems and interpretations. For some, the crucial issue is the persistence of altruism in an age of narcissism. What seems notable from this perspective is the continuing willingness of some individuals, families, and firms to maintain their participation in a tradition of giving (cf. Karl, 1986; Odendahl and Boris, 1986; Odendahl et al., 1987; Galaskiewicz, 1985, 1986). To others, the critical issue is the use of philanthropy to sustain privilege, its focus on the funding of a society and value base designed to sustain structures of capitalist inequality (cf. Alchon, 1985, 1986; Berman, 1983, 1986; Schervish, Herman, and Rhenisch, 1986).

Thus Karl (1986) notes that: "Foundations have been viewed as both conservative supports of a reactionary Capitalism and as Trojan horses carrying left wing ideology into the center of the camp of American free enterprise" (p. 109). He concludes: "It is difficult to assign class consciousness" to the first generation of American donors who developed our great foundations (p. 118). Clearly, what impresses Karl most about foundations is their persistence in the face of the alternative uses to which money might be put. And it is the declining rate at which new foundations are being formed that concerns Odendahl and Boris, in spite of the perception of "America's wealthy" that "their charitable giving [is] essential to the maintenance of society" (Odendahl and Boris, 1986, p. 42).

In contrast, research into the history of 20th century philanthropy convinces Alchon (1986) of "the depth and extent of the technocratic and anti-democratic impulses animating to this day large areas of liberal capitalism's political culture" (p. 81). Echoing this theme, Berman (1986) notes that "foundations have promoted modes of intellectual inquiry that preclude or minimize investigation of the structural properties of American society, particularly the organization of the economy and the polity and the composition of the ruling class. Their funded studies focus instead on the marginal issues of system maintenance and the techniques required to effect incremental reform" (p. 91).

Schervish, Herman, and Rhenisch (1986) note that the problem of philanthropic influence is not a trivial one: "Through concerted philanthropic efforts, the wealthy, for good or for ill, for progressive or conservative ends, actually produce (rather than simply run or influence) the organizational world at the cutting edge of society" (p. 226). Philanthropy involves, they assert, an "intricate interplay between structure, culture, and practice" (p. 227).

The contemporary phenomenon of "celebrity voluntarism" provides a telling instance of the kind of intricate interplay that emerges between the four major sectors in modern society. Such philanthropic events as the "We Are the World" recording, the "Live-Aid" and "Farm Aid" concerts, the worldwide "Run for Africa," the "Hands Across America" connection, the restoration of the Statue of Liberty, and the provision of "Comic Relief" all took place in the mid-1980s with film and music performers playing leading roles, the media providing organizing services and heavy coverage, and corporations capitalizing on the goodwill accompanying their contributions. The practice of "cause-related marketing," which earmarks a portion of sales to a particular charity, has been identified as pernicious by Gurin (1987), who argues that it leads to a decline of established patterns of corporate philanthropy.

Ostensibly, such activities should be considered instances of voluntary action. They involve the financial and time contributions of many thousands, or even millions, of participants. They receive support in terms of released time and financial contribution from economic enterprises. Leading politicians, even the President, join in supporting and participating in the activities. And the events are organized by hastily constructed nonprofit organizations led by charismatic broker-administrators, often on leave from well-paying positions as entertainment brokers.

The four sectors clearly join hands in such activities. Business, government, voluntary organizations, and the household are linked by the common nexus of the mass media and the arts they purvey, particularly rock music and film. The structure of such events involves a number of identifiable characteristics: 1) the entertainment industries, mediated particularly by television and its prominent corporate advertisers, provide the vehicle for the realization of this form of action; 2) front-end costs are considerable*; 3) direct appeals are made to American values and culture in the activ-

---

* *The Wall Street Journal* (July 8, 1986) noted that of the $9 million raised by the first Farm Aid concert, $2 million went toward expenses. A second concert yielded only $505,000 for charitable purposes after its production costs of $1.8 million were met.

ity; 4) political and government figures play largely symbolic roles in the activities (though not necessarily insignificant ones); 5) nonprofit organizations specially chartered for the events, rather than established organizations, organize and control the events.

Such activities are controversial forms of voluntary action, subject to satire and question. Humorist Garrison Keillor makes use of his "Jack Schmidt, Arts Administrator," a former "private eye," whose practice maintains the same seedy standards of that ilk in the pulp of novels of an earlier era. *Newsweek* asks: "Can millions of Americans really help the nation's hungry and homeless by joining hands for 15 minutes? Was it Woodstock Without Guilt—or the stirring of something deeper?" (June 2, 1986, p. 18). And in Britain, a principal organizer of the 1970s "Rock Against Racism," David Widgery (1986), offers the following critique of the work of Live-Aid organizer Bob Geldof:

> Under the punk trappings, Band Aid faces the oldest of the fundraiser's problems. It is bound to think in terms of aid rather than political change. And that very thought process, central to the charitable approach, undermines the recipients to the exact degree it ennobles the donors. We could feed the world, plant the Sahara with peaches and potatoes, control the weather, harness the elements and protect against the locusts and the droughts. But this involves taking power out of the hands of the tiny elite who govern the world, east and west, rather than giving to those who, at present, endure the consequences of their irresponsible rule.

The gains of celebrity voluntarism are found in the awareness it creates of the magnitude of social problems, the opportunities (however fleeting) it provides for the manifestation of concerns and the joining with others of similar inclination in an expression of those concerns, and in the (highly variable) proceeds generated that actually reach and improve the lot of those suffering under the problem at hand.

Moreover, if one believes in "going with the flow" of social change, then why not "privatize" philanthropy as well as everything else in society? If the business of America is business, why not hawk philanthropy along with everything else? As a recent "society figure" who became a "celebrity" for running a house of prostitution put it when asked if the public revelation of her past had ruined her life: "Do you know how much better my life is? The number and quality of opportunities open to me now so far exceed those that would have been available to me had I gone down another road. I'm sure it upsets people when they hear me say that. . . . They think, 'here is someone who did something bad and she is making out like a bandit.' But hey, that's America."*

---

* Jill Gerston, "Success from Scandal." *The Philadelphia Inquirer,* September 22, 1986, p. E-1.

The costs of celebrity volunteerism may be identified, as sociologist Robert Hunter has perceptively noted (personal conversation, 1986), in an interruption of the "social problems cycle." Rather than a problem moving from stages of awareness and initial response to organization and resolution, action may become immobilized in the false belief that a single event has sufficed to resolve a problem. "Compassion fatigue" or the sense of being "aided out" may emerge, further slowing the course of social change. And corporate giving may be increasingly channeled only to causes that provide widespread advertising of the benevolence of the donor, thus reducing corporate interest in providing less visible philanthropy than that which provides it access to such venerated, and widely viewed, symbols as the Statue of Liberty. Thus, by 1986, leaders of African relief organizations had begun to point to a widening gap between need and charitable resources, as the problem of African famine fell from the narrow peak of public and media concern.

Celebrity voluntarism, with its aura of faddishness and its close ties to the entertainment industry, may itself peak as a trend. Straws in the wind may be discerned in the contemporary search for alternatives to the "charity ball" (one nonprofit organization trade journal has suggested as a new idea for fundraising the "non-ball"). After all, even the wealthy enjoy not dressing up and spending an evening at home, at least now and then.

In a scholarly study to the point, Susan Ostrander (1984) explores the interaction between class and gender as the upper-class women she studied approched voluntary action. One of her respondents, Mrs. Holt, "expressed the generally shared view that private money is somehow less constrained than public money: 'Private contributions are necessary in a democracy. It has a freer hand than public money.' At the heart of volunteerism the role of private money in protecting the 'American Way' is the issue of private control, or private power" (pp. 132–133). Ostrander continues: "These women are highly conscious of class. They have a genuine class analysis that they use to make sense out of their own lives, and they speak highly of the joys of their material standard of living and the freedom it gives them. They enjoy the pleasures of coming from well-known and well-respected families. And they appreciate the advantages of having direct and informal access to persons in positions of power who are their class, if not gender, equals" (Ostrander, 1984, p. 152). Volunteerism and philanthropy do indeed stand as part of an intricate interplay between structure, culture, and practice.

The contemporary reemergence of philanthropy as a field for scholarly study and interpretations returns us to the theme of the manifold nature of social science. As lines form between scholars on the basis of ideological interpretation and methodological proclivity, the five familiar perspectives begin to reappear: Berman adopts the social democratic perspective, while

Johnson (1973) uses the language of the economist and writes of the "charity market"—presaging a neo-corporatist perspective. Bellah holds the lines for the idealist view; Odendahl and Boris note the emergence of a populist tradition among change-oriented children of the wealthy; and Karl stakes out the centrist ground of the pluralist.

The meaning of philanthropy—altruistic concern or manipulative protection of privilege and position—continues to rage as a debate among voluntary action scholars. Like other issues that involve the major perspectives at contest among social scientists, this one will not be resolved simply by waiting for "the facts." It is actively linked to the ways in which we define voluntarism, and to the boundaries we draw about it.

CONCLUSION: THE IMPACT OF TECTONICS AND CLIMATE ON THE BLURRING OF BOUNDARIES

If it is most appropriate to develop theories of voluntarism that comprehend the three physical forces of surface structure, tectonics, and climate, as Meister, the developers of social economy theory, and the argument of the last three chapters contend—then it will be necessary to show how an awareness of tectonics and climate contributes to the fuzziness of conventional boundaries between the three (or four) major societal sectors, and the interdependence of their activities. The argument of this chapter has shown the boundaries to be blurred and the activities of sectoral organizations to be interdependent. Now, can the argument be sustained that the blurriness and interdependence relate to tectonic and climatic forces—that is, to forces of deep structure or values in society?

One way to make the argument is by noting the static nature of the conventional three- (or four-) sector conceptions. If the organizational world is divided into three (or four) sectors, we are given no indication of why each sector takes the form and magnitude that it does. Nor are we given any cue as to why one or another sector might expand, contract, or be subject to organizational stress. And evidence of blurriness between the sectors similarly stands incapable of explanation by the conventional approach.

Once tectonic forces are introduced into the map or model, an important dynamic is provided. Now it becomes possible to relate the structure of the voluntary sector to prevailing and emerging forces at work in the political and social economies of differing societies. The relative expansion or contraction of levels of national wealth, of tax policies, of spending priorities, and of governmental capacity may now be assessed and added to our understanding of the shifting boundaries between the major sectors. The blurring of boundaries becomes understood as a function, at least in part, of shifting forces in the basic political and economic substructures of society.

Moreover, when the climatic forces that comprehend the prevailing and emerging values of society are added to our consideration, important understandings present themselves regarding the workings of the voluntary principle in society. Now we begin to understand how the predisposition toward societal concern can infuse not only voluntary organizations but governmental and economic institutions. The blurring of boundaries is thereby explained in yet a greater part by understanding the ways in which differing conceptions of valued action wax and wane with the shifting societal climate.

Figure 1 depicts these relationships graphically, and it suggests the superiority of the three-level model to the flat cartography of conventional representations. Chapter 9 then provides a practical test for these conceptions, examining the contemporary quest for achieving viable and effective organizational partnership.

FIGURE 1. A THREE-LEVEL MAP OF SECTORAL RELATIONS

Climate:
dominant values

Self-absorption:
privatism

Voluntarism:
concern for others

Surface topography:
organizational forms

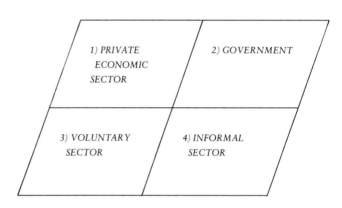

1) PRIVATE
ECONOMIC
SECTOR

2) GOVERNMENT

3) VOLUNTARY
SECTOR

4) INFORMAL
SECTOR

Tectonics:
socio-economic forces

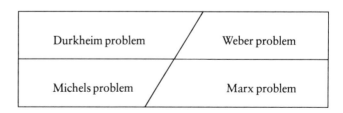

Durkheim problem

Weber problem

Michels problem

Marx problem

9

The Quest for Partnerships

> The private sector can address the tough social problems of special concern to minority Americans, and I believe that we will soon see a torrent of private initiative that will astound the advocates of big government.
>
> —Ronald Reagan, Speech to National Alliance of Business (1981)

INTRODUCTION

Few themes have seemed more compelling to the organizational politics of the 1980s than the quest for effective partnerships. While rarely specified by either theory or canon of practice, this theme appears to appeal to a widespread desire to "do more with less," to create "win–win" relationships, and to "get to yes."

The quest for partnerships has straddled the various boundaries between the major institutional sectors. Faced with a governmental crisis occasioned by the desire to augment military spending at the expense of domestic support, the Reagan administration gave its blessings to the concept of "public–private partnerships," or the joint assumption by businesses, nonprofit corporations, and governmental bodies of responsibilities of mutual concern.

Stuart Langton (1983) observes that, on the surface, "the idea of partnerships appears simple, sensible, and benign. Quite simply, the idea suggests greater cooperation between government, business, nonprofit groups, and individual citizens in addressing community needs. In an era of strained government resources and uncertainty about the role of the state in addressing social problems, such an approach seems like a promising way to go" (p. 3). But, as Langton examines the concept further, he concludes that it is generally unexamined and accepted uncritically by otherwise hard-headed individuals. He calls for the development of criteria, "such as effectiveness, efficiency, and impacts," to be used when judging the value of partnership efforts.

Members of the Reagan administration have been accused of speaking of "partnerships" when they really mean "divestment"; this thrust has been seen to be part of an overall strategy of privatization of formerly public responsibilities. Nelson Rosenbaum (1982) points to the error of this assumption, noting that: "only in cases where the city and the private corporation jointly plan an activity and in which both the city and the corporation independently invest resources in implementing the activity, do privatization agreements fall within the partnership framework" (p. 3).

Sheldon Wolin (1981) has viewed such efforts to imply consensus as cynical and manipulative means of asserting the dominance of the first sector:

> When the economy becomes the polity, *citizen* and *community* become subversive words in the vocabulary of the new political philosophy. The ultimate achievement of this form of politics is that it completely reverses Lord Acton's dictum. Instead of power corrupting, this politics manages to corrupt power by divorcing it from its grounding in political community. The necessary condition of a political ground to power has been stated and restated for about 2,500 years: power becomes political when it is based; not when a victor emerges and imposes his will, but when shared and common concerns are discovered through a process of deliberation among civic equals and effected through cooperative action. Which is not only why the new public philosophy cannot rise to a genuinely political plane, but also why it will continue to need the backing of the moral and religious conservatives. In their fury over welfare, abortion, sex, women's rights, and school prayers, they furnish a substitute for politics, replete with solidarity, a sense of community, and a glow of moral superiority. And they leave the entire structure of power, inequality, hopelessness, and growing repression wholly untouched (p. 36).

Several boundaries between the major sectors have been loci for partnership efforts in recent years. Among the most interesting is the boundary between the household and the third sector. As we saw in Chapter 9, family- and community-linked volunteering is a major source of social service in American life. The reality of problem-anchored helping networks must be recognized as a vital link between the individual and the larger society.

The family foundation presents an important instance of another link between household, voluntary sector, and the broader political economy. As Odendahl and Boris (1986) discovered in their research, the rate of formation of small family foundations has been decreasing in recent years. They write: "The strongest motivation across all sizes of foundations was the donor's personal philosophy. It is an important part of an altruism factor that includes a concern for the welfare of others, religious heritage, a belief in social responsibility and concern for the welfare of others" (p. 51).

The boundary between corporations and voluntary organizations has been the location of a set of shifting positions on the partnership issue. Historically through the 1950s in American society, it was expected that corporations would act as private, inwardly focused organizations. Individual entrepreneurs like Andrew Carnegie or John D. Rockefeller would assume personal responsibility for the contributions of their companies, but the focus of giving remained on individual initiative rather than institutional expectation. Indeed, through the 1950s there was little noticeable demand by the public for corporations to change their relationship to society.

In the 1960s, however, the consensus on behavior that was characteristic of earlier years dramatically broke down. Among the relationships challenged in this decade was the relationship of the corporation to society. As protests of civil rights, the Vietnam war, and environmental pollution escalated, the business sector was accused more and more of social guilt. During this period, profit margins remained high, fueling public frustration and contributing to public expectations that corporations could reduce negative externalities and yet remain profitable.

Popular demands for corporate accountability in the late 1960s and early 1970s culminated in political support for new forms of regulation of corporate actions. This period saw an expansion of government regulation unlike any since the 1930s, and greater in scope than ever before. Aimed at protecting consumers and the environment, regulation during that decade included passage of the Water Quality Act, the Clean Air Act, and the Truth-in-Lending Amendments, among others. As many pressing public problems received address by federal law, demands by the public for further legislation and action abated. The level of public unrest that had characterized the 1960s declined throughout the 1970s.

At first, given the public pressure and optimistic economic climate of the early 1970s, corporations reacted in a positive way. An increase in corporate sponsorship of social programs occurred, accompanied by some acceptance of the new government regulations. In 1971, the Committee for Economic Development (CED), composed of 200 top-level corporate executives, issued a report on the "Social Responsibilities of Business Corporations." This report was notable because it acknowledged that voluntarism is not sufficient to ensure socially responsible corporate behavior. Rather, the CED endorsed the use of a combination of government incentives and disincentives to encourage positive social performance by business, in addition to supporting traditional voluntary programs.

In succeeding years, however, economic conditions worsened in the face of the oil embargo of 1973 and the end of the Vietnam war. Inflation and stagflation became the order of the day, and corporate profit margins declined along with the public demand for social change. In response, corporations returned to the rhetoric and practice of self-regarding profit, as they struggled with new governmental restrictions in a declining economic environment. They increased their political outreach activities throughout the decade, in a defensive response to the widespread public demands for corporate involvement heard in previous years. By the end of the 1970s, over 80 percent of the Fortune 500 companies had established public affairs offices that oversaw community relations programs, allocated philanthropic thropic contributions, and (most significantly) directed media and governmental relations efforts. By the 1978 congressional election, 40 percent of those companies had established federally registered political action committees (Useem, 1984).

An examination of the statements issued by the CED eight years after its landmark 1971 statement reveals the extent to which attitudes toward social responsibility had shifted in less than a decade. In retrospect, the 1971 statement can be viewed as a capstone of an era rather than as a prediction of future trends. The 1979 CED statement, "Redefining Government's Role in the Market System," marks the shifting of national attention away from social concerns and toward economic goals. The statement suggests that government involvement produces negative economic impacts and supports market incentives as a preferred method to reach the nation's social and economic goals. While both the 1971 and 1979 statements support social voluntarism by corporations, the 1979 report clearly indicates a reversion to the more traditional relationship between business and the rest of society.

By the 1980s, few corporate leaders remained as forthcoming as Aetna's chairman John Filer, who continued to declare that "the pursuit of social goals can significantly strengthen a corporation's capacity to achieve its primary corporate purpose of being profitable" (Committee for Economic Development, 1982, pp. 82–83). And the President's Task Force on Private Sector Initiatives, on which Filer served, at least gave lip service to that concept. In the 1980s the concept of "corporate philanthropy" and "public–private partnerships" emerged to replace the earlier theme of "corporate social responsibility" (cf. Brooks, Liebman, and Schelling, 1984).

While it is obvious that the first sector will not assume anything near full responsibility for meeting community needs that result from government cutbacks or reductions in monies from any other source, corporate leaders continue to express some obligation to confront their public responsibilities. Meanwhile, a weak economy and limited revenue sources inhibited any second sector initiatives for employment and/or training programs in the first sector (Churma, 1982, p. 42). However, if the first sector does not make some type of commitment of either money or effort, the community that surrounds it will inevitably suffer (Ehrmann, 1978, p. 12). In light of the Gramm-Rudman-Hollings Bill, which would lead to severe cutbacks, business organizations continued to be asked what they could realistically contribute to their communities.

The role of the third sector in partnership activities has been identified as important in light of responsible spatial planning (Beauregard and Holcomb, 1984, p. 219), reduction of later complaints (Ehrman, 1978, p. 5), long-term community support (Committee for Economic Development, 1982, p. 13), and accurate impact assessment (Langton, 1983, p. 16). However, the tendency of corporations to merge into transnational entities whose perspective no longer rests on any single community structure gives rise to the possibility that only large-scale units will be chosen for partnership. The rise of global economics, where business is transacted on a "limitless plain" in which localism means nothing and the mobility of labor and capital is all, contains implications that are only beginning to be sorted out. Among them are the reduction of the prospect of nuclear war (Naisbitt, 1982) and the neglect of community political and voluntary structures (Warren, Rosentraub, and Weschler, n.d.).

Partnership proposals have boomed in recent years within organizations, whether corporate or governmental. Experiments to reform the workplace have emerged from sources as varied as Japanese culture and guild socialism. The dictates of "Theory Z," derived from Japanese practice, gave rise to experiments with quality circles and other forms of task-centered workers' participation. Issuing from a more egalitarian perspective, the theme of worker ownership and workers' control sought ways to involve employees not only in decisions of how to act at work but also how to assume ownership of the workplace in both its products and processes (cf. Dahl, 1984; Dreier, 1980; Rothschild-Whitt, 1979; Toscano, 1981).

Each of these innovative proposals for reforming the boss-controlled authoritarian workplace involves the development and empowerment of voluntary organizations at the workplace. Varying the scope and scale of decision-making power allocated to them, or taken by them, these voluntary organizations all participate in some fashion in making decisions traditionally left to the boss or the manager.

The future of the "political economy of cooperation," to use Clayre's term (1980), is uncertain at best. Partnerships take many forms, ranging from the genuinely collaborative to the cynical pseudo-partnership, dominated by corporate purpose and power and often created largely to allow for policy support or gains of tax exemption. We know that partnerships can fail, and that the common strands in successful partnerships include cooperation, support, basic respect for the needs of each sectoral actor, active involvement on the part of government in planning and managing the partnership, and a degree of trust between the partners (cf. Langton, 1983; Brooks, Liebman, and Schelling, 1984). Whether this knowledge will lead to the development of an effective developmental tool or just another political shibboleth remains to be seen. Nevertheless, it is undeniable that the partnership vision appeals to something deep in the American character. It is closely related to the ideas of teamwork, fair play, and productivity. It also reflects a basic truth about the way Americans have structured the provision of governmental services. This tradition of "coproduction" deserves closer attention.

COPRODUCTION AS A REALITY IN THE AMERICAN SOCIAL ECONOMY

When political scientists sought to develop explanations of how public services are delivered in cities and towns, the concept of coproduction was developed. Rick Wilson (1981) defines the term clearly when he writes: "Coproduction involves the direct transformation of a product by citizen consumers and hired producers. The contribution of resource inputs by both citizens and producers to production constitutes an elemental linkage between the two" (p. 43).

Thus, "public order" in a city is produced not only by the actions of municipal employees—police, courts, and corrections officials—but also by the interaction of those officials with an alert and watchful citizenry. As Jane Jacobs (1961) has noted, the parent watching his or her child at play in the street below, or the neighbor seemingly idly chatting on the front steps, play important roles in the provision of urban order. Their very presence dissuades the criminal or vandal from striking. The vigilance of the urban citizenry performs the tasks of street surveillance with far greater efficiency than the limited ranks of police personnel, who may therefore concentrate their efforts on quick response to reported crimes.

As with public order, so with nearly every other municipal service. The cleanliness of streets results from both the proper disposal of trash and its effective collection. The minimization of loss by fire results from citizen attention to prevention and prompt reporting, as well as from the skills of the fire department. The provision of adequate shelter involves the attention of homeowners and tenants to the maintenance of property, as well as the regulatory attention of city-enforcers and licensers. The maintenance of public health results from the prevalence of proper diets and habits adopted by individuals, as well as from the availability of doctors, nurses, hospitals, and medicine.

The list of services to which coproduction may be applied can be extended to include drug abuse, family planning, and nutrition. Programs in each of these areas depend "as much on the efforts of clients to secure and utilize information" as they do upon the abilities of staff members. "Similarly," writes political scientist Richard Rich (1981: 60–61), "one frequently hears that the amount of education a child actually derives from public school attendance is determined at least as much by his or her own effort to learn and parents' support of educational norms as by the efforts of classroom teachers and school administrators."

The enforcement of retrenchment in human services occasioned by public policy provides a unique opportunity to reorganize these services with greater attention to the gains of coproduction. Consider first the opportunities in the area of day care of young children and able elders.

Models of day care for children and elders developed in the past 20 years assure that the facilities will be separate, and that clients will be staffed in mandated ratios by paid service providers. Thus, fifty children will be cared for by ten or fifteen service providers, and activities for able elders will be provided on a somewhat higher ratio, say one service provider to ten.

If, however, the concept of coproduction is applied to such a situation, new images of institutional structuring begin to emerge. When children and elders become viewed as more than passive clients incapable of being "empowered," they may begin to appear as coproducers of services. Several thousand years of recorded human life would suggest that, if the relationships between grandchildren and their elders are reflected upon.

Children, after all, are not mere clients, but possess unique abilities to delight and occupy elders. And most elders possess unique skills and long experience in relating to children. If these service-creating skills are joined, and parts of the senior center merge with the children's center, it becomes plausible to assume that some proportion of the elders would willingly occupy themselves as "child care volunteers," such that they would come to see the children as their own "service providers" while simultaneously looking after the interests of their charges.

A second example was suggested some years ago by disability activist Deborah Stewart, who proposed that disabled individuals be teamed to provide for greater mobility and intellectual expression. A team consisting of a person who is mentally retarded but possessed of able locomotion and a person who is physically weak, but clear of mind, might shop together, perform housekeeping and personal care, and cope ably with many other challenges of modern life—while requiring far fewer hours of professional and custodial care and supervision.

Loretta Schwartz-Nobel (1981) has described the way in which the gleaning of otherwise wasted food involves the coproduction concept. In Sacramento, California, 1200 senior citizens set up a nonprofit organization that managed to support its members with food and also to serve 45 other charitable organizations: "They did it quite simply—by collecting the food that the rest of society was throwing away." These "Gleaners" go into the fields of nearby farms after the machines and migrant workers have finished their work, and they harvest any food left behind to rot. Farmers, who can get Internal Revenue Service credit for giving food to a charity, are usually pleased to have the Gleaners come: often they save the part of the crop that they can't sell so that the Gleaners can collect it (Scwartz-Nobel, 1981, p. 205). One member of the group told Schwartz-Nobel (p. 206), "Our moral commitment is to avoid waste."

Many other ideas for social service coproduction may be developed, but the concept should now be clear. Service coproduction affords a powerful tool for redefining the client into a productive citizen, permitting many social services to be redefined so that they will not suffer in proportion with the ongoing budget cuts for their provision.

Coproduction is a concept that applies more broadly than to services alone. It can be used in the neighborhood to facilitate the development of cooperative projects for growing food or collecting solar energy; in the community, to impress upon owners of businesses and industries their responsibility to provide employment; and in the nation, to address pressing problems of public policy that do not receive the full attention of officials. The widespread nature of the "nuclear freeze" initiative suggests one such issue, as citizens seek to coproduce peace in the face of apparent disregard for this value on the part of several prominent officials in the United States and elsewhere.

Coproduction is also an idea well fitted to our times. It implies the need for new partnerships, and for an awareness that our future is filled with perils and pitfalls unlike those faced by any previous society. A vast debate, scholarly and public, exists over the likelihood of continuing economic weakness and social decay. This debate will be joined in Chapter 11 of this book; for now, it seems safe to say that the future cannot be known with certainty, and that gloomy images of the future certainly can be cast with plausibility.

These are dangerous times, and societal forces of great weight are seemingly nearing the limits of their control. Arthur Blaustein (1982) has written powerfully about some of these dangers:

> There is a very real price to be paid for the reduction of human and social services. These cutbacks will not reduce crime; they will increase it. They will not reduce drug abuse; they will increase it. They will not reduce physical and mental illness; they will destabilize it. They will not reduce alcoholism; they will increase it. They will not increase respect for the law; they will weaken it. They will not reduce local taxes; they will increase them. These painful realities have not been factored into the administration's game plan (p. 25).

If partnerships are to be entered, it is important that the stakes of the game being played are understood. To talk of coproduction in a time of social crisis is to set about building new social institutions: community eco- -nomic ventures of a variety of sorts, worker-owned stores and factories, neighborhood-based cooperatives, all set on a legislative base sufficient to restrain the flight of capital from region to region, or beyond our shores. Such people-run economic enterprises will require capital, management experience, and political support. They will, in short, be coproduced between local governments, voluntary organizations, and those corporations and holders of capital determined enough to venture into new and uncharted social and economic waters.

TOWARD GENUINE PARTNERSHIPS

Some years ago, introducing a Special Issue of the *Journal of Voluntary Action Research* on "Interagency Collaboration," Ronald Lippitt and I (1981) sought to identify a number of steps through which all collaborative efforts must pass if they are to succeed. These steps may usefully be rehearsed here, for they imply the development of criteria for evaluating partnership relations.

Lippitt and I began by noting that: "Collaboration begins with a dream, a vision, or a fantasy, or an idea—about how something in the world would be better if two or more organizations were to work more closely in resolving a problem of mutual concern." This may be seen as the first step toward building a genuine partnership—establishing the preconditions of collaboration.

The second step involves testing the collaborative waters. Here we find four tests that need to be applied to the vision and passed, in a "mental experiment" conducted by the potential proposer: 1) it must be clear that the collaboration will not threaten the turf or "domain" controlled by either partner; 2) the collaboration must be shown not to threaten the organizational autonomy of either partner; 3) an image of potential "domain consensus" or vision of potential collaboration must be able to be plausibly sketched; and 4) the impact on any already-existing collaborative networks needs to be considered.

In the third step, the potential collaborator can now approach the chosen partner. This is a delicate step, and "the literature on failed collaboration is replete with instances in which parties to the process did not clearly see collaboration as a vehicle for problem-resolution." As Isidro Ortiz (1981) has noted in a study of a Hispanic coalition in California, organizations may be very chary of the initiator of a collaborative idea. This is a time for being quite sensitive to the danger that one may be perceived as an "empire-builder," for demonstrating how collaboration may extend the use of resources, and for sharing quite openly the way in which the collaborative vision has emerged.

The fourth step toward collaboration involves the definition of the proposed partnership. Here we find the need for a clearly defined collaborative team, whose members demonstrate, when needed, that they can act independently of their home-base loyalties. Such "boundary-spanners" come to take on a new identity—loyal to their own organization but possessed of the broader vision that comes from working closely with trusted colleagues of somewhat different experience and perspective.

A fifth step is that of invigoration, for the maintenance of a working partnership, as with any marriage or liaison, has its moments of boredom, fatigue, and disillusionment. Here we find strength in the partnership between diverse organizations, who seem to be able to draw upon unique strengths to carry a partnership through its rough days. Smaller numbers of partners seem to be more able to weather such seas more successfully than very large, broad-based coalitions.

The sixth step that Lippitt and I identified is that of evaluation.

> The validity of the initial dream that brought the collaboration into existence requires renewal and review. Even more important, the contributions that may have emerged as gains, whether anticipated or unanticipated, of the process need to be recorded and shared both back home and in the collaborative milieu. Of course, not all collaborative experiences do meet their goals; nor do all create serendipitous gains that no one anticipated. Those collaborative ventures should be abandoned, their participants knowing that another day may bring another dream.

So the question presents itself: how, in light of setbacks and failed partnerships such as those I have mentioned, can genuine partnerships be created in this time of economic deterioration and social malaise? Or to put it another way, how can visions be converted into the kinds of partnerships that will meet the tests of true collaboration?

In speeches to practitioners of voluntary sector adminstration, I have from time to time sought to present, in a rather folksy manner, a few simple rules for creating successful partnerships between voluntary sector organizations, on the one hand, and corporations, governmental units, or foundations, on the other:

> 1. First, make certain that you have done your darndest to assure that the potential partner understands that you intend to address a problem that is mutual. It is astounding how often otherwise intelligent persons who deliver voluntary services are willing to pretend that the problems they seek to resolve are their own responsibility, and no one else's.
>
> We must be very clear that we are all in this predicament together. The viability of our nation's social fabric is every bit as important to the health and viability of a corporation that exists to sell cameras, or automobiles, or computers, as it is to the agency that seeks to help pregnant teenagers make sense of their lives and

the future. The issues of the day are those of national rededication to the preservation of domestic tranquillity and productivity. Such issues, if not resolved, threaten the health, and indeed, the very survival, of almost all our institutions, as well as the futures of those who hold paying positions within those institutions.

Partnerships begin with a process of accepting ownership of a problem. The search for any partnership that does not begin with such a process of finding and accepting mutual interest and responsibility becomes "mere charity"—the less than responsible granting of small sums to assure that a problem will stay hidden from us. We are far too deeply enmeshed in social and economic turmoil in our land to settle for such a palliative. As Elliot Liebow (1967) reminds us in the conclusion of his study of ghetto life: "We must love each other or die."

2. This takes me to Van Til's second law: partnerships are two-sided things. The question is not just: "OK, volunteers, what can we do for you?" It is also: "What can you help us do to be more effective in meeting the profound domestic needs of our times?"

Here, obviously, I believe we can build upon the conceptual and practical strengths of our practice to assist large, bureaucratic institutions to learn the arts of coproduction and to benefit from the structural magic of mediating structures.

Let us not sell ourselves short: Those who practice voluntary action are among the few in this society who know how to relate directly to people. We know how to identify their needs, to help them rise toward self-esteem and self-sufficiency, and to embody a caring respect for the uniqueness of each individual. Those who seek to spend their lives convincing us that we need to buy the particular deodorant their company manufactures or to elect them to the Congress because their hair is attractively styled and the members of their families appear devoted in a fifteen-second TV spot have much to learn from voluntary sector practitioners about what people really need and want, as well as how to work with people in a context of mutual respect, rather than one-sided manipulation.

A danger to democracy and reason exists in the modern world, and that is the specter of corporatism—the political theory that asserts that all important decisions should be made by three sets of bureaucratic forces acting in unison: the state, the corporation, and labor unions. Those members of society who are left out of these councils—most notably nearly all citizens and most persons active in the voluntary sector—must learn to speak and act decisively against this pernicious and destructive theory.

3. The final lesson involves learning that no single institution or sector of society possesses all the resources, all the wisdom, or all the energy to create the kind of healthy society we all seek. Waldemar Nielsen (1979) has pointed us in this direction in noting that the voluntary sector "does not offer a substitute for the social and humanitarian programs of the modern welfare state. But it does offer a means of supplementing and stimulating them and of lessening some of the most dangerous fiscal, psychological, and political side-effects of excessive bureaucratization, centralization and depersonalization of governmentally administered programs" (p. 251).

Nielsen's measured perspective reminds us that it does as little good to rail against the unproductivity of government or the sterility of corporations as it does to inflate claims for voluntarism. We need to have all our major institutions—churches, corporations, national government, voluntary social service organizations, schools, small businesses, local governments, neighborhood organizations, colleges and universities, labor unions, citizen cooperatives, and on and on—working in concert, to meet our pressing needs. Our task, then, is to regroup and reinspire forces rather than to fantasize that one set of institutions can lead the way to the future we desire.

CONCLUSION: PARTNERSHIPS IN AN EFFECTIVE SOCIAL ECONOMY

The partnership vision, with all its allure, requires evaluation by the varieties of theory that have been explored in this work. Returning to a consideration of the five configurations of three-sector relationships identified in Chapter 5, it is apparent that partnerships are likely to be seen in dramatically different ways from these varying perspectives:

- the neo-corporatist viewing partnerships as a good way of doing business
- the pluralist identifying partnerships as the embodiment of democracy in action
- the populist suspecting that many partnerships are means by which large institutions coopt authentic forces of participation
- the idealist worrying that the pragmatic nature of partnerships may overwhelm the goals of deliberative decision-making
- the social democrat asserting that partnerships are simply one more tool for those who control economic structures to manipulate opinion and policy.

The study of partnership experiences calls for their evaluation by the criteria of these five perspectives. And that requires that we see the voluntary sector participants in such activities acting as both bearers of the voluntary tradition and as representatives of voluntary associations.

The five traditions provide a personal style for the voluntary partner to assume, and evaluation of the five perspectives requires us to choose that personal style. My own preferences are to the blending of the pluralist's quest for collaboration, the populist's insistance on participation, the idealist's assertion of quality, and the social democrat's focus on the goal of justice. I reject for myself the neo-corporatist's deference to established powers, choosing rather the more democratic styles of voluntary leadership. Other potential partners, obviously, will find styles congenial to their own values and preferences.

As we act out the transactions of partnering, however, it will be important to be aware of the ways in which our personal values are affected by the social climate of our times. Conversely, it is part of the genius of the voluntary principle that we also can know of the ways in which our own lives and choices affect and build those socio-cultural values. At the level of values, the volunteer or voluntary organization leader plays a vital social role. It is here that ideas take organizational form, and movements emerge and develop that may transform larger social institutions and structures.

These ideas, at the same time, relate to the slow movement of society's tectonic plates. As new economic, political, and global forces exert their influence on the surface of society, the social equivalents of volcanic eruptions and earthquakes begin to be felt, as do the effects of the slower, barely perceptible lifting or settling of the terrain. We all sense social change, but only some are able to understand it and redirect their lives and maintain a solid footing. The final section of this book addresses some of the directions and manifestations of these forces as they may emerge in the years ahead.

PART IV

Voluntarism and the Future: Policies and Practice

Introduction

Thus far in this volume, a number of central points have been made, and argumentation provided for their support. Principal among these points are the following:

1. The third sector is an interdependent, rather than an independent, arena of action. Boundaries between third sector organizations and organizations in the other sectors (government, business, household) are permeable, blurred, and laced with intersectoral connections.

2. The concepts "voluntary organization" or "nonprofit organization" alone are not sufficient as bases for a theory of third sector activity. If the full significance of voluntary action in modern life is to be understood, central attention needs to be paid to the individual act of volunteering itself, as well as to the social forces that buffet and shape organizations. Individual volunteering can take place within voluntary and nonprofit organizations, and also within governmental, corporate, and household structures. And the social forces that help shape organizations are at work among voluntary and nonvoluntary groups alike.

3. The concept of "social economy" represents well the unique combination of purpose and organization involved in effective voluntarism. This concept draws fully on the democratic theories of populism, idealism, pluralism, and social democracy. It clarifies a position for voluntary organizations in society, and it suggests a variety of productive roles for individuals, both inside and outside of formal organizations.

4. The significance of voluntary and nonprofit action can best be understood by means of a three-level map, in which the topographic form of the action as an ecology of organizations is seen in the context of both values and individual action (climatic

forces) and deep structural forces (tectonics). Such a map integrates the major insights of social theory toward voluntarism, and the previous efforts of contemporary theorists of voluntary and nonprofit organizations.

Several implications follow from these points. Among the principal ones are the following:

1. We should avoid hypostasizing concepts of "the sector" in our research, and be wary of them in our action. Voluntary and nonprofit organizations are not independent in their activity; nor are their acts necessarily clothed in a special robe of virtue. They are human endeavors, and like the rest of them, require questioning, evaluation, and, at times, even regulation.

2. Criteria are required for the analysis and evaluation of voluntary and nonprofit organization. They need to be developed; and both volunteers and organizations should be held accountable for their realization.

3. As with other organizations, process must be balanced by outcome in assessing the merits of voluntary action. If process is appropriate and strong, this should surely be celebrated. But it is not enough; this is a world with many problems, and they shout for resolution. No principal avenue of organization in society can justify itself on process alone.

This, the final section of this book, seeks to achieve three remaining tasks. These are addressed in three chapters oriented toward the study of present and future trends in American voluntary action.

- Chapter 10 seeks to clarify the "special role" of voluntary action in the shifting authority bases of contemporary societies.
- Chapter 11 peers into the future of voluntary action, developing criteria for the analysis and evaluation of voluntary and nonprofit action and organizations.
- Chapter 12 begins to specify policies to guide the development of voluntary and nonprofit professional practice in the years ahead.

10

The Three Sectors and Changing Authority Patterns

It reminded me of something Bobby Jo had said in a taxicab in Rio, where we were attending a five-day conference on the need for a comprehensive system of evaluating arts information. "It's simple, J.S.," she said. "The problem is overhead. Your fat cats will give millions to build an arts center, but nobody wants to donate to pay the light bill because you can't put a plaque on it. They'll pay for Chippewa junk sculpture, but who wants to endow the janitor?"

"Speaking of endowments," I whispered hoarsely, and leaned over and pressed my lips hungrily against hers.

—Garrison Keillor, "Jack Schmidt, Arts Administrator" (1983, p. 10)

INTRODUCTION

Jack Schmidt, the fast-dialing Arts Administrator, is the first nonprofit organization manager to play a leading role in American literature (unless you want to include Elmer Gantry). Schmidt moved into this profession from his former avocation as a private detective, and administers his chain of thirty-seven organizations "from the Anaheim Puppet Theatre to the Title IX Poetry Center in Bangor" (Keillor, 1983, p. 4) with the panache of a highwayman. Schmidt is sometimes slowed, but never vanquished, as when told that matching funds will be required for a grant:

> Matching funds! The perpetual curse of the arts administrator! Fifteen thousand dangled before my eyes but before the load comes down my chute I have to scrounge up fifteen more. The girl says yes, but first I have to find a date for her ugly sister (p. 86).

Jack Schmidt, Arts Administrator, may be telling us that something is changing in American life. Not only Democratic Party hopefuls for the presidency have a way with women; not only late-night TV talk-show guests have a way with words: voluntary sector administrators can also contribute to the greed and coarseness toward which so many societal authority patterns seem to be slipping. And, as Jack would put it so effectively: "Speaking of slipping authority patterns . . . ."

This chapter addresses the question of how authority is structured in contemporary society. The problem is both scholarly and applied. As a problem in social science, it is important to discover in what ways institutional systems are affected by changing cultural orientations. Examining authority patterns in change should provide clues about the adequacy of the various social theories that have been examined in this work. Which forms of theory serve best as descriptors of the contemporary direction of modern societies? Which forms provide the best guideposts for the direction society should take in organizing its three sectors?*

On a practical level, the problem of shifting authority patterns will be of obvious importance to leaders in the voluntary sector, as well as to persons involved in the functioning of governmental and corporate organizations. This is, as we have seen, an era in which we hear much about the need for "partnerships" between leaders of the three sectors. And the road to successful partnerships may be strewn with pitfalls if contrasting images of proper modes of decision-making and organizational participation are not understood, and their implications recognized, by aspiring partners.

In this chapter, "authority" is taken to mean "shared beliefs about the power or the influence of an organization or individual representing that organization" (Heller, 1985, p. 488). Trudy Heller (1984) has described authority as being in "crisis" in the contemporary United States:

> No aspect of societal transformation is more apparent within organizations than the change in authority patterns. Middle-aged managers can remember when employees were more obedient and docile, more respectful of authority. Senior executives may recall the days when employees unquestioningly conformed to organizational directives, even when sacrifice of family or personal life was involved.
>
> The pervasiveness of this change extends not only to authority figures, such as "the boss," but also to society's organizations and institutions. Watergate, Abscam, and criminal dealings by corporate executives have undermined the public trust in both organizations and those who lead and represent them. The result is an erosion of the authority of these institutions (p. 88).

In this chapter the impact of this putative "decline in authority" is traced in the three major institutional sectors (corporate, governmental, and voluntary). For each sector, evidence is reviewed regarding changes in authority patterns, and assessment is made of the receptivity to such changes of lead-

---

* Authority patterns are, of course, rarely static in a complex society. Authoritarian religion, politics, and corporate organization have shown considerable strength in the 1980s and may continue to develop, fueled by, among other forces, a "New Victorianism" occasioned by fear of the AIDS virus (cf. Cornish, 1986).

ership in the sector at hand. Thus it is asked: How have authority patterns changed in each sector? How are these changes evaluated, through the medium of scholarship, by institutional participants?

Once the state of authority is assessed, we shall be able to compare patterns within the three sectors. The problem of educating leaders and managers of voluntary and nonprofit organizations will then be examined. The chapter will conclude with a perusal of possible future developments in the evolution of authority both within our broader cultures and our major societal institutions.

CHANGING AUTHORITY PATTERNS IN CORPORATIONS

In the corporate sector, a decline in authority has been described as existing on the level of the corporation in society, and on the level of superior-subordinate relations within the corporation (Heller, 1985). Trudy Heller describes the development of this pattern:

> The Industrial Revolution's image of the corporation likened the power/ authority of the corporate owner to that of God. As God had created the universe and man to serve Him, so the creators/owners of the corporations had created the industrial organization and the employees to serve themselves. The next image of the corporation emerged after World War I —that of the corporation as an organism. The organization and its leaders maintained, during this phase, a fairly lofty position but lost their God-like status: "Management was characterized as the brain or head of the firm and employees as its organs" (Ackoff, 1981, p. 27). During the post-World War II period, the current image of the corporation emerged. Here the corporation is an open system and managers mere jugglers of stakeholders' competing interests (p. 489).

Public opinion polls indicate an acceleration in the decline of the authority of the corporation in recent years. Heller (1985, p. 490) notes that the authority of the boss has diminished in recent years as a result of a "double loss: loss of the motive to manage and be the boss on the one hand, and loss of willingness to submit to authority and be bossed on the other." In the transformation of authority from divine right to bureaucratic modes, we tend to follow our bosses less willingly, and we tend to avoid the role ourselves. The result can be seen as a crisis of both leadership and followership (Heller, Van Til, and Zurcher, 1986).

In partial response to this crisis of authority in corporate organizations, experiments are occasionally undertaken that involve less hierarchical authority patterns. Developments such as the importation of Japanese management, quality of work life, autonomous work groups, worker buy-outs, matrix structures, union representation on corporate boards, and in-house entrepreneurial teams all involve tinkering with authority patterns.

Nonetheless some of these tinkerings seem promising, perhaps, in part, because they mesh well with contemporary attitudes toward authority. For example, William Foote Whyte (1986, p. 39) has described the efforts of organizations in Philadelphia to develop employee ownership, and he notes that: "Among the main benefits of employee ownership are enhanced learning opportunities, with a consequent increase in personal confidence and self-esteem." The student of voluntarism will note that the Philadelphia experiment in worker-ownership was stewarded by several active and innovative nonprofit organizations, in partnership with a major labor union.

Most corporate organizations, however, have chosen to suffer through the problems occasioned by the new worker, rather than suffering with their workers toward the development of alternative structures of organization. Fortified by images of entrepreneurial leadership, managers of even the largest corporations have assumed the role of omnipotent celebrities, guardians of the "bottom line," and claimants of the quality of products made under their apparent supervision (Lee Iacocca of the Chrysler Corporation is a prominent example here). What Louis Zurcher (1973) called "bureau-charisma" has become a predominant corporate tool for maintaining control of both markets and workers in the 1980s. This response is not greatly dissimilar from the choices made by many government leaders in the same period.

AUTHORITY WITHIN GOVERNMENT: THE CENTER HOLDS

Public concern with the organization of governmental activity has in recent years focused on a single major issue—the "problem" of bureaucracy. Lynn (1981, p. 36) puts the matter starkly: "However much Max Weber believed bureaucracy to the be most efficient form of social organization, with the bureaucratic specialist a natural successor to the unqualified amateur, in American political life bureaucracy is perceived as a problem, even a danger."

The supposed inefficiency of bureaucracy, and particularly the presumed sins of bureaucrats—their arrogance, their casual work habits, their unionized rules and collectively negotiated wages—have come to dominate political discussion of governmental administration in the contemporary United States. Blaming the bureaucrat has become an easy path to the White House for such political "outsiders" as Jimmy Carter and Ronald Reagan.

The public distrust, and even disgust, with bureaucracy seems quite uncoupled with any systematic reform agenda. Opinion polls show that governmental authority has fallen at least as far as corporate, union, religious, or educational authority.

Faced with this disenchantment with public authority, students of public administration tend to stand firm in defense of the established order. Herbert Kaufman (1981), for example, in his Brookings Institution study of the behavior of six federal bureau chiefs, writes that they "probably could have survived by simply drifting with the current. . . . But they did not elect to behave in this fashion. Instead, they hurled themselves into the fray they could have avoided, striving to influence the course of events despite the limitations under which they had to labor" (pp. 134–135).

In Kaufman's eyes (1981), these leaders of bureaucracies assume extraordinary leadership qualities. Describing the success of Food and Drug Administration Commissioner (now President of Stanford University) Donald Kennedy's successful effort to right the image and practice of his agency, he writes:

> The consensus among informed commentators on the FDA seems to be that he accomplished this remarkable feat by the sheer force of his intellect, personality, and style. Even his adversaries came to admire him. . . . Having seen him at congressional committee hearings, press conferences, personal interviews, appearances before interest groups, and a variety of meetings, I fully concur in these judgments. His performance glittered (p. 146).

The resurrection of the "great man" theory of leadership by Kaufman is reflected in his consideration of the role of chief in motivating his organizational charges: "The chiefs delivered inspirational extemporaneous speeches in the fashion of football coaches firing up their teams between halves. They lauded the achievements, conceded the deficiencies, urged greater efforts, and indicated generally where improvements were needed and how they might be effected" (1981, p. 82).

Against this thoroughly charismatic rendition of the theme of bureaucratic leadership, concepts of participatory management are brusquely dismissed. Lynn referees a debate between advocates of the "hard" (executive leadership) and "soft" (organizational development) paths of governmental management, and sides with the former. The soft path is limited by pressures of time, does not enhance productivity, and ignores the protective functions of bureaucratic rigidity. As former Secretary of Commerce Juanita Kreps put it, the soft path is too "precious" for bureaucratic realities.

Lynn (1981) concludes the debate with the "most fundamental objection" to employee-centered management reforms: "They violate the principle that government organizations exist to serve the public, not their employees" (p. 96). Similarly, Warwick, in his *A Theory of Public Bureaucracy* (1975, ch. 9), provides a full explanation of "why bureaucracy stays," citing the external resistance to change of congressional orientations, agency turf, statutory and system-wide rules, interagency linkages, and interest groups, and the internal resistance provided by leadership discontinuity, careerism, administrative orthodoxy, and organizational goals.

The conclusion that emerges from the studies of federal bureaucracy, then, is that bureaucracy is here to stay, barring some kind of miraculous transformation in the orientations of the public, political leaders, and bureaucrats themselves (see Warwick, ch. 11). We may query this scholarly orthodoxy by noting the introduction of such innovations as flexible work hours and quality circles into some corners of federal structure, or by following the suggestion of students of street-level bureaucracies that new age values are sometimes accommodated in patterns of superior–subordinate interaction. (Perhaps the contrast between the camaraderie of "Hill Street Blues" and the corporate-macho tyrannies of "Dallas" suggests a greater cultural openness to bureaucratic reform than to corporate reform—but these speculations will be left to the rumination of the readers.)

The image of J.R. Ewing does, however, suggest a brief discussion of experiences in the Reagan presidency toward governmental reform. Political scientist Sheldon Wolin (1983) observed that: "When Reagan appointees are asked about the difference between working for the government and for private business, their principal response is that in business an executive can expect an order to be obeyed promptly, while in government an executive encounters only frustration" (p. 3). The cases of the Environmental Protection Agency under Anne Gorsuch and the Department of the Interior under James Watt, both of which outlasted their administrator's efforts to debilitate them, bear comparison to the less bureaucratic National Security Council as administered by Admiral John Poindexter while the Iran-Contra dealings evolved in 1985 and 1986. When Poindexter was succeeded by Frank Carlucci in 1987, the NSC required a thorough reconstruction. The ability of a more bureaucratic organization to resist destructive leadership sometimes may prove to be one of its most endearing qualities.

VOLUNTARY SECTOR MANAGEMENT: THREADBARE AND/OR ADAPTIVE?

From the point of view of management authorities, the voluntary sector often appears to be a poor and weak sister. Indeed, the same combination of charity, pity, and patronizing we lavish on our unfortunate kin seems the common stance of many corporate and governmental leaders, as well as their scholarly admirers, toward voluntary sector administrators. As Robert David (1986) puts it:

> In the literature of the last two years the business attitudes toward NFPs [not-for-profit organizations] are blatantly faultfinding. In general, it is believed that NFPs could be improved if they were taught how to manage, businesslike ways, better management, how to hire better personnel and retain top quality employees, better recruitment techniques, how to charge for their services, management orientation to determine their market

position, how to deliver services effectively, how to cooperate with other NFPs, how to maintain consistent quality, procedures to receive more earned income, financial planning, how to evaluate the programmatic value of their services, and tax planning and contract negotiating (p. 364).

Few of these corporate biases toward nonprofit organizations, David continues, take into account the "special organizational characteristics" of organizations in the third sector. These characteristics are recognized, if not entirely charitably, by marketing specialists Christopher Lovelock and Charles Weinberg (1984), in their list of characteristics of nonprofit organizations (pp. 3–7). This list includes: the nature of products, the dominance of nonfinancial objectives, the need for resource attraction, the presence of multiple constituencies, the tension between mission and customer satisfaction, the presence of public scrutiny, the realities of nonmarket pressures, the ability to obtain free or inexpensive support, and the presence of "duplicate management" structures. The last condition is viewed by the authors as "perhaps the worst situation of all" (p. 7).

The somewhat bemused contempt of voluntary sector management may reflect a preference for things over people. Thus, management theorist Theodore Levitt, who has sought to interpret the "third sector" to a corporate readership, writes that "manufacturing has outperformed service because it has for a long time thought technocratically and managerially about its functions. Service has lagged because it has thought humanistically" (quoted in Lynn, 1981, p. 91). In a more charitable approach, Wortman (1981) has identified much voluntary management as existing in a "prebureaucratic" state.

When looked at in terms of shifting authority patterns, however, the voluntary sector appears particularly permeable. The voluntary sector is, of course, the locus of social movements in society. As such movements begin to form around the nucleus of a new configuration of values, they become the organizational force to advance the values shift. Thus the civil rights movement, the black power movement, the gay rights movement, the women's movement—and the list can be greatly expanded—all come to embody the definition and advocacy of new rules and new orientations.

Other parts of the voluntary sector are far more resistant to such changes. The Michels problem remains to trouble many voluntary associations, even those committed to the principle of democratizing all organizations. Additionally, many established organizations hold firm to traditional values, responding to change in defensive and reluctant fashions (cf. Gusfield, 1963). Yet other organizations may respond much as a corporation or a bureaucracy to shifting values—keeping their eye on the product of their labors, and adjusting the process as conditions require.

Indeed, some denizens of the voluntary world are essentially agents of government, deliverers of publicly funded services who operate under the permissive aegis of "paper" boards of directors. Such participants in "third-party government," as Lester Salamon (1983) identifies them, are essentially entrepreneurs under contract. But the full breadth of the nonprofit sphere, as discussed in Chapters 6 and 7, can only be comprehended by retaining the many varieties of non-religious charitable institutions, religious institutions, membership benefit institutions, umbrella organizations and trade associations, and fundraising institutions and foundations.

Michael O'Neill and Dennis Young (1986, p. 4) have searched for ways in which nonprofit organizations are a distinctive arena for management, and they identify five characteristics:

- the ambiguity of their performance criteria and the complexity of their management-related values;
- the legal and financial constraints under which they operate;
- some of the sources from which they derive economic sustenance;
- the kinds of personnel they employ;
- their governance structures

Bruce Vladeck (1986, p. 6) underlines the last O'Neill–Young point when he notes that the "relationship between board chairman and the chief salaried officer is . . . the single most important relationship within a nonprofit." And Cecily Selby's observation that nonprofits typically involve three parallel hierarchies—those of paid staff, volunteers, and professionals— is cited by O'Neill and Young (1986, p. 10) as a factor to reckon with in essaying the interpersonal skills of the nonprofit manager. Brian O'Connell (1986) has called for attention to the training of boards and for a careful attention to the degree to which values are actually advanced by nonprofit organizations.

Paul DiMaggio (1986) and Simon Slavin (1986) have noted important differences between nonprofits on the basis of their "core technology" or field of interest. And Jonathan Cook (1986) sees size of organization as an important point of differentiation among not-for-profits. Studying individual organizations within this vast voluntary world, Jone Pearce (1980 and 1982), David Adams (1983), and Arlene Kaplan Daniels (1986) illustrate the wide range of organizational styles that may be found in the voluntary sector. Adams has conducted detailed research on a Red Cross Chapter, and the image of that agency that appears in his writing is of a carefully controlled and highly structured bureaucracy. Within the "elite" and "lower" roles of this organization, workers go about their various production and governance tasks. Like a corporation, there is a product—blood—and it is the job of volunteers and paid staff within the organization to "manufacture" as much of that product as they can in the most cost-effective ways.

Pearce also regards the voluntary association from an essentially economic perspective in her research, which focuses on the compensation, or rewards, of voluntary participation. The organizations she studies (a student newspaper, a poverty relief clinic, a family planning center, and a volunteer fire department) appear to be less secure and stable than Adams's Red Cross chapter. Within these organizations, Pearce (1980) finds few rewards, whether in the form of power or status, accompanying the assumption of leadership roles. Nor does she find a stable authority structure prevailing among volunteers: "Volunteers in the organizations were much more likely to work when they wanted and in the manner they wanted [than were paid employees]" (1982, p. 390).

Daniels (1986, p. 12), in a study of career patterns among foundation employees, finds that chief executive officers emerge from a variety of personal and organizational backgrounds:

> The CEOs of foundations are a varied lot; they come from very diverse backgrounds and serve very different types of organizations. They range from secretaries promoted up from handmaiden status to eminent former college presidents; and their responsibilities range from personal service for a family board, dispensing funds of a few hundred thousand a year to large national and international foundations that can give millions away.

Despite this variation, Daniels identifies a number of career patterns, grouped by gender. Males are found in four categories: "The Eminent Man," "The Successful Male CEO at Mid Career," "The Male CEO in an Ambiguous Position," and "The CEO at or Near Retirement." Female types include "The Eminent Woman," "The CEO from a Volunteer Background," "The Ambiguous Woman CEO in a Small Organization," "The Personal Assistant to the Board," and the "Rising Secretary."

Eva Schindler-Rainman has sought in her work (1980) to both comprehend and control shifting authority patterns in the voluntary sector: "This is and will continue to be a time of changing values, moving from an emphasis on conformity to an acceptance of pluralism . . . from an emphasis on quantity to one on quality . . . from an acceptance of authority to one of confrontation" (p. 160).

In such an era of change, Schindler-Rainman and her colleague Ronald Lippitt clearly see both the decline of former patterns of authority and the emergence of new configurations. Of decline they write (1975, p. 22):

> Youth's faith in the ability of the older generation to give guidance in coping with the present and the emerging future will continue to decline. Female confrontations of the male-dominated political and economic functions will intensify, as will the attack on the double standard in sexual mores. A coalition of all racial minorities is likely to confront the racial majority. The poor are developing an increasing sense of potency and outrage in their growing conflict with the affluent.

The reader need only reflect on the challenge the National Organization of Women (NOW) presented to women on the significance of their volunteering, or the daily struggle of voluntary agencies to stay current regarding the role of the disabled or those of same-sex preference to appreciate the sensitivity of leaders in this sector to shifting authority patterns. One anecdote that offends a client category, and one risks the loss of both one's staff and one's clients. The costs of insensitivity are high in the voluntary sector, and the result is an openness to change.

It should not be surprising, then, that many voluntary sector leaders do not long dwell on changes in authority patterns as a problem of "decline," or "erosion," but rather see these changes as an integral part of their work milieu. Bruce Vladeck (1986), President of the United Hospital Fund of New York, writes:

> The gap between one's ultimate and instrumental goals can be narrower in nonprofit management than in almost any other job one can imagine. For many nonprofit managers, of course, their occupational activities are directly a result of religious or moral convictions; it is, quite literally, a vocation. For secular humanists, on the other hand, it's the closest they can come to doing God's work (p. 18).

From this perspective, even rapid changes are often viewed as challenges, to be integrated and recombined into new patterns of adaptive organizational authority. As Schindler-Rainman and Lippitt write: "The necessary interdependence between polarized groups . . . requires the development of new models of creative compromise which integrate the dimensions of conflict in the meeting of needs and the solving of problems" (p. 23).

And this reconstruction of authority can be embodied in a voluntary organization if it can face up to the manifold challenges of the new order, challenges that include finding ways to use the services of temporary volunteers and developing positions for them that will mesh with their own values and needs. "It is important," Schindler-Rainman writes (1980), "for human service professionals to become familiar with some of the literature and practices of the corporate work place. Many of these participatory ways of work can be adapted in the Volunteer Agency field" (p. 160).

Just as volunteer leaders can learn much from corporate innovation, so, the work of Jone Pearce implies, can corporate managers learn from the experience of volunteer leaders. Pearce (1982, p. 393) suggests that the problems of unwilling leaders and undependable volunteer followers represent part of a much larger problem, that of decreasing employee dependence. More and more paid employees are acting like volunteers by losing their will to manage or their desire to submit to authority. This pattern represents a part of what we have been calling a "crisis of authority."

Many voluntary organizations have sought to cope directly with shifting authority patterns. Among the mechanisms are the following:

- By using volunteers as a large portion of their labor force, voluntary organizations can protect themselves from sudden, or even long-term, financial shortfall (cf. Hirschhorn et al., 1983).
- By appealing to a wider range of motivations than employing organizations, voluntary organizations have the potential of energizing a highly motivated work force while directly facing the possibility that they will lose those workers who become bored (Pearce, 1982).
- By combining both self-regarding and other-regarding interest in their work, voluntary organizations are well positioned to spearhead "coproductive" approaches to the resolution of problems, in which "win-win" outcomes replace "zero-sum games" (cf. Van Til, Culleton, and Margolin, 1982).
- By legitimating the achievement of ideological goals as an outcome of organizational activity, voluntary associations may be particularly enabled to reorient their organizational patterns of cultural preference (say in the area of sensitivity to rights of the disabled or expectations regarding the family responsibilities of the father, or any of a hundred other rapidly changing fields of sociocultural definition).

Rather than being a "poor sister" when it comes to reorienting authority, then, many voluntary organizations may provide models worthy of emulation by corporate or governmental agencies. Commerce between the three sectors may be a far more egalitarian set of transactions than may first appear.

THE SEARCH FOR NEW FORMS OF AUTHORITY

The moral of our search should by now be clear: we must all seek ways of creating viable authority patterns or we shall all suffer. And no one has yet found the one way. Furthermore, we should avoid the pitfall of equating a decline in hierarchical authority patterns with an absolute decline in authority. What we may be witnessing is, rather, a shift to alternative authority patterns—patterns that may be better adapted to a postindustrial society characterized by high levels of complexity and rapid change.

The challenge to contemporary institutions facing the future is to discern the leading edge. Here one's definition of the problem determines the solution of choice. Hence, in the corporate literature, where the problem is defined as an erosion or decline in hierarchical authority patterns, solutions involve ways and means to reconstitute past arrangements—except in dire situations when concern for survival may prompt experimentation. In government, where the problem is defined as a weakening or inefficiency of official structures, we have reviewed proposals to reinvigorate the bureaucratic forms by the placement of energetic and "great" men in positions of power. And, while many organizations in the voluntary sector follow either the corporate or the bureaucratic model, other voluntary institutions define the problem as one of adaptation to attitudes toward authority which are shifting in the society at large. Here is a climate that is "right" for innovation.

Faced with the need to re-establish authority in a time of rapid sociocultural change, some leaders turn to the cultivation of charisma while others initiate the search for management reforms that will allow for effective organizational planning. I suspect that each of these approaches has its uses but that neither forms a full solution to the problem of reconstituting authority in a time of change. Rather, I sense that the development of authority patterns adequate for the sustenance of our society in change will be a multifaceted process—a process in which the very best will be required of both people and their institutions.

As for corporate futures, Robert Reich (1983, pp. 18–19) may yet to be proven accurate with his forecast that: "The enterprises that will dominate the economics of advanced nations in the future depend on participation and thus on security and equity." Such enterprises are rather highly egalitarian, provide for secure employment, and depend on consultation and negotiation for their decision-making. Reich asserts that: "only when skills, knowledge, and responsibility are widely diffused can employees build on one another's strengths in responding to new problems and opportunities; only when employees feel relatively secure from arbitrary job loss and on an equal footing can they collaborate spontaneously. In this setting industrial change does not have to be 'sold' to the work force; change is promoted and carried out by the work force."

To conclude the present chapter, however, let us recognize the possibility that the principles of participation, and even democracy and equality, that many for-profit corporations will adopt in order to survive in the transnational future will also come to characterize, though at a slower pace, the evolution of many governmental organizations. It then becomes possible that these very principles that have infused so powerfully the development of a great deal of voluntarism will come to greater influence in areas other than voluntary and nonprofit organizations.

In short, it is voluntarism as a behavioral principle, as discussed in Chapters 6–9, that may yet prove to be a potent force in the forging of new patterns of authority in postindustrial society. Embodied initially in the forms of contestation–participation outlined by Meister, this principle may extend itself into the arenas of official participation. Like a long-term shift in the climate, an infusion of the voluntary principle into economic and governmental life would transform these institutions. And when time is found for the great institutions to learn from each other about coping with changing authority patterns, they may each approach the table with the sense that all have much to learn from each of the others—and that the collaboration of all three sectors is required for building a society that will allow for institutional development and societal growth.

11

Voluntarism and the Future of Complex Societies

The declining importance of empiricist philosophies of natural science is recognized to have profound implications for the social sciences also. It is not just the case that social and natural science are further apart than advocates of the orthodox consensus believed. We now see that a philosophy of natural science must take account of just those phenomena in which the new schools of social theory are interested—in particular, language and the interpretation of meaning.

—Anthony Giddens, *The Constitution of Society* (1984, p. xvi)

INTRODUCTION

Social scientists do not share a single paradigm for their studies, as was seen in the review of the multiple perspectives on voluntary action theory discussed in Chapters 3 and 4. Individual social scientists vigorously cleave to such divergent theoretical views as presented by neo-Marxism or neo-conservatism. To try to argue that a single paradigm prevails is to find oneself embroiled in argument with colleagues whose sense of what is known, and how and why, is radically different.

Nowhere is the divergence among social scientists more clearly shown than in their orientation toward the study of the future. While some social scientists turn with considerable interest to the systematic study of those futures that are plausible, possible, and predictable, others shun this area of study as indeterminate and unscientific.

The past several decades have seen the gradual emergence of futures studies as a reputable field for scholarship. This maturation has been reflected in the development of methodologies and approaches both more cautious and more sophisticated than those of the Utopians—Plato, Augustine, Thomas More, Edward Bellamy, Aldous Huxley, and George Orwell—whose work typifies the main strand of futurism in Western thought. New approaches now seek to avoid the pitfalls of straight-line forecasting and do not assume that the future will simply be an extension and magnification of present trends. The best of contemporary futurists tend to rely on the development of alternatives for the unfolding of future trends, observing ways in which multiple factors may emerge in mutual interaction.

This chapter will probe the future of voluntary action in contemporary society, concluding with the development of a set of criteria that might usefully guide that development. It begins, however, with an examination of the sources of diversity in social theory, diversity that applies to the study of both the present and the future of societal development.

SOCIAL THEORY AND VOLUNTARY ACTION

The paradigms employed by social scientists are used differently in the various fields within the social sciences. While a variety of theoretical perspectives may be developed on voluntary action, what researchers actually do is quite a bit more limited than what they might develop. For example, the area of voluntary action research evinces few presentations derived from any coherent overall theoretical perspective. Such theory as exists in the field overwhelmingly reflects the implicit assumption of pluralist or neo-corporatist perspectives.

While many researchers persist in the quest for a "scientific" social science in which the facts speak for themselves, more and more influential thinkers in the field have come to recognize the potency of these widely different paradigms. Some thinkers, like the prolific British theorist Anthony Giddens (1984), see this plurality of perspectives as a result of the fact that social scientists study people, who themselves construct varying images of reality (theories).

As this diversity becomes an ineluctable part of social science, so can it be seen to characterize the world of policy. In a major recent statement, Alford and Friedland (1985) have argued that three major perspectives (pluralist, managerial, and class) inform almost all political sociology and political science, and that these perspectives approach mutual exclusivity as they are commonly employed. Slowly, it seems to dawn upon self-styled "empiricists" and "Marxists" and "phenomenologists" and "humanists" alike that they do not share common assumptions about the bases of their knowledge and their craft. Gradually, they begin to see that however they seek to impose in the name of "science" or their discipline an orthodoxy of theory or method, they are engaged in the political process of changing someone else's mind, rather than in the scientific process of testing for the presence of truth.

Burrell and Morgan (1979) have demonstrated the existence of four archetypal modes of defining the field of organizational theory, a scholarly field notable for the efforts of its practitioners to assume and enforce a single methodological and theoretical orthodoxy. Drawing broadly on the philosophical traditions underlying social and political theory, Burrell and Morgan argue that social scientists differ profoundly among themselves on both the nature of their task (social science) and the nature of their field of study (society itself).

Some social scientists define their task as essentially "subjectivist." That is, they adopt an *ontology* of nominalism (focusing on concepts and labels) rather than realism. They assume an *epistemology* of antipositivism (relating what is known to the knower, rather than searching for universal laws) as against a positivistic belief. They hold to a view of *human nature* as voluntaristic (free-willed) rather than as determined. They take on a *methodology* of ideography (focusing on first-hand experience) rather than a nomothetic one.

Other social scientists adopt the opposite position. They may be seen as "objectivists." Their beliefs are those of *realism* (a hard, knowable, certain social world exists), *positivism* (laws can be discovered), *determinism* (by the environment rather than by free-willed behavior), and the *nomothetic method* (using systematic research techniques).

Not only do social scientists differ among themselves on these fundamental questions of how to know about society, Burrell and Morgan argue that they also differ on their assumptions about the nature of society itself. Some adopt a position that emphasizes values of order or integration: societal stability, integration, functional coordination, and consensus. Others approach society from a conflict perspective, seeing change, conflict, disintegration, and coercion as basic social processes.

Combining the subjectivist and objectivist dimensions, Burrell and Morgan derive four resulting paradigms: 1) the functionalist (objective in methodology, oriented to the sociology of regulation); 2) the interpretive (subjective in methodology, oriented to the sociology of regulation); 3) the radical structuralist (objective in methodology, oriented to the sociology of radical change); and 4) the radical humanist (subjective in methodology, oriented to the sociology of radical change). Applying the Burrell-Morgan typology to the study of voluntary associations and nonprofit corporations, I have developed the following five propositions:

1. *The study of voluntary action and nonprofit organizations may be approached from each of the major paradigms of social science study.* This point seems true *ceteris paribus*. If social scientists choose one of these four paradigms for their intellectual home, then that subgroup of social scientists who study voluntary action will, by necessity, face the same choice. Thus Alperovitz and Faux (1984) and Kramer (1984) develop typologies that highlight the range of voluntary responses to political economy, ranging from change (social democracy, nationaliza

tion) to regulation (neo-corporatism, reprivatization). Gamwell (1984) has developed a philosophical justification for focusing on the "public-regarding" subsector of the nonprofit sphere as "teleologically prior," using a subjective methodology that ranges between the interpretive and radical humanist approaches identified by Burrell and Morgan.

2. *Both regulation and radical social change paradigms raise central themes of voluntary action and nonprofit organizational behavior.* Thus, a review of Smith's influential listing of voluntary sector impacts (1973) reveals the regulatory themes of social integration, play (need satisfaction), value preservation (status quo), economic networking (social order), and latent goal-attainment (consensus). Smith's list also includes a number of radical change impacts: nurturing challenging ideologies, embodying mystery and the sacred (potentiality), and liberating individual expression (emancipation).

Two other impacts combine themes from both societal views: developing societal innovations and providing feedback for system change and correction. Both of these impacts may be seen, from the perspective of open systems theory, as involving either regulation or radical change.

3. *Studies of voluntary action tend to focus most centrally on the use of the functionalist paradigm.* This proposition is more clearly subject to empirical test than the first two. And to test it, a preliminary analysis was conducted of all articles published in the *Journal of Voluntary Action Research* during an eight-year period. The analysis—which must be considered "interpretive" in light of the fact that I now edit the journal and have published in it (three "interpretive" articles)—shows that 78% of the articles published in the journal took the functionalist approach to social science, while 21% approached their task from the interpretive perspective. During the eight-year period, only two articles employed a radical social change perspective (both "structuralist," rather than "humanist").

4. *When studies of voluntary action address change organizations from the functionalist paradigm, a "mobilization of bias" may be discovered such that some organizations are considered "dangerous and deviant" while others are "acceptable and appropriate."* By the term "mobilization of bias," political scientists have indicated the tendency of organizations to create assumptions that things are always and properly done the way they are presently being done within that organization.

David Horton Smith (1973) argues that this position may prove short-sighted: the voluntary sector often provides "the social risk capital of human society," and can play the role of "gadfly, dreamer, and moral leader in society" (pp. 388–389). Those who seek to apply the label of "deviant" or "un-American" to an organization, then, run the risk of foreclosing an option for society that may prove invaluable to its development.

5. *The development of trans-paradigmatic theories (open systems theory, "transformational" theory) may be useful in creating an appropriately catholic, broadly based science of voluntary action.* Open systems theory may bridge the gap between theories of regulation and those of radical change. A similar hope is held by many students of societal transformation (cf. Harman, 1979; Ferguson, 1980). The persuasive development of such transcendent paradigms, however, awaits expansion.

THE CHANGING CONTEXT OF VOLUNTARY ACTION

What occurs in the voluntary sector will have its impact on the course of societal development, but the broader societal forces will also constrain the development of voluntarism. A consideration of the environmental forces affecting the future of voluntary action gave rise to a list of eleven factors in the Report of the National Forum on Volunteerism (cf. Rydberg and Peterson, 1980). These factors were identified as follows:

1. Inflation
2. Motivations of volunteers
3. Impact of government
4. Energy shortage
5. Empowerment of unempowered people
6. Changing workplace conditions
7. Demographic changes
8. Stance of the helping environment
9. Corporate involvement
10. Litigious society
11. Degree of democratic pluralism.

In both my own contribution to the National Forum on Volunteerism (Van Til, 1980) and a separate study of ways in which energy patterns might affect the shape of our cities and towns (Van Til, 1982), I found it useful to consider three possible images of the future, or views of societal development. I called these images "Good Luck," "Continuity," and "Hard Luck." We must hope for the best, I wrote, but plan for the worst.

It is possible, I argued, that the future might come to be as gloomy as all this:

• Galloping inflation
• Feelings of self-centeredness, privatism, and competitiveness
• Government as captive of the wealthy
• Severe energy shortfall and dislocations in pricing and supply
• Setbacks in empowerment of the disaffected, with severe social dislocation and conflict
• Rise of permanently unemployed masses
• Failure of welfare state, accompanied by economic dislocation
• Inability of helping establishment to ameliorate distress
• Rise of revolutionary and repressive political-economic forces
• Exacerbation of litigiousness
• Demise of pluralistic democracy and active society.

Such a hard-luck situation is not probable, but it certainly is possible. With the exception of the relatively good luck we have enjoyed in maintaining energy supplies at steady prices and in reducing inflation over the past several years, the other factors in this hard-luck setting are in place at least in part, at this time. Unemployment, poverty, interest rates, corporate domination of government, a whittling away at the role of citizen participation, and a decline in interest in the empowerment of minorities certainly have characterized both public policy and economic trends during the Reagan era.

It is also possible that the factors listed above might assume the configuration of a "good-luck situation," and look more like the following pattern:

• Inflation at historically low levels
• Feelings of predictability and human interrelatedness
• Governmental action as responsible planner
• Adequate energy supply without price shocks
• Continuing extension of the empowerment of minorities
• Adequate provision of employment
• Capacity to cope with demographic change
• Ability of helping establishment to provide service
• Preservation of balance between corporate and entrepreneurial activity
• Avoidance of litigious society
• Flourishing of democratic pluralism.

Such a good-luck future has been developed in the futures literature along two major lines, one relatively traditional and the other explicitly transformational. The traditional image, held by such conservatives as Ronald Reagan, assumes that the institutions of modified capitalism can lead us to the promised land of wealth and happiness for all. The transformational image, as developed by futurists like Willis Harman, Marilyn Ferguson, and Alvin Toffler, posits a widespread change in values, which then ushers in a new age of simple living and societal creativity.

Betwen the extremes of the good-luck and hard-luck futures lies the third, and most probable, image of the emerging U.S. future, which I identify as the "continuity" future. This image assumes that the future will be much like the recent past, or at least will develop along lines that are visible. In it, the eleven factors sort out along the following pattern:

- Inflation at moderate levels, with occasional bursts above 10%
- Struggle between attitudinal forces of materialism and meaning
- Struggle between role of government as planner and steward of elites
- Incremental rise of reliance on renewable energy sources
- Slowing in rates of empowerment of the disaffected
- Allaying of high unemployment rates by mid-1990s
- Demographic change in the context of search for community
- Self-help strengthening beleaguered helping establishments
- Continued corporate domination of society
- Extension of litigious society
- Continuing struggle to advance forces of democratic pluralism.

The continuity future, it is apparent, involves a standoff on a number of key issues, such as the choice between materialism and meaning in values and the choice between planner and steward of elites by government. Its indeterminacy represents current reality, as fundamental questions of the role of government or of cultural development are not likely to be resolved in the remaining years of the 20th century. While these questions do not receive decisive resolution, they will surely continue to excite the commitment and concern of many citizens organized into voluntary associations in the years ahead.

IMAGES OF THE FUTURE OF VOLUNTARY ACTION

Voluntary responses of citizens will play a part in shaping any societal future while at the same time being affected by those futures. To help see the kinds of issues that may emerge regarding the role of voluntarism in society, let us proceed and sketch three possible images of the future of voluntary action in society.

A Hard-Luck Future for Voluntarism

The hard-luck situation posits a downward cycle of deprivation and frustration, and disorganization is propelled by energy dislocations and rampant inflation. Like many other conventions of civility and urbanity, voluntarism will be jolted, reshaped, and severely strained in such an era. This future would be a time of widespread discontent and severe unemployment, concentrated among those unable to gain access to a shrinking set of entry-level jobs at both the middle and the bottom of the socioeconomic pyramid. These unemployed and underemployed persons will have available to them a large amount of free time in which to perform nonwork activity. At the same time, those fortunate enough to retain employment will be increasingly pressured to search for additional income in nonworking hours, as will ever-rising numbers of mothers of children of all ages. Time available for volunteer activity will therefore decline for the employed, and increase only for the two groups of "unemployable" persons.

For the first of these groups, the overtrained, volunteering will be seen more and more as a necessary step in the search for access to employment. "Experience" will be required of all entry-level job seekers, even beyond the mandatory national youth service that will have been implemented in an attempt to reduce the numbers of job seekers. Such experience will most readily be provided by certified volunteering, which will become an important step in the "rat race" for jobs that characterizes the hard-luck future.

Not all the overtrained will choose to compete for volunteer positions aimed at the rat race, and many will drift into other forms of voluntary activity. As in the 1960s, the challenge of protest groups will once more be joined by the emergence of violent and revolutionary cadres. Those shut out from entry-level jobs at the bottom of the economy will also be subject to volunteer recruitment and certification, but the combination of their lack of personal discipline and virulent disaffection will lead many of them to be perceived as "unmanageable" by professional volunteer administrators, who will even more heavily represent white, upper-middle-class women as employed positions decrease and salaries fall rapidly behind inflation.

In this scene, the "dark side" forces of voluntarism emerge in their full powers. In an effort to restore order to society, corporations join government agencies in promoting volunteer work on themes of self-interest and required altruism. National volunteerism organizations break off ties established in previous years to neighborhood and advocacy movements in an attempt to preserve corporate support for their own dwindling budgets. These budgets are ravaged by the withdrawal of governmental monies and a decline in foundation and corporate support itself occasioned by falling levels of profits and return. In such a climate, the voluntary sector becomes even more disparate and disputatious than at present, split between the overwhelming demands on the provider of services, the quest for eventual employment, and the realities of the needs for social change.

Continuity Future for Voluntarism

The continuity future involves a number of indeterminacies and presages the slow and painful choice of a sustainable societal future. For the voluntary sector, such a time will involve a critical set of choices of direction that will not only involve its own future but also its ability to contribute to the shaping of critical elements of society.

If voluntarism keeps to the path it has hewn thus far in the American experience it is likely that its role in the future will be to do the following:

- Keep alive the tradition that the giving of volunteer effort to alleviate social and economic distress is valued and necessary
- Foster an intermittent reconsideration of the responsibility both governments and corporations must assume for the construction of a society in which opportunity and achievement match aspiration and possibility
- Join in the consideration of a reconstructed social contract, capable of sustaining trust and productivity in an era of constraint
- Organize on a community and national level programs and activities designed to meet a variety of educational, cultural, and leisure needs.

A significant contribution of such voluntarism involves its nurturance of the sense that individual action itself is important, that the actions of people working together can make a difference. It is quite possible that this historic commitment to voluntarism might broaden in the years ahead to see the emergence of a continuing dialogue and selective partnership between volunteer-interested associations and those whose primary focus lies in such areas as neighborhoods, self-help, personal liberation, economic democracy, political involvement, and citizen participation. Broadly based conferences are held in which leaders in these many realms of voluntary action participate, share perspectives, and develop concerted collaborative action. Sector-serving organizations, such as INDEPENDENT SECTOR, continue to grow in their reach and influence.

This path contains considerable possibilities for an expanded role of voluntarism in the American future. As links become more clearly perceived among the varying practitioners of voluntary action, organized around emerging academic and applied specializations in nonprofit management and voluntary sector leadership, the idea that voluntary action is a principle of organization may begin to spread. A set of transformations in the structure of American voluntarism, and the broader society as well, then become possible. In this fashion, voluntarism may contribute significantly to the emergence of a good-luck future.

A Good-Luck Future for Voluntarism

Good-luck images of the future, it will be recalled, take either traditional or transformational forms. In the traditional image, voluntary action will blossom as a means of problem-solving and the alleviation of remaining societal distress. Problems will be resolved at the level of household, neighborhood, and workplace, and will rarely overheat into the arena of confrontation, either on the local or national level. This is a "cornucopian" image of the future, in which economic plenty is assured, and (to change the metaphor) a rising tide lifts all boats. It is a time of good feelings and the achievement of the American dream.

In the transformational future, one that most futurists find both more preferable and more likely than the cornucopian image, voluntarism takes on a much more considerable role than merely being an alternative, and cheaper, way of providing social services. In this future, a "voluntary society" is created, and individuals join with their neighbors and fellow citizens in the development of a "pluralistic commonwealth" in which problems are discussed and resolved and solutions conceived and implemented. In this vision, troubling problems of distributive justice are confronted and resolved, and a new era of individual and social creativity is achieved.

The role of voluntarism in the transformational future rises to a principle of societal organization. It becomes the embodiment of freedom in action and achieves the goals of autonomous and intelligent social construction so often mentioned in the classic literature reviewed in Chapter 1. Voluntary action becomes, in this image of the future, a critical tool for the construction of the good, or active, society. The shape of such voluntarism has been identified by many previous writers, including the following:

- Amitai Etzioni's brilliant construct of the "active society" (1968), in which individuals and communities identify needs and proceed to resolve problems with the confidence that they themselves and what they do matters.

- Ronald Lippitt and Eva Schindler-Rainman's vision of the "collaborative community" (1980), in which the barriers that separate us are removed in a collective process of trust-building and problem-resolution. (It should also be noted that this volume contains an extremely wise chapter on "the motivational dynamics of voluntarism.")

- Willis Harman's image of "societal transformation" (1979), in which the basic longings of persons for meaning are harnessed to the powerful engines of science and communications.

- Marilyn Ferguson's observation that an "aquarian conspiracy" (1980) is abroad in this land, by which individuals find ways to connect with each other and ways to regain control of the organizational forces that threaten both sanity and civility in a world in chaos.

- My own argument that "citizen coproduction"—the emerging partnerships between individuals and communities, on the one hand, and economic and political organizations, on the other, both to define what is needed and how it can most sensibly be produced—will characterize much of our energy, food, security, and social peace processes in the years ahead.

CRITERIA FOR PERVASIVE VOLUNTARISM

The forces identified by Etzioni, Lippitt, and the other scholar-practitioners of voluntarism just cited tend to be meteorological, according to the three-fold image of societal forces derived in Chapter 7. If a genuine role for voluntarism is to be found in society, such meteorological forces will have to join with basic topographic and tectonic realities. Thus a clear eye will be required to assure that the three sectors are not hypostasized, but are recognized as being overlapping and even occasionally blurred constructs on the landscape of human endeavor. And a simultaneous concern will be required to assure that the deeper forces of economic development, decay, control, political guidance and decisions, and cultural signification and shift are attended as well.

Recognizing that the institutional topography of modern societies does not permit an easy distinction between what is corporate, government, third sector, and household is a beginning. The third sector, we have seen, is closely linked to each of the other sectors. At times it takes a form not dissimilar from a business; at other times it exercises the functions of government; and on the neighborhood level, it blends with the household in the meeting of local and family needs.

This blurring of the sectors gives voluntarism an opening to permeate the other sectors, introducing them to the transforming powers of democratic control, concern with values, and the courage to create change. When the corporate executive calls upon the skilled volunteer to help develop structures for employee participation and control at the workplace, the powers of pervasive voluntarism will be seen. When the political leader calls upon the neighborhood associations to develop an agenda for legislative change that will then be supported, then the powers of pervasive voluntarism will be exercised. When the working mother calls upon the United Way to recognize that the future of her children depends upon the quality of after-school care and emergency illness care, then the powers of pervasive voluntarism will become real.

The contribution that voluntary action can make to society depends critically upon our ability to understand and even direct the awesome tectonic forces that shape the structure of modern societies. If the lessons of classic social theory are remembered, our chances of controlling these forces will be increased. With Tocqueville and Durkheim, we shall need to recognize that pluralism requires participation to be fully democratic—that the aspirations of populist and idealist thinkers must be applied to the modern polity. With Weber and Michels, we shall need to recognize that voluntary associations, like economic, governmental, and even family organizations, are subject to atrophy and corruption, and that the democratic structure must be renewed to keep pace with the values it proclaims. And with Marx, we shall need to recognize that voluntarism never exists in a vacuum, but is subject to the blandishments and rewards of economic structure and control.

It would be highly desirable to possess a set of criteria to apply to the evaluation of particular forms of voluntary action. While, as shown in Chapter 1, voluntarism is seen by its defenders as a seamless web of social virtue and productivity, there is also a dark side to voluntary action, and clear distinctions are required to guide our evaluations.

The development of criteria, however, is no simple process. Criteria themselves vary in their forms and implications with the social theory held by the evaluator, as a cursory review of the legacy of the French and Anglo-American Revolutions will make clear. Whether our criteria are "liberty, equality, and fraternity," "life, liberty, and property," or some other set of values, it is likely that they will refer to values of democracy, justice, achievement, social bonding, and personal meaning.

As a beginning effort to develop a set of criteria, the following list is presented of forms of voluntary action that, embodied in individual and organizational life and commitment, identify most clearly those forms of voluntarism that are "teleologically prior." The work of volunteers, and voluntary and nonprofit organizations, is most important, productive, and valuable, I assert, when it:

1. Builds habits of the heart.
2. Is constructive of community.
3. Recognizes both regulation and social reform.
4. Assures democracy and restrains authoritarianism.
5. Seeks to develop genuine partnerships.
6. Begins to pervade corporate and governmental structures.
7. Enhances social justice by addressing the difficult questions of how to eliminate unjustified inequalities.
8. Enables understanding of society.
9. Solves problems by means of an effective internal structure.
10. Demonstrates both good leadership and effective management.

Let me elaborate on each criterion, not asserting that all nonprofit organizations do meet, or ought to meet, each of them. Rather, I would suggest them as desirable goals to aim for as voluntary action is structured by individuals and organizations.

Builds Habits of the Heart

This criterion has been central to almost all perspectives on the phenomenon of voluntary action. Provided a persuasive empirical base by the work of Bellah and associates (1985), this criterion insists that voluntary action generate sentiments of interpersonal identification on the parts of both the donor and the recipient in the voluntary relationship. Problematic in an age of mediated and bureaucratic social relations, this criterion nonetheless insists that it is possible to build a society in which people care about each other and manifest that caring in their everyday actions.

Constructs Community

Closely related to the first criterion is the generation of widespread social solidarity as a result of manifold individual acts of caring and concern. The identification of an overarching societal interest in solving problems and improving the quality of life of all its members is a first step in the creation of community. From that point emerges a social pattern in which common interests rise to the surface and competitive interests are subdued. Whether in the context of family, neighborhood, or mass society interactions, a society in which community has been achieved is one that manifests a greater presence of civil interactions and deeper intergroup understandings.

Recognizes Regulation and Reform

A key value of voluntarism involves its deference to central principles in both the conservative and liberal traditions. With most conservatives, the criterion of regulation recognizes that cultures evolve glacially and that values and structures achieved over generations are altered at the risk of creating less adequate institutional means: personal and social needs for stability and predictability are critical in this perspective. On the other hand, this criterion understands a central component of the liberal tradition: that social institutions can typically be improved in order more fully to meet the needs of individuals and to fit the changing conditions of the time. Both "holding fast to that which is good" (the conservative principle) and seeking to build a truly just society (the liberal principle) are elements of a fully functioning voluntary contribution to society.

Assures Democracy and Restrains Authoritarianism

By developing basic forms of democracy, voluntary action is frequently said to make a critical contribution to the building of a democratic society. Perhaps the most difficult of the criteria to subject to empirical test, it is nonetheless defended by a long tradition of political theorists of a variety of ideological persuasions. One way that nonprofit organizations can advance this criterion is by embodying principles of humane and democratic organization. Studies of effective nonprofit structuring are beginning to be conducted and should be carefully attended to assess the costs and gains of participative structuring. Clearly, nonprofit organizations have become central actors in the contemporary political scene. I believe they can affect the battle between forces of democracy and authoritarianism that rages at many levels of modern institutional life.

Fosters Genuine Partnerships

A fully developed voluntarism will distinguish clearly between genuine and pseudo partnerships, employing criteria like those developed here. This criterion insists that voluntary organizations respect the basis of their own vision and mission and not succumb to the temptation to become just one more tax-free business organization. Identifying, and then living out, the principles of valuing and organizing that are particularly characteristic of the voluntary principle becomes the central task generated by this criterion. Dennis Young's research is particularly appropriate here, with its identification of the orientations that most distinctively characterize actors in the nonprofit arena: believers, conservers, poets, searchers, and professionals. These skills are critical in the shaping of effective partnerships, and in bringing the resources of major societal actors to bear on the resolution of pressing problems. The role of voluntary organizations in conceiving, brokering, and implementing problem-solving partnerships is a critical one in society.

Pervades Corporate and Governmental Structures

This criterion, rarely articulated in the literature, follows the preceding one in its insistence that voluntary associations possess a special and distinctive quality among the social institutions of modern society. With their vision of community and their mandate for conservation and change, participants in nonprofit organizations have much to offer to governmental and corporate leaders in the way of structure and process. The corporate world, particularly, is often urged to adopt voluntary means (e.g. quality circles, participatory management) to improve its own operations. It is at least plausible to suggest that voluntary sector leaders might provide useful input to the restructuring of over-bureaucratized and hyper-authority-centered organizations in the other two sectors.

Enhances Social Justice

The work of voluntarism meets this criterion by addressing the difficult questions of how to eliminate unjustified inequalities. This is probably the most difficult criterion, reflecting ancient divisions regarding charity, philanthropy, and voluntarism. On the one hand stand those who see the voluntary sector as clearly tilted toward the righting of distributive wrongs in society—the ally of the poor and unempowered; from this perspective injustice is built into some social institutions and needs to be confronted and removed. On the other hand stand those who view voluntary action as a matter of assisting those temporarily down on their luck; from this perspective the institutions of society are basically fair—it is only chance and the lack of motivation that prevent individuals from achieving success. Positions located between the extremes of the Marxist and the Smithian invisible hand might agree that injustice is sometimes a matter of structured inequality and at others a result of rotten luck. Voluntary sector institutions might do well to dispense both change and Band-Aids, depending on the occasion at hand.

Enables Societal Understanding

Voluntary sector organizations should clarify rather than obfuscate the nature of society. The field of voluntarism has long been plagued with boosters, who attach bloated value to concepts that cannot withstand their weight. Voluntarism has frequently been identified as virtue itself in the American tradition. Contemporary scholarship has come particularly to question the wisdom of identifying a distinct "third sector," removed from other sectors in terms of both its putative independence and its merit. Similarly, the distinction between public and private is often inaccurately drawn in order to conform to particular ideological preferences. The best voluntary action research should raise questions that sharpen the practice of voluntarism, rather than serve as chants for the cheerleaders of the trade.

Solves Problems by Means of an Effective Internal Structure

As in business and government, there is no free lunch in the voluntary sector. The "bottom line" confronts any organization, and costs and gains are assessed in terms of human resources as well as financial ones. The emergence of academic and applied professional subspecializations in nonprofit management during the past decade signals a welcome attention to the finer points of problem-solving in the third sector.

Involves Good Leadership and Effective Management

Leadership and management are sometimes seen as competing values in the administration of effective voluntarism. Positing opposition between these two concepts seems a particularly unproductive, and probably false, dilemma. Both strong leadership (and good "followership" as well—I refer to a recently published volume called *Leaders and Followers: Challenges for the Future* that Trudy Heller, Louis Zurcher, and I edited)—and effective management are required of voluntary sector practitioners. As a criterion, the effective blending of the two invaluable aspects of organization is required.

CONCLUSION: APPLYING THE CRITERIA

The criteria for voluntarism developed in this chapter may be applied to the work of any voluntary organization, be it a group of neighbors joined to express a concern regarding the safety of their streets or a large service organization seeking to reexamine its role in modern society. They stand as goals for developing voluntary organizations that make a positive contribution to the achievement of basic social and democratic goals of liberty, justice, and community. The degree to which these goals are achieved should be the concern of researchers, activists, nonprofit managers, and citizens alike. As contemporary societies evolve, they will surely require spirited and effective voluntary action, as well as the strong and wise contribution of its third sector to its growth and change. The final chapter examines the role "professionalization" might play in this process.

12

The Professionalization of the Third Sector

Training in an MBA curriculum permits the nonprofit manager to employ facilely technical terms and techniques that baffle trustees and staff alike and to bask in the halo of the purportedly more efficient proprietary sector.

—Paul DiMaggio (1986, p. 30)

INTRODUCTION

The third sector has heard a good deal of talk about professionalization over the past 20 years. In the 1970s, attention focused on the development of "volunteer administration" as a profession; in the 1980s principal attention has focused on the emergence of "nonprofit management." This chapter examines the joys and perils of the professionalization process, and pays central attention to the role of colleges and universities and their faculties in shaping this process.*

THE VOLUNTARY SECTOR AS A LOCUS OF EMERGENT PROFESSIONALISM

The Nature of Professionalism

Professionalism is one of the looser words in the contemporary lexicon, often connoting little more than an ability to do most anything competently, as in the phrase, "he's (she's) a real professional." The social scientist has placed a stricter construction on the term, and the place to start is with the definitive work of Magali Sarfatti Larson (1977). Professions, Larson (1977, p. 208) informs us, are "organizations of producers of relatively scarce and mostly intangible skills." In modern societies they are organized on a market model designed to exchange services for a price. Central to the

---

* Of course, the development of a profession is affected by many other actors besides university-based faculty. In the cases reviewed in this chapter, practitioners, providers of technical assistance, funders, and principals of sector-serving organizations all play central roles. For a fuller discussion of the emergence of nonprofit management as a profession, see Block (1987).

historical evolution of the concept are the ideas of "training and tested competence," which evolve over time into the principle that excellence "can be measured by 'units of training' and by series of objective examination. . . . In our century, the generalization of bureaucratic patterns of recruitment reinforces the apparent equivalence between competence and length of training: while the use of IQ and other tests spreads at the lower and middle levels of the occupational hierarchy, expertise at the technical, professional and managerial levels tends to be equated with years of schooling and numbers of credentials" (Larson, 1977, p. 211).

The core of the concept of the professional, then, lies in the possession of skills that are "relatively scarce and mostly intangible." The professional develops and employs these skills with a dedication to them that, ideally, transcends organizational corruption and the vagaries of social power. Thus, as Robert Lifton (1986) writes, the active involvement of physicians in Holocaust programs of euthanasia "was viewed as the most shameful of all Nazi behavior" by Germans as well as survivors and scholars worldwide. "No wonder that it still haunts German medicine, and has only recently begun to be confronted by contemporary German physicians."

The presumption that the professional will provide services at a price to those able to pay, while also assuring service to those unable to pay, undergirds not only the familiar "sliding fee" scale but also traditions of "pro bono" service for those not able to pay. The concept of professionalism is thus linked, at least in logic, to concepts of voluntarism, for both assert the right of all to the receipt of professional service. In actual practice, the rise of the welfare state and the bureaucratization of professions have both served to modify that link.*

Modern society sees the formation of vast "organizational professions," as Larson (1977, p. 179) calls them. She identifies two categories of these professions:

> The first category is generated by the concentration of administrative and managerial functions under corporate capitalism. Hospital administrators, "professional" business administrators, management analysts, school superintendents, college presidents and the like illustrate this type. Here, the claim of specialized or "professional" expertise for technobureaucratic functions which are unspecific and polyvalent does not aim at asserting independent professional status; rather, it borrows from the general ideology of professionalism to justify technobureaucratic power.

---

* Larson comments (1977): "This aspect largely accounts for the 'residual' persistence of a traditional ideal of service in the *contemporary* ideology of profession: the ideal of moral obligation to the collectivity is the main ideological response of a profession to the contradiction between socially produced knowledge and its private appropriation. It appears, at the same time, as a justification and as a guarantee that such competence will, indeed, be 'returned to society.' Such an idealistic guarantee is not necessary, however, in a society where the large majority of people must sell their labor power in order to survive, and where special competencies are sought with a view toward their sale" (p. 223).

Significantly, subordinate professionals are included among the relevant publics to which this claim is addressed.

The second category derives directly from the expansion of the state's functions and attributions. Teaching at all levels, counseling of different types in public or semipublic agencies, social work, librarianship, city planning, and museum curatorship are essentially connected with education, welfare, and regulatory mechanisms "in the service of the public," even if these functions may be fulfilled by private institutions of charity or culture. For these aspiring occupations, the claim of expertise—sanctioned by external sources of credentialing—represents a possibility of acquiring countervailing power vis-à-vis the bureaucratic hierarchy of the organizations in which they are contained.

Professional training is assumed to take place most centrally in universities, and particularly in profession-oriented graduate schools. Such training offers not just a grounding in basic skills, but also socialization into a career, "a pattern of organization of the self" (Larson, 1977, p. 229).

> For most recognized professions, an orderly career begins with training in professional schools or universities. The authoritative and authoritarian framework of relations between teachers and students is a fundamental element of institutionalized professional socialization. . . . Prestige filters down, from the "great men" in a field to those who study or work under them. . . .
> The content of professional education is, in part, a function of its length. . . . It is almost impossible to distinguish the real from the ideological effects of this overtraining (Larson, 1977, pp. 229–230).

This selective review of the theory of professionalism suggests that the recent experience in the voluntary sector offers a rich lode for study and prescription. Let us briefly review what has been happening in the areas of volunteer administration and nonprofit management over the past few decades.

THE PROFESSIONALIZATION PROCESS IN THE THIRD SECTOR

Volunteer Administration

Before 1970, few would have known that the activity of "volunteer administration" existed, much less that it aspired to be a profession. Throughout the decade of the 1970s, however, the job title "volunteer administrator" began to appear more frequently in hospitals and other institutions of social service. Encouraged by a series of national organizations that attracted increasing support from community elites and foundations (among them, the National Information Center on Volunteerism, the National Center for Voluntary Action, and the Association of Volunteer Bureaus), volunteer administration became a rather clearly identified field for activity and employment. By the mid-1970s the Association of Administrators of Voluntary Service (AAVS) was holding national conferences, and by the decade's end, renamed the Association for Volunteer Administration (AVA), it was busily engaged in the process of certifying its members for practice.

Harold Stubblefield and Leroy Miles (1986) have recently surveyed volunteer administrators, and note that they are overwhelmingly drawn from the ranks of white women (89% are women; 96% are white). While 28% held a master's degree, and 1% a Ph.D., only 6% thought that a graduate degree should be the minimum educational requirement for entrants to the field. Stubblefield and Miles (1986) caution:

> The results of this and other studies suggest that universities should proceed cautiously in formulating the nature and extent of their role in volunteer administration. . . . The principal concern of volunteer administrators as expressed through one professional association (AVA), has been the certification of competencies for those persons already employed and not on career preparation. The AVA position is that how a volunteer administrator acquires the competencies is unimportant; the critical factor is that they can demonstrate they possess the competencies. The picture of volunteer administration that emerges from this study is that of an occupational practice still in the process of defining itself and who its practitioners should be (p. 11).

The central findings of the Stubblefield–Miles research indicate clearly that volunteer administration has adopted a distinctive path toward its own professionalization. Rather than seeking to advance its claims to professionalism by encouraging the development of university-based curricula, AVA increasingly distanced itself in the 1980s from the academic organization (the Association of Voluntary Action Scholars) with which it had previously shared management of a "practitioner's journal." AVA assumed full responsibility for the publication of its own journal (the *Journal of Volunteer Administration*) and established its own Research Committee. Agreements for the collaborative co-location of annual meetings previously established between AVA and the scholars' organization were not renewed, to the expression of some relief on both sides. By mid-decade the AVA credentialing process was well-established, but no viable graduate or undergraduate program had emerged for the education or training of volunteer administrators. Nor does the emergence of such programs seem at all likely in the foreseeable future.

The commitment to a path of self-certification rather than academic certification can be explained in large part by the domination of the field of volunteer administration by women of diverse practical experience who tended to see little relevance in professional graduate education to the work they performed. Among the forces influencing these women was the strong feminist ideology of the 1970s, which cautioned women against submitting themselves to the male-dominated academy. Even after the Association of Voluntary Action Scholars came to elect a woman as its president in 1981, the administrators' choice to "go it alone" was not subject to reconsideration. In conformance to the times, as foundation support for the field of volunteerism dwindled and the limits of paid possibilities in the area became clear, the choice of a self-certification process for those already employed appears to have made a good deal of sense.

Nonprofit Management

In the age of Reagan, volunteerism became something to which lip service was given, but nonprofit management was deemed worthy of more serious concern and support. The combination of federal defunding of nonprofits and the tougher corporate attitude toward philanthropy (both factors discussed earlier) gave rise to a frequently articulated call for the development of management capacity in the third sector. Universities heard this call and began to see in the field of nonprofit management a far more receptive constituency than had emerged among volunteer administrators. The nonprofit rubric offered a clientele more often possessed of a college degree, most often male, and quite often backed by organizations seen to pay comfortable salaries and able to assume the formidable costs involved in graduate tuition.

Paul DiMaggio (1986) correctly observes that nonprofit managers, "almost without exception," refer to their occupation as a "profession" (and do so in a manner more assertive than volunteer administrators—JVT). "Yet this self-characterization is frequently contested," DiMaggio continues, "and not without reason. Nonprofit managers . . . do not control the market for their services; in most fields they do not maintain codes of ethics; nor do they offer credible claims of disinterested public service. To confuse matters more, many nonprofit managers are, in fact, members of professions that are distinctly nonmanagerial."

The resolution to this dilemma, DiMaggio notes, is to agree with Larson that nonprofit managers, when they act as managers per se, are "techno-bureaucratic" professionals in Larson's terms—and belong in the first of her two categories of organizational professions. And the problem of being in that category is that one's claim there rests on a base of expertise that, DiMaggio continues:

> . . . is far from obvious. Professional knowledge, to represent an effective claim to authority, must be at least partially codifiable, monopolized, acquirable through formal education, and sufficiently tacit to require a combination of both apprenticeship and rote training [here DiMaggio cites Larson]. Managerial knowledge, by contrast, is poorly defined, widely dispersed, and commonly viewed as experiential (p. 28).

DiMaggio brings us to an important choice by his analysis. On the one hand, we may conclude that nonprofit managers and volunteer administrators, like other managers, are "would-be" or "pseudo" professionals at best, and should abandon their claim to professional competency, certification, and practice. On the other hand, we might follow DiMaggio's argument to the point that modern organizational practice, with its increasing complexity, requires the development of technobureaucratic managerial professionalism and its base in expertise, even if that task is neither simple nor evident.

Up until this point, organizational scholars have almost entirely ignored the professionalization experiences recounted in this chapter. But the results of research not being in—indeed, not even being contemplated*— has not discouraged entrepreneurial academics from essaying the development of programs aimed toward the education of nonprofit managers. In 1984, Case Western Reserve University announced the formation of the Mandel Center for Nonprofit Management, funded to the tune of several million dollars by several Cleveland philanthropies. A notable Ph.D. program was dispensing graduate training for nonprofit managers at the University of Colorado in Denver throughout the decade. By 1985, well over 100 universities were willing to indicate that they had a graduate program or track in the general area of nonprofit management (Sandra T. Gray, 1985). And by 1986, important research centers in the field were established at the Graduate Center of the City University of New York and at Duke University, to be joined by the Center on Philanthropy at Indiana University in 1987.

By late 1986 the obvious need to examine what had become a boomlet in academe† gave rise to an invitational conference at the University of San Francisco. The conference was organized by nonprofit management educators Michael O'Neill and Dennis Young, and was funded by the Sloan Foundation. The centerpieces of the conference were the presentation of eleven papers by leading academics, heads of sector-serving organizations, and prominent nonprofit managers. The papers are notable both for what they said, and for what they chose to ignore. A summary of inclusions and exclusions are the subjects of the next two sections of this chapter.

THINGS ARE REAL IF DEFINED AS REAL

The celebrated dictum of sociologist W. I. Thomas, "Things are real if they are defined as real in their consequences," may usefully be applied to the process of professionalization among nonprofit managers. For writers and

---

* An exception is the research in progress of Stephen R. Block on the emergence of nonprofit management as a profession.
† The academic trade journal *The Chronicle of Higher Education* identified the opportunities in this area in a widely read 1984 article.

scholars positioned to influence such a process, it is a time of high energy, occasional controversy, and a not inconsiderable personal interest. Careers may be affected or deflected in such times; a field is being defined and organized.

The theme of definition is accompanied by a sense of discovery: "Belatedly," write Keane and Merget (1986), "institutions of higher education have recognized a new professional cadre in our society. The third sector . . . has matured well beyond the stereotype of its personnel and managers as volunteers and amateurs" (p. 1). The desirability of taking action, even as others in power choose not to recognize this need, is asserted: "to have no explicit attention paid to this sector by the mainstream management education 'establishment' seems on the face of it less than sensible . . . ." (O'Neill and Young, 1986, p. 2). There will be problems, but they should be confronted vigorously so that need can be met: "Of course, there remains the question of whether the nonprofit sector is in some sense a coherent entity. . . . [Nevertheless,] the fact that such organizations fall not only outside the sectors of business and government, but also outside the functional disciplines that attend to the education of administrators, appears to argue for some new, more comprehensive approach to nonprofit management education" (O'Neill and Young, 1986, p. 2).

A review of the conference papers identifies a number of themes that gain widespread approval, and are not contradicted by any presentations. These themes include the assertions that: 1) nonprofit management is an important and diverse endeavor, and an appropriate field for designed improvement; 2) management education is an appropriate function of the graduate faculties of universities; 3) education for nonprofit managers should provide both professional and managerial competencies; 4) business schools are definitely the wrong place to site graduate programs for nonprofit managers; 5) a pluralistic approach toward graduate education of nonprofit managers is indicated at present. Let us review these contentions one by one.

1. *Nonprofit management is an important and diverse endeavor, and an appropriate field for designed improvement.* The importance of the field of nonprofit management, and the likelihood that it can be improved by an educational intervention, is taken as an assumption by all the conference writers. Typically, this observation is followed by some worrying about the diversity of the field. For example, O'Neill and Young (1986, p. 14) note that the "population of nonprofit organizations is highly diverse," but conclude that this diversity is itself an argument that nonprofit management education should be developed, since gaps remain between the areas covered by the few professional schools that do address the subject. And Vladeck (1986, p. 3) seems a bit uncomfortable with his task when he writes, early in his paper: "I

don't believe that all nonprofits are alike in most critical ways, but the discussion in this paper will essentially assume that they are, unless otherwise noted."

Other writers emphasize elements of diversity in the field: Cook concludes that size of organization is an important differentiating variable among nonprofits. DiMaggio finds considerable differences among nonprofits by the specializations of their work. And Daniels identifies a rather wide range of career patterns among managers in one type of nonprofit organization, foundations. But the awareness of this diversity does not lead any of these authors to question the wisdom of discovering one or more ways to enhance the education and capacity of nonprofit organization managers, though it does modify some of their recommendations, as will be seen in point 5, below.

2. *Management education is an appropriate function of the graduate faculties of universities.* This point also typically takes the form of an assumption in the papers, although it is briefly argued by O'Neill and Young (1986), McAdam (1986), Keane and Merget (1986), and Cyert (1986). O'Neill and Young briefly review the literature on professional education (pp. 20–21), and Cyert offers a brief history of the development of management education in its path from industry-specific to general approaches.

3. *Education for nonprofit managers should provide both professional and managerial competencies.* With this point, the authors move beyond a common core of assumptions toward the development of their original assertions. Borrowing a term from Perrow, DiMaggio (1986, p. 10) distinguishes between the "core technology" of the field of application of the nonprofit organization (e.g. its "professional field"—be it art museum, hospital, community service) and the generic management skills applicable to all nonprofit organizations. Cyert (1986, pp. 10; 38–39) and Slavin (1986, p. 11) concur with this point, the latter noting that: "One deals with managerial science and related organizational theories and concepts. The other relies on respective professional theories and concepts and related social and behavioral science."

DiMaggio (1986, p. 29) observes that professional insiders are: "by and large, better able to navigate among their staff than are outsiders to the field," but also notes that they will need to compensate with management acumen for the loss of professional status occasioned by their removal from their former fully professional position. Thus the professor who becomes a dean may understand the university better than an outside administrator, but will need to show skills beyond those of the teacher or scholar to retain the respect of those who formerly considered themselves peer or colleague. Among the skills expected from such an administrator will be, as Vladeck (1986, pp. 8–9) implies, the ability to choose from the management armory approaches that will be valid in the particular situation, rather than simply imposing the latest fad or gimmick.

Armed with these observations, the writers move to a strong consensus that the curriculum for nonprofit managers should treat centrally both the professional specialization and the learning of generic management skills. Slavin (1986, p. 13) observes that the "essential function of the administrator is to chart and monitor the life of the organization," a task requiring both professional and managerial skills. Cyert (1986, pp. 38–39) notes that "we do need some material in the curriculum . . . that emphasizes the institutional differences" between nonprofit organizations. And, McAdam (1986) asserts a point also mentioned by Cyert (p. 39) that the curriculum should also pay attention to "applied or specific nonprofit sector management education," treating topics such as fund accounting, volunteer management, and fundraising.

The question now arises of where to place the responsibility for educating nonprofit managers within the university, keeping in mind McAdam's observation that a good deal of training will continue to be provided by nonprofit organizations themselves, along with sector support centers and independent consultants. The authors do not, however, contradict McAdam's observation (1986, p. 7) that such programs "will not have the same prestige of a program which is university based." The authors are nearly unanimous in their view that there is one place where such a curriculum should not be based, and that place is the school of business.

4. *The business school is not the right place for nonprofit management education.* The judgment that graduate programs for nonprofit managers should be housed elsewhere than in schools of business reflects in part the observation of O'Neill and Young (1986, p. 4), previously discussed, that the nonprofit arena is distinct from those of government and business. Moreover, as DiMaggio notes, the principal product of graduate programs of business, the MBA degree, is typically provided absent a context appropriate to the nonprofit organization, although it does provide certain quixotic advantages to its holder.*

A more sober insider's view is offered by Cyert (1986, p. 40), a committed defender of generic management education: "There is extremely strong evidence that a program for nonprofit managers

---

* See the quote at the beginning of this chapter.

should not be in the business school. . . . The evidence is very strong that nonprofit management curricula become lost in a business school." Like those who designed the program at George Washington University (cf. Keane and Merget), Cyert sees a role in such programs for business school courses and faculty, but believes that such programs might best be centered in schools of public policy, public administration, or urban affairs. And that is about as specific as the San Francisco authors are prepared to be about the locus of such programs at this time.

5. *A pluralistic approach toward graduate education of nonprofit managers is indicated at present.* Not moving to any single model of graduate education for nonprofit managers seems advisable for a variety of reasons. McAdam (1986, p. 3) observes that "the basic approach used and the degree of enthusiasm demonstrated by the host would appear to be far more important (for the siting of programs in this field) than the actual identity of the host unit." Keane and Merget note that in one case the program developed under the rubric of a college of public administration, but with strong participation from faculty in business administration and management science as well. There is no reason to believe that schools of social work, communications, and fine arts could not contribute well to such programs, or that an appropriate base might not be found in programs in urban affairs or public policy.

DiMaggio and Cook point to further dangers inherent in premature institutionalization of this field. Universities, DiMaggio reminds us, are themselves nonprofit organizations, and being such, and large as well, as Cook (1986, pp. 19–20) asserts, they can fall prey to ossification, such that:

1. The organization prospers but the clients are overlooked except as tools of the institution.
2. Glamour services are installed, despite an increase in costs to the overall client base.
3. Many different kinds of services and programs are undertaken.
4. Opulence becomes the standard.
5. Employees become the living dead.

In many respects, the field of nonprofit management education takes on the character of a social movement. It is a new idea; it is exciting to contemplate new vistas in program and process; it involves the creation of new networks between practitioners, academics, and leaders of sector-serving organizations. But this movement, like any other, can fall prey to the pitfalls of excessive zeal and overpromising. It is surely best to proceed with both an optimistic spirit and a prudent sense of reflectiveness, and to examine carefully the stamp of the first footprints in the field.

SOME OTHER QUESTIONS WORTH SERIOUS EXPLORATION

As a new field begins to be defined, among the most important questions are often those that are not asked. The shape of an agenda sets the development of a field, and questions not asked tend almost surely not to get on that agenda (Bachrach, 1967). In an effort to assure that as many right questions as possible are asked about the emerging field of nonprofit management education, it will be useful to scan the five major approaches to the study of voluntarism that have been developed in earlier chapters: pluralist, populist, idealist, social democratic, and neo-corporatist.

The pluralist, it will be recalled, values the articulation of interests in political society and welcomes voluntarism as an enabler of these many voices. But a major flaw in the pluralist's heaven, as E.E. Schattschneider put it so pointedly (1960), is that the chorus sings with so decidedly an upper-class accent. A truly pluralistic voluntarism will enable as many organizational voices as possible and will seek to assure that the blessings of advanced study are available to the executives of a wide variety of organizations—large and small; rich and poor; suburban, urban, or rural; majority and minority. The question of access is central to the pluralist in assuring that the system is indeed fair and just. Designers of educational programs, if they choose to follow the pluralist's judgment, will need to assure that access as they build tuitions, residency requirements, and scholarships into their programs.

The populist's main value, previous chapters indicate, is the direct representation of the voice of the people. This value reminds the designer of programs of nonprofit management education of the importance of community and citizen organizations to the democratic society. Definitions of nonprofit organization should be carefully reviewed to assure that they do not exclude associations and groups that do not rank high in the level of their funding, although they may strongly attract the commitment of citizens and volunteers. The populist also reminds us of the need to educate board members and volunteers, and not just managers. The exclusion of community-based organizations and citizen-governed voluntarism from the world of nonprofit management education, on whatever grounds (ranging from the amorphousness of the goal of "advocacy" to a general sense that ordinary people do not share in the kind of opulent style that raises money nonprofitwise) is a grave injustice from the populist perspective.

The idealist, whose central value is the quality of public dialogue in society, reminds those who create educational programs of the importance of reflective thought and thoughtful action in society. The idealist stands foursquare with Brian O'Connell (1986)* in focusing on the development of

---

* O'Connell's position is most directly an idealist one, focusing on the values of a "truly free society," though there are strong elements of pluralism in it as well. Managing the INDEPENDENT SECTOR organization as long and ably as he has indicates his ability to forge a creative balance between these two approaches.

leadership as the principal goal in educating managers of nonprofit organizations. And the idealist would note that it is in the curricula of undergraduate colleges and secondary schools, as well as in the lives of families and communities, that the values of leading and caring are instilled and developed.†

The social democrat, whose central value aims toward the assurance of social justice in society, reminds us that not all nonprofits are created equal. Some are richer than others; and some speak directly for those who seek to sustain the privilege of the few over the aspirations of the many. If, as Gamwell has contended, some associations are "teleologically prior," the social democrat would argue that they are those that do not relegate the value and practice of social justice to a secondary rank.

Finally, the neo-corporatist, whose central values aim toward the protection of social stability among principal economic and political concerns, reminds us that nonprofit organizations exist in a delicate interdependence with the megastructures of the first and second sectors. Questions of which organizations get funded, which individuals get credentialed, and who gets which jobs are centrally raised by an analysis of the neo-corporatist ideology. Nonprofit organizations can easily be targeted by first and second sector organizations to do their bidding. The specter of neo-corporatism reminds us of the need for nonprofit organizations to sustain as much of their independence as they can.

The five main perspectives on voluntarism, then, remind us of questions that are not obvious when we first confront the subject of educating leaders and managers in the third sector. They suggest that we develop curricula that see the third sector, in its efforts to build a "truly free society," as engaged in a long and always problematic struggle. What educators have come to call courses in "social realities" could be central to such curricula, as would a process of education that effectively presents profiles in voluntary leadership for examination and at least partial emulation. Bruce Vladeck (1986, p. 17) calls for nonprofit managers to learn the very difficult task of institutionalizing charismatic roles, and sees this task as one that they "have to do better and must be taught to do better."

A vision of the nonprofit leader as an agent of social change differs considerably from that of the nonprofit manager as the effective bureaucrat. Combining the two perspectives into a single style of leadership and management, and successfully imparting those difficult and yet vital skills, seems a challenge to colleges and universities well worth the time and energy it will consume. Such programs will need to respond to the question: knowledge

---

† McAdam attends to the role of undergraduate colleges, advocating a curriculum much like the ones encouraged by the "Program on Studying Philanthropy" of the Association of American Colleges, launched in 1986. That program, which initially funded eight colleges to develop new courses in philanthropy, received 51 proposals in the first round. A key desideratum in developing this program was the encouragement of courses "that outline a broad and interdisciplinary exploration of philanthropy in the spirit of liberal education" (Association of American Colleges, 1986).

for what? (Lynd, 1939). And that requires consideration of the research agenda that will most appropriately accompany the professionalization of the third sector.

A RESEARCH AGENDA FOR A PROFESSIONALIZING FIELD

Among the professionalizing forces in the third sector is research itself, as reflected in a variety of university- and agency-based activity that has become more visible in recent years. This thrust is well represented by such university-based programs as the Program on Nonprofit Organizations at Yale, by such organizational programs as the Research Division of INDE-PENDENT SECTOR, and by such academic journals as the *Journal of Voluntary Action Research.*

It is not my intention to recount the development of this field, but it is obvious that research, like any other form of program development, has been buffeted by the various forces involved in the process of professionalization. At this juncture, the outlines of a research agenda may be discerned that would allow increasing numbers of academic and association-based scholars to join in the exploration and definition of the field.

Among the tasks such scholars might address are the following:

1. Development of research protocols that allow the application of criteria, like those developed in the present work, to the organizational realities of voluntary associations and their work throughout society is an important task on the future agenda of social scientists. As voluntary action research emerges as a significant field of research, an agenda may be identified to guide the work of scholars. As the criteria for voluntary action are refined and applied, we will need to know more about the lives of extraordinary volunteers, those who identify tasks beyond the routine and accomplish beyond the norm. We need, in short, a study of volunteer "Profiles in Courage" that details what it is that people can do to serve others, challenge injustice, and build a better society.

   I suspect that far too many of our diurnal pronouncements on volunteering are, in fact, mere boosterism. Abstractions such as "private-sector initiatives" or "independent sector activity" are often only distantly related to the reality of the lives of those who actually practice volunteering. These concepts need to be rooted firmly in reality lest they remain mere ideological fluff in an age of image, display, and PR.

2. Another important research task involves learning from those who have succeeded in building effective volunteer communities and organizations. We need to know how people can learn both to enjoy each other's company and to achieve valued ends. Volunteering is

not merely "unpaid work"; nor is it pure socializing. Rather, it is a unique combination of the two, and we need to know more about its organizational chemistry and how to produce it more regularly.

3. We also need to develop methods of "action research" that identify the needs and aspirations of those who volunteer, and feed back to those individuals and their organizations useful information and assistance. Such research might give us a fuller picture of the size and power of the voluntary sector within a city or state. It could also provide an invaluable means of building effective collaborative networks among discrete organizations (cf. Lippitt and Van Til, 1981).

4. Finally, we need to pay much more attention to what it means to aspire to the creation of an "active society." As the potential citizen volunteer faces the manifold decisions to act or not to act, he and she will benefit from reviewing summaries of the thinking and action of others (by which I mean research) that are concrete, reality-based, and actionable. Such research often studies matters of policy, an issue which an author publishing in a presidential election year may be pardoned for addressing in the concluding section of his work.

CONTEMPORARY POLICY ISSUES IN VOLUNTARISM

Several major areas of policy concern appear to be waxing at the current time in the American political economy. They represent areas in which reasonable persons do indeed disagree reasonably, often with regard to the conflicting paradigms of social thought and analysis. They are also issues on which candidates for public office, from the presidential level to the local level, might properly be asked for opinions for which they would be held accountable upon election.

Among the more important of these policy areas are: 1) the question of how "business-like" the voluntary sector should be; 2) the issue of professionalism; 3) the question of leadership vs. management; 4) the problem of partnering; 5) the questions of tax reform and budgetary policy; and 6) the selection of clientele.

1. The first issue involves the degree to which the voluntary sector should adopt a "business-like" stance in the conducting of its affairs. Here positions range from the "regulation" position adopted by the American Management Associations (cf. Borst and Montana, 1975, pp. 1–2) to the "radical change" position that warns of cooptation of the third sector by corporate interests.

A possible resolution of the question of how business-like the voluntary sector ought be lies between the two polar positions. One can recognize, as do Rosenbaum and Smith (1983, p. 254), that "the voluntary sector is clearly moving toward a more businesslike, unsubsidized posture." But Young's warning warrants consideration as well: "a nonprofitization policy may be expected to improve industry-level performance but also to obfuscate the character and trustworthiness of the nonprofit sector" (1983, p. 144). It seems best to me to be business-like in the operation of third-sector organizations, but not wholly "like a business."

2. The second policy issue involves the centrality of "professionalism," another value, like "business-like," that receives wide support in current American life. Here positions can be found ranging from the enthusiastic development of volunteer professionalism to dire warnings of the consequences of the loss of splendid amateurism.

The regulatory consequences of professionalism are noted by Kosters (1983): "The tendency toward professionalization in describing problems and in prescribing problems and credentials for those involved is a prominent feature in many regulations" (p. 408). This tendency may be a chilling factor for change of any sort, as well as on the chances for the creation of community, as Stuart Butler argues (1983):

> The growth of professionalism within nonprofit organizations and government service agencies has been extremely damaging in many instances. It has led to a concentration of research on the *deficiencies* of communities (with the assumption that these can only be corrected with more money and professionals), and to the establishment of a plethora of credentialling requirements and "standard-setting," which has enabled expensive professional providers to crowd out local volunteers (p. 379).

Researchers have tended to soft-pedal this problem, Butler argues, because they themselves "constitute an element of the problem. Given that most researchers sympathize with the perspective of the professionals, public policy analysts are generally presented with an imbalance of information" (1983, p. 379).

Professionalism, then, would seem a societal force that the third sector will need itself to regulate. Often a requirement of governmental grantors, this factor itself needs to be tempered with the essential insight of voluntary action that, often, people know best. To some degree then, the professionalism question raises basic issues regarding the role of citizens in contemporary decision-making (cf. Petersen, 1984).

3. The third policy issue to be noted is one already figuring in discussions of the role of "management" in voluntary sector affairs. As the pressure to be business-like increases, both as a requisite for corporate support (see *Wall Street Journal,* May 21, 1984) and as a consequence of diminished governmental support (cf. Rosenbaum, 1981), those who have proved useful to corporate and governmental management have increasingly sought to make their knowledge and services available to third sector organizations (cf. Moyer, 1984).

One way of phrasing the issue is a bald one, as provided by accountant Herbert Heaton (1983): "Leadership has gone out of fashion and management has taken its place. What's the difference? Leadership puts people first. But the mission of nonprofit service organizations is serving people and their development" (p. 483).

Heaton's warning requires careful attention, because once again here the extreme positions of "management is all" or "leadership is all" are both suspect. An effective nonprofit sector will be well managed, but it will also be directed by leaders and leadership structures that are democratic, open, and participatory (which latter are, after all, aspects of some images of "good management"; cf. Lippitt, 1982).

4. A fourth policy question involves the role of various "partnerships" between corporate, governmental, and voluntary organizations. A necessary aspect of the new political economy, in Bruce Smith's terms, partnerships have been the subject of both ecstatic prose and dire warnings in recent years. I strongly believe that partnerships should only be essayed when they have a significant chance of achieving the criteria for voluntarism presented in Chapter 11.

5. A fifth set of contemporary policy issues surrounds the questions of tax reform and budgetary policy. Should the charitable deduction be restored to all taxpayers, or limited only to itemizers? Will the lowering of the maximum tax rate in the 1986 tax law provide a formidable disincentive to charitable giving for the well-off? Will the Gramm-Rudman budget-balancing bill lead to a continuing abandonment of the federal role in domestic affairs, further complicating the financial crisis of voluntary organizations?

Policy questions like these are perennials in the blurred boundaries between the governmental and the voluntary sectors. Neither liberals nor conservatives have clearly defined positions on them, and they are generally resolved in the melee of contemporary interest group politics and the increasingly desperate efforts on the part of the federal government to keep its debt off the brink of economic disaster. They are, however, issues on which government and voluntary sector leaders work toward intelligent solutions, for they vitally affect the fiscal standing of both sets of organizations.

6. The final policy issue involves the question of clientele. Traditionally, the voluntary sector has attended as a major concern the interests of those least fortunate in society. The primacy of that focus is under considerable contemporary reconsideration as the voluntary sector copes with the withdrawal of federal funding.

Again, it is Lester Salamon whose research is most definitive. The Urban Institute Nonprofit Sector Survey, which he directs, has found that voluntary organizations serving the neediest suffered overall revenue losses in the 1980s. The reason for this pattern is obvious: as the newly "business-like," "autonomous," and "professionalized" non-profit organizations turn increasingly to fees and product sales to replace lost governmental funding, they find that the most needy cannot afford their services. And so the organizations that grow are those that cater to people who can afford to buy more of their services. Current growth areas in the third sector are health, institutional and residential care, culture and the arts, and mental health. Losing ground are legal services, employment and training, and social services.

In a society that is learning to live with its growing poverty population, it is perhaps not surprising that voluntary organizations are similarly abandoning their service of the needy. But, as Salamon notes, such a trend undermines much of the sector's *raison d'être* in the process. If voluntarism is to be something more than simply a way of doing business tax-free, it will have to rediscover a way to address the needs of those deemed superfluous in contemporary society. Of all the challenges in contemporary voluntarism policy, this is perhaps the most significant.

Questions like these, joined with others of like ilk over the years, assure us that voluntarism will remain on the agenda of policy concerns. An important part of the U.S. political economy, voluntary sector organizations are part of the way in which Americans define and resolve their common and specific problems. Voluntarism is now a public issue, and it will remain one in the years ahead.

However we approach these questions—as policy-shapers or associational leaders or researchers, or simply as citizens—we need to be able to know how it is possible to act responsibly in an interdependent world. We need to know how to maintain individual autonomy in an era of corporate and political megastructures. And we need to learn how to sustain the sense that if we are to survive, it will be by caring about each other as well as ourselves. When we know these things we may be able to build a society as good as our remarkably enduring willingness to volunteer, and to create associations and organizations that will surely advance the goals embedded in the values of our voluntarism.

REFERENCES

Ackoff, Russell L.
1981   *Creating the Corporate Future.* New York: John Wiley and Sons.

Adams, David
1980   "Elite and Lower Volunteers in a Voluntary Association: A Study of an American Red Cross Chapter." *Journal of Voluntary Action Research,* 9: 95–108.

Adams, David
1983   "Selection, Socialization, and Four Types of Members in the Red Cross Chapter: A Typology of Voluntary Association Members." *Journal of Voluntary Action Research,* 12 (April–June):31–45.

Adamson, Walter L.
1980   *Hegemony and Revolution: A Study of Antonio Gramsci's Political and Cultural Theory.* Berkeley: University of California Press.

Alchon, Guy
1985   *The Invisible Hand of Planning: Capitalism, Social Science and the State in the 1920s.* Princeton: Princeton University.

Alchon, Guy
1986   "Foundations, Social Sciences, and the Origins of American Macroeconomic Planning." In *Working Papers for the Spring Research Forum: Philanthropy, Voluntary Action, and the Public Good* (pp. 75–84). Washington, D.C.: INDEPENDENT SECTOR.

Alford, Robert R., and Roger Friedland
1985   *Powers of Theory.* Cambridge: Cambridge University Press.

Allen, Natalie, and William Rushton
1983   "Personality Characteristics of Community Mental Health Volunteers: A Review." *Journal of Voluntary Action Research,* 12 (January–March): 36–49.

Alperovitz, Gar
1973   "Notes Toward a Pluralist Commonwealth." In Staughton Lynd and Gar Alperovitz, eds., *Strategy and Program: Two Essays Toward a New American Socialism* (pp. 49–109). Boston: Beacon.

Alperovitz, Gar, and Jeff Faux
1984   *Rebuilding America.* New York: Pantheon.

Anderson, John C., and Larry Moore
1978   "The Motivation to Volunteer." *Journal of Voluntary Action Research,* 7 (July–December, 1978):51–60.

Anderson, Robert T.
1971   "Voluntary Associations in History." *American Anthropologist,* 73: 209–219.

Arnove, Robert S., ed.
1982   *Philanthropy and Cultural Imperialism: Foundations at Home and Abroad.* Bloomington: Indiana University Press.

Association of American Colleges
1986   "Program on Studying Philanthropy." Washington, D.C.: Association of American Colleges.

Austin, David M.
1981   "The Political Economy of Social Benefit Organizations." In Herman Stein, ed., *Organization and the Human Services* (pp. 37–88). Philadelphia: Temple University Press.

Bachrach, Peter
1967   *The Theory of Democratic Elitism: A Critique.* Boston: Little Brown.

Bakal, Carl.
1979   *Charity U.S.A.* New York: Times Books.

Banfield, Edward, and James Q. Wilson
1963   *City Politics.* Cambridge, MA: Harvard University Press.

Banton, Michael
1968   "Voluntary Associations: Anthropological Aspects." In David Sills, ed., *International Encyclopedia of the Social Sciences,* (Vol. 16, pp. 357–362). New York: Macmillan.

Barnekov, Timothy K., Daniel Rich, and Robert Warren
1981   "The New Privatism, Federalism, and the Future of Urban Governance." *Journal of Urban Affairs,* 3:1–14.

Basso, Jacques-A., and Michele Ruffat, eds.
1985   "Les Groupes d'Interet et le Pouvoir." *Problemes Politiques et Sociaux,* 511:1–39.

Beauregard, Robert, and Briavel Holcomb
1984   "City Profile: New Brunswick, New Jersey, U.S.A." *Cities,* 1(3):215–220.

Bellah, Robert N., and William Sullivan
1981   "Democratic Culture or Authoritarian Capitalism." *Society,* 18 (September–October):41–50.

Bellah, Robert N., Richard Madsen, William M. Sullivan, Ann Swidler, and Steven M. Tipton
1985   *Habits of the Heart: Individualism and Commitment in American Life.* Berkeley: University of California Press.

Beresford, Peter, and Suzy Croft
1984   "Welfare Pluralism: the New Face of Fabianism." *Critical Social Policy,* 9 (Spring): 19–39.

Beresford, Peter, and Suzy Croft
1986   *Whose Welfare?* Brighton, England: The Lewis Cohen Urban Studies Center at Brighton Polytechnic.

Berger, Peter L., and Richard J. Neuhaus
  1977   "To Empower People: The Role of Mediating Structures in Public Policy."
         Washington, D.C.: American Enterprise Institute.

Berle, Adolf A., Jr.
  1959   *Power Without Property: A New Development in Political Economy.* New
         York: Harcourt, Brace.

Berman, Edward H.
  1983   *The Ideology of Philanthropy.* Albany: State University of New York.

Berman, Edward H.
  1986   "Critical Perspectives on Philanthropy at Home and Abroad." In *Working
         Papers for the Spring Research Forum: Philanthropy, Voluntary Action, and
         the Public Good* (pp. 85–102). Washington, D.C.: INDEPENDENT SECTOR.

Billis, David, and Margaret Harris
  1986   "An Extended Role for the Voluntary Sector: The Challenge of Imple-
         mentation." Program of Research and Training into Voluntary Action.
         Uxbridge, England: Brunel University.

Blaustein, Arthur
  1982   "Moral Responsibility and National Character." *Society,* 19 (May–June):
         25–31.

Block, Stephen R.
  1987   *The Academic Discipline of Nonprofit Organization Management: Past,
         Present, and Future.* Ph.D. dissertation, University of Colorado (Denver).

Body–Gendrot, Sophie N.
  1985   "French and American Cities: Restructuring Processes and Grass-Roots
         Mobilization." Presented to the Society for the Study of Social Problems
         meeting, Washington, D.C.

Boonin, Leonard
  1969   "Man and Society: An Examination of Three Models." In J. Roland Pen-
         nock and John Chapman, eds., *Voluntary Associations* (pp. 69–84). New
         York: Atherton.

Borst, Diane, and P.J. Montana, eds.
  1975   *Managing Nonprofit Organizations.* New York: AMACOM.

Boulding, Kenneth
  1973   *The Economy of Love and Fear.* Belmont, CA: Wadsworth.

Boyte, Harry C.
  1984   *Community is Possible: Repairing America's Roots.* New York: Harper
         Colophon.

Boyte, Harry C.
  1980   *The Backyard Revolution: Understanding the New Citizen Movement.*
         Philadelphia: Temple University Press.

Bradfield, Richard Maitland
1973   *A Natural History of Associations.* 2 vols. London: Duckworth.

Bremner, Robert H.
1960   *American Philanthropy.* Chicago: University of Chicago Press.

Brenton, Maria
1985   *The Voluntary Sector in British Social Services.* London and New York: Longmans.

Brooks, Harvey, Lance Liebman, and Corinne S. Schelling, eds.
1984   *Public-Private Partnership: New Opportunities for Meeting Social Needs.* Cambridge, MA: Ballinger.

Brudney, Jeffrey L., and R. England
1983   "Toward a Definition of the Coproduction Concept." *Public Administration Review,* 43:59–65.

Bruyn, Severyn T.
1977   *The Social Economy: People Transforming Modern Business.* New York: John Wiley and Sons.

Bulmer, Martin.
1987   "Privacy and Confidentiality as Obstacles to Interweaving Formal and Informal Care: The Boundaries of the Private Realm." *Journal of Voluntary Action Research,* 16 (January–June):112–125.

Burrell, Gibson, and Gareth Morgan
1979   *Sociological Paradigms and Organizational Analysis.* London: Heinemann.

Buss, Terry F., and F. Redburn Stevens
1983   "Religious Leaders as Policy Advocates: The Youngstown Steel Mill Closing." *Policy Studies Journal,* 11:640–647.

Butler, Stuart
1986   "Research into the Impediments to Voluntarism." In *Working Papers for the Spring Research Forum: Philanthropy, Voluntary Action, and the Public Good* (pp. 369–382). Washington, D.C.: INDEPENDENT SECTOR.

Cass, Rosemary H., and Gordon Manser
1976   *Volunteerism at the Crossroads.* New York: Family Service Association of America.

Chapman, John
1969   "Voluntary Association and the Political Theory of Pluralism." In J. Roland Pennock and John R. Chapman, eds., *Voluntary Associations* (pp. 87–118). New York: Atherton.

Churma, Thomas
1982   "Local Government and Community Partnerships." *Journal of Community Action,* 1:41–44.

Clark, Robert
1980   "Does the Nonprofit Form Fit the Hospital Industry?" *Harvard Law Review,* 93:1416–1489.

Clayre, Alasdair, ed.
1980   *The Political Economy of Cooperation and Participation: A Third Sector.*
Oxford: Oxford University Press.

Cole, G.D.H.
1945   "A Retrospect of the History of Voluntary Social Service." In A.F.C.
Bourdillon, ed., *Voluntary Social Services: Their Place in the Modern State*
(pp. 11–30). London: Methuen.

Committee for Economic Development
1982   *Public-Private Partnership: An Opportunity for Urban Communities.*
Washington, D.C.: Committee for Economic Development.

Commission on Private Philanthropy and Public Needs
1975   *Giving in America: Toward a Stronger Voluntary Sector.* Washington, D.C.:
U.S. Department of Treasury.

Connolly, William E., and Michael Best
1981   *The Politicized Economy.* Lexington, MA: D.C. Heath.

Cook, Jonathan B.
1986   "Managing Nonprofits of Different Sizes." In Michael O'Neill and Dennis
R. Young, eds., *Educating Managers of Nonprofit Organizations.* San Francisco: University of San Francisco.

Cornish, Edward
1986   "Farewell, Sexual Revolution. Hello, New Victorianism." *The Futurist,* 20
(January–February):3 ff.

Cornuelle, Richard
1983   *Healing America.* New York: G.P. Putnam's Sons.

Cummings, Laurie Davidson
1977   "Voluntary Strategies in the Environmental Movement: Recycling as
Cooptation." *Journal of Voluntary Action Research,* 6 (July–December):
153–160.

Cyert, Richard M.
1986   "Nonprofit Management's Place in the Menu of Higher Education." In
Michael O'Neill and Dennis R. Young, eds., *Educating Managers of Nonprofit Organizations.* San Francisco: University of San Francisco.

Dahl, Robert A.
1984   "Democracy in the Workplace." *Dissent,* 31:54–60.

Daniels, Arlene Kaplan
1986   "Career Scenarios for Nonprofit Managers." In Michael O'Neill and
Dennis R. Young, eds., *Educating Managers of Nonprofit Organizations.*
San Francisco: University of San Francisco.

David, Robert L.
1986   "Perceptions of Management Effectiveness Between Corporations and
Not-For Profit Organizations." In *Working Papers for the Spring Research*

Forum: *Philanthropy, Voluntary Action, and the Public Good* (pp. 101–118). Washington, D.C.: INDEPENDENT SECTOR.

Davies, Bleddyn, and David Challis
1986   *Matching Resources to Needs in Community Care.* Brookfield, VT: Gower Publishing Co.

DeLaat, Jacqueline
1987   "Volunteering as Linkage in the Three Sectors." *Journal of Voluntary Action Research,* 16 (January–June):97–111.

Delors, Jacques
1985   "Quelle Société Voulons-Nous Construire?" Fonda Lettre d'Information #29–30. Paris: Nouvelles Pratiques de l'Emploi, 1985.

Dewey, John
1927   *The Public and Its Problems.* Denver: Alan Swallow.

DiMaggio, Paul
1983   "Non-Economic Theories of the Independent Sector." In *Working Papers for the Spring Research Forum: Since the Filer Commission* (pp. 101–118). Washington, D.C.: INDEPENDENT SECTOR.

DiMaggio, Paul
1986   "Nonprofits in Different Fields of Service." In Michael O'Neill and Dennis R. Young, eds., *Educating Managers of Nonprofit Organizations.* San Francisco: University of San Francisco.

Dolbeare, Kenneth M., and P. Dolbeare
1976   *American Ideologies.* Chicago: Rand McNally.

Donnison, David
1984   "The Progressive Potential of Privatisation." In Julian Le Grand and Ray Robinson, *Privatisation and the Welfare State* (pp. 45–57). London: George Allen & Unwin.

Douglas, James
1987   "Political Theories of Nonprofit Organization." In Walter Powell, ed., *The Nonprofit Sector: A Research Handbook* (pp. 43–54). New Haven: Yale University Press.

Dreier, Peter
1980   "Socialist Incubators." *Social Policy,* 11 (May–June):29–34.

Dunn, William N.
1981   *Public Policy Analysis.* Englewood Cliffs, NJ: Prentice-Hall.

Durkheim, Emile
1958   *Professional Ethics and Civic Morals* (translated by Cornelia Brookfield). Glencoe, IL: Free Press.

Ehrmann, Michael
1978   *Making Local Rehabilitation Work: Public/Private Relationships.* Wash-

ington, D.C.: National Association of Housing and Redevelopment Officials.

Ellis, Susan J., and Katherine Noyes
1978 *By the People: A History of Americans as Volunteers.* Philadelphia: Energize.

Etzioni, Amitai
1968 *The Active Society.* New York: Free Press.

Feagin, Joe R.
1975 *Subordinating the Poor: Welfare and American Beliefs.* Englewood Cliffs, NJ: Prentice-Hall.

Ferguson, Marilyn
1980 *The Aquarian Conspiracy: Personal and Social Transformation in the 1980s.* Los Angeles: J.P. Tarcher.

Ferrand-Bechmann, Dan
1986 "Moderniser Le Benevolat." Unpublished paper.

Flynn, John P., and Gene Webb
1975 "Women's Incentives for Community Participation in Policy Issues." *Journal of Voluntary Action Research,* 4 (July–December):137–146.

Fremont-Smith, Marion
1983 "Since the Filer Commission: Constitutional and Other Legal Issues." In *Working Papers for the Spring Research Forum: Since the Filer Commission* (pp. 417–432). Washington, D.C.: INDEPENDENT SECTOR.

Froland, Charles
1980 "Formal and Informal Care: Discontinuities in a Continuum." *Social Science Review,* 54: 572–587.

Fuller, Lon L.
1969 "Two Principles of Human Association." In J. Roland Pennock and John R. Chapman, eds., *Voluntary Associations* (pp. 3–23). New York: Atherton.

Galaskiewicz, Joseph
1985 *Social Organization of an Urban Grants Economy.* Orlando, FL: Academic Press.

Galaskiewicz, Joseph
1986 "The Environment and Corporate Giving Behavior." In *Working Papers for the Spring Research Forum: Philanthropy, Voluntary Action, and the Public Good* (pp. 141–154). Washington, D.C.: INDEPENDENT SECTOR.

Gallagher, Orvoell R.
1957 "Voluntary Associations in France." *Social Forces,* 36:153–160.

Gallup Poll
1981 *Volunteering in America.* Princeton, NJ: Gallup.

Gamwell, Franklin I.
1984   *Beyond Preference: Liberal Theories of Independent Association.* Chicago: University of Chicago Press.

Gartner, Alan, and Frank Riessman
1974   *The Service Society and the Consumer Vanguard.* New York: Harper and Row.

Gaylin, Willard, et al.
1978   *Doing Good: The Limits of Benevolence.* New York: Pantheon.

Gerard, D.
1983   *Charities in Britain: Conservatism or Change?* London: National Council for Voluntary Organisations.

Giddens, Anthony
1984   *The Constitution of Society.* Berkeley: University of California Press.

Gidron, Benjamin
1983   "Sources of Job Satisfaction Among Service Volunteers." *Journal of Voluntary Action Research,* 12 (January–March):30–35.

Gidron, Benjamin
1977   "Volunteer Work and its Rewards." *Volunteer Administration,* 11:18–32.

Gilbert, Neil
1983   *Capitalism and the Welfare State: Dilemmas of Social Benevolence.* New Haven: Yale University Press.

Gilder, George
1981   *Wealth and Poverty.* New York: Basic Books.

Gladstone, Francis
1982   *Charity, Law and Social Justice.* London: National Council for Voluntary Organisations.

Gladstone, Francis
1979   *Voluntary Action in a Changing World.* London: National Council for Voluntary Organisations.

Glaser, W.A., and D.L. Sills, eds.
1963   *The Government of Associations: Selections from the Behavioral Sciences.* Totowa, NJ: Bedminister Press.

Gluck, Peter R.
1975   "An Exchange Theory of Incentives of Urban Political Party Organization." *Journal of Voluntary Action Research,* 4 (October–December):104–118.

Goldschmidt, Maure L.
1969   "Rousseau on Intermediate Associations." In J. Roland Pennock and John R. Chapman, eds., *Voluntary Associations* (pp. 119–137). New York: Atherton.

Goldsmith, William W., and Harvey M. Jacobs
1982 "The Improbability of Urban Policy: the Case of the United States." *Journal of the American Planning Association,* 48 (Winter):53–66.

Goodwyn, Lawrence
1978 *The Populist Moment.* New York: Oxford University Press.

Gordon, C. Wayne, and Nicholas Babchuk
1963 "A Typology of Voluntary Associations." In W.A. Glaser and D.L. Sills, eds., *The Government of Associations: Selections from the Behavioral Sciences.* Totowa, NJ: Bedminister Press.

Gorman, Robert F., ed.
1984 *Private Voluntary Organizations as Agents of Development.* Boulder, CO: Westview Press.

Gorz, Andre
1967 *Strategy for Labor.* Boston: Beacon Press.

Gottlieb, David
1974 "The Socialization and Politicization of VISTA Volunteers." *Journal of Voluntary Action Research,* 3 (January–March):1–9.

Gray, A. C. Gregory
1985 "Nonprofits in Competition with Private Enterprise: Where Is It Leading?" *Nonprofit World,* 3 (November–December):12–14.

Gray, Bradford, ed.
1986 *For-Profit Enterprise in Health Care.* Washington, D.C.: National Academy Press.

Gray, Sandra T.
1985 *An Independent Sector Resource Directory of Education and Training Opportunities and Other Services.* Washington, D.C.: INDEPENDENT SECTOR.

Graycar, Adam
1983 "The Interrelationship of Voluntary, Statutory and Informal Services." *British Journal of Social Work,* 13:379–393.

Greene, Susan
1977 "To Promote Voluntarism." New York: Association of Junior Leagues.

Gronbjerg, Kirsten A.
1987 "Patterns of Institutional Relations in the Welfare State: Public Mandates and the Nonprofit Sector." *Journal of Voluntary Action Research,* 16 (January–June):64–80.

Gronbjerg, Kirsten A.
1982 "Private Welfare in the Welfare State: Recent U.S. Patterns." *Social Service Review* 56 (March):1–26.

Gross, Bertram
  1980   *Friendly Fascism: The New Face of Power in America.* Boston: South End Press.

Gurin, Maurice G.
  1987   "Cause-Related Marketing." Discussion Paper presented to the American Association of Fund-Raising Counsel board meeting, Dallas.

Gusfield, Joseph
  1963   *Symbolic Crusade: Status Politics and the American Temperance Movement.* Urbana: University of Illinois Press.

Hadley, Roger, and Stephen Hatch
  1981   *Social Welfare and the Failure of the State.* London: George Allen & Unwin.

Hadley, Roger, and M. McGrath
  1980   *Going Local: Neighbourhood Social Services.* London: Bedford Square Press.

Hall, Peter Dobkin
  1982   *The Organization of American Culture, 1700-1900: Private Institutions, Elites, and the Origins of American Nationality.* New York: New York University Press.

Hansmann, Henry B.
  1980   "The Role of Nonprofit Enterprise." *The Yale Law Journal,* 89:835–901.

Hansmann, Henry B.
  1983   "Economic Theories of the Nonprofit Sector." In *Working Papers for the Spring Research Forum: Since the Filer Commission* (pp. 23–40). Washington, D.C.: INDEPENDENT SECTOR.

Harman, John D., ed.
  1982   *Volunteerism in the Eighties: Fundamental Issues in Voluntary Action.* Washington, D.C.: University Press of America.

Harman, Willis W.
  1979   *An Incomplete Guide to the Future.* New York: W.W. Norton.

Harrington, Michael
  1968   *Toward a Democratic Left.* New York: Macmillan.

Hatch, Stephen
  1980   *Outside the State: Voluntary Organizations in Three English Towns.* London: Croom–Hall.

Hatry, Harry
  1983   *A Review of Private Approaches for the Delivery of Public Services.* Washington, D.C.: Urban Institute.

Heaton, Herbert
  1983   "Search and Research for Productivity in the Nonprofit, Service Sector."

In *Working Papers for the Spring Research Forum: Since the Filer Commission* (pp. 469–486). Washington, D.C.: INDEPENDENT SECTOR.

Heimovics, Richard, and Robert Herman
1986 "Characteristics of the Higher Performing Managers in Not-for-Profit Organizations. In *Working Papers for the Spring Research Forum: Philanthropy, Voluntary Action, and the Public Good* (pp. 347–362). Washington, D.C.: INDEPENDENT SECTOR.

Heller, Trudy
1984 "Authority: Changing Patterns, Changing Times." In John Adams, ed., *Transforming Work* (pp. 88–95). Alexandria, VA: Miles River Press.

Heller, Trudy
1985 "Changing Authority Patterns: A Cultural Perspective." *Academy of Management Review,* 10:489–495.

Heller, Trudy
1986 "A Meeting of the Minds and Other Dramatic Rites of Organizational Life." Paper presented to the Eastern Academy of Management meeting, Philadelphia.

Heller, Trudy, Jon Van Til, and Louis A. Zurcher, eds.
1986 *Leaders and Followers: Challenges for the Future.* Greenwich, CT: JAI Press.

Henderson, Charles S.
1895 "The Place and Functions of Voluntary Associations." *American Journal of Sociology,* 1:327–334.

Henton, Douglas C., and Steve A. Waldhorn
1983 "The Role of the Independent Sector in Governance Reform." In *Working Papers for the Spring Research Forum: Since the Filer Commission* (pp. 163–177). Washington, D.C.: INDEPENDENT SECTOR.

Herman, Edward S.
1981 *Corporate Control, Corporate Power.* Cambridge: Cambridge University Press.

Hirschhorn, Larry, et al.
1983 *Cutting Back: Retrenchment and Redevelopment in Human and Community Services.* San Francisco: Jossey–Bass.

Hoch, Charles, and George Hemmens
1985 "Linking Informal and Formal Care: Trouble Along the Pathway of Support." Paper presented to the Society for the Study of Social Problems meeting, Washington.

Hodgkinson, Virginia Ann, and Murray S. Weitzman
1984 *Dimensions of the Independent Sector: A Statistical Profile.* Washington, D.C.: INDEPENDENT SECTOR.

Hogan, Harry
  1981 "Philosophic Issues in Volunteerism." *Journal of Voluntary Action Research*, 10 (January–March):90–102.

Horowitz, Irving L.
  1982 "The New Fundamentalism." *Society*, 20 (November/December):40–47.

Hougland, James G., and James A. Christenson
  1982 "Voluntary Organizations and Dominant American Values." *Journal of Voluntary Action Research*, 11 (October–December):7–26.

Hougland, James G., and Jon Shepard
  1985 "Voluntarism and the Manager: The Impacts of Structural Pressure and Personal Interest on Community Participation." *Journal of Voluntary Action Research*, 14 (April–October):65–78.

Howard, A., and D.W. Bray
  1980 "Continuities and Discontinuities between Two Generations of Bell System Managers." Paper presented to the American Psychological Association meeting, Toronto.

Hyman, Drew
  1984 "On the Dialectics of Community Theory and Action." Paper presented to the Association of Voluntary Action Scholars annual meeting, Blacksburg, VA.

INDEPENDENT SECTOR
  1983 *Working Papers for Spring Research Forum: Since the Filer Commission.* Washington, D.C.: INDEPENDENT SECTOR.

INDEPENDENT SECTOR
  1986 *Working Papers for the Spring Research Forum: Philanthropy, Voluntary Action, and the Public Good.* Washington, D.C.: INDEPENDENT SECTOR.

INDEPENDENT SECTOR
  1987 *Working Papers for Spring Research Forum: The Constitution and the Independent Sector.* Washington, D.C.: INDEPENDENT SECTOR.

Jacobs, Jane
  1961 *The Death and Life of Great American Cities.* New York: Random House.

James, Estelle
  1983 "Comparisons of Nonprofit Sectors Abroad." In *Working Papers for Spring Research Forum: Since the Filer Commission* (pp. 539–556). Washington, D.C.: INDEPENDENT SECTOR.

Jeantet, Thierry
  1986 *La Modernisation de la France par l'Economie Sociale.* Paris: Economica, 1986.

Jenner, Jessica Reynolds
  1982 "Participation, Leadership and the Role of Volunteerism Among Selected Women Volunteers." *Journal of Voluntary Action Research*, 11 (October–December):27–38.

Johnson, David B.
1973   "The Charity Market: Theory and Practice." In *The Economics of Charity.* London: Institute of Economic Affairs.

Kanter, Rosabeth Moss
1968   *Commitment and Community.* Cambridge, MA: Harvard University Press.

Kariel, Henry
1981   *The Decline of American Pluralism.* Stanford: Stanford University Press.

Karl, Barry D.
1984   "Lo, the Poor Volunteer: An Essay on the Relation Between History and Myth." *Social Service Review,* 58:493–522.

Karl, Barry D.
1986   "The Moral Basis of Capitalist Philanthropy." In *Working Papers for the Spring Research Forum: Since the Filer Commission* (pp. 539–556). Washington, D.C.: INDEPENDENT SECTOR.

Kaufman, Herbert
1981   *The Administrative Behavior of Federal Bureau Chiefs.* Washington, D.C.: The Brookings Institution.

Kaufmann, Jean-Claude, and M. Laigneau
1984   "French Urban Sociology: Problems and Prospects." *Urban Affairs Quarterly,* 19:287–302.

Keane, Mark, and Astrid Merget
1986   "Management Education as a Mid-Career versus Entry-level Program." In Michael O'Neill and Dennis R. Young, eds., *Educating Managers of Nonprofit Organizations.* San Francisco: University of San Francisco.

Keillor, Garrison
1983   "Jack Schmidt, Arts Administrator." In Garrison Keillor, *Happy to Be Here* (pp. 3–14). New York: Penguin.

Kelley, Dean M.
1984   "The Supreme Court Redefines Tax Exemption." *Society,* 21 (May/June): 23–28.

Kelso, William Alton
1978   *American Democratic Theory: Pluralism and its Critics.* Westport, CT: Greenwood Press.

Kerr, Clark
1983   *The Future of Industrial Societies: Convergence or Continuing Diversity?* Cambridge, MA: Harvard University Press.

Kesselman, Mark
1983   "From State Theory to Class Struggle and Compromise: Contemporary Marxist Studies." *Social Science Quarterly,* 64:826–835.

Knoke, David, and James R. Wood
1981   *Organized for Action: Commitment in Voluntary Associations.* New Brunswick, NJ: Rutgers University Press.

Knoke, David, and David Prensky
1984   "What Relevance do Organization Theories Have for Voluntary Associations?" *Social Science Quarterly,* 65 (March):3–20.

Knowles, Malcolm S.
1972   "Motivation in Volunteerism: Synopsis of a Theory." *Journal of Voluntary Action Research,* 1 (April–June):27–29.

Koch, Frank
1979   *The New Corporate Philanthropy: How Society and Business Can Profit.* New York: Plenum.

Kornhauser, William
1959   *The Politics of Mass Society.* New York: Free Press.

Kosters, Marvin
1983   "Government Regulation, Non-Commercial Activities and the Public Interest." In *Working Papers for the Spring Research Forum: Since the Filer Commission* (pp. 403–416). Washington, D.C.: INDEPENDENT SECTOR.

Kouchner, Bernard
1986   *Charité Business.* Paris: Le Pré aux Clercs.

Kramer, Ralph M.
1984   *Voluntary Agencies in the Welfare State.* Berkeley: University of California Press.

Kramer, Ralph M.
1985   "The Future of the Voluntary Agency in a Mixed Economy." *Journal of Applied Behavioral Sciences,* 21:377–391.

Kuttner, Robert
1984   *The Economic Illusion: False Choices Between Prosperity and Social Justice.* Boston: Houghton Mifflin.

Lakoff, Sanford A.
1969   "Private Government in the Managed Society." In J. Roland Pennock and John R. Chapman, eds., *Voluntary Associations* (pp. 170–201). New York: Atherton.

Landauer, Carl
1983   *Corporate State Ideologies: Historical Roots and Philosophical Origins.* Berkeley: University of California Institute for International Studies.

Landy, Mark K., and H.A. Plotkin
1982   "Limits of the Market Metaphor." *Society,* 19 (May/June):8–17.

Lane, Robert E.
1981   "Personal Freedom in a Market Society." *Society,* 18 (March/April): 63–76.

Langton, Stuart
1982   "Reaganomics and the Plight of the Nonprofits." *Citizen Participation* (March/April):11 ff.

Langton, Stuart
  1983 "Public–Private Partnerships: Hope or Hoax?" *National Civic Review,* 72: 256–261.

Larson, Magali Sarfatti
  1977 *The Rise of Professionalism: A Sociological Analysis.* Berkeley: University of California Press.

Lasch, Christopher
  1979 *The Culture of Narcissism: American Life in an Age of Diminishing Expectations.* New York: Warner.

Lasch, Christopher
  1982 "The Prospects for Social Democracy." *democracy,* 2 (July:1982): 28–32.

Layton, Daphne Niobe
  1987 *Philanthropy and Voluntarism: An Annotated Bibliography.* New York: The Foundation Center.

Lerner, Michael P.
  1973 *The New Socialist Revolution: An Introduction to Its Theory and Strategy.* New York: Dell.

Levitt, Theodore
  1973 *The Third Sector: New Tactics for a Responsive Society.* New York: AMACOM.

Liebow, Elliott
  1967 *Tally's Corner.* Boston: Little, Brown.

Lifton, Robert Jay
  1986 *The Nazi Doctors: Medical Killing and the Psychology of Genocide.* New York: Basic Books.

Lindblom, Charles E.
  1977 *Politics and Markets.* New York: Basic Books.

Lindgren, H. Elaine
  1987 "The Informal–Intermittent Organization: A Vehicle for Successful Citizen Protest." *Journal of Applied Behavioral Science,* 23 (3): 397–412.

Lippitt, Ronald
  1982 "The Changing Leader–Follower Relationships of the Eighties." *Journal of Applied Behavioral Science,* 18:395–404.

Lippitt, Ronald, and Jon Van Til
  1981 "Can We Achieve a Collaborative Community?: Issues, Imperatives, Potentials." *Journal of Voluntary Action Research,* 10 (July–December): 7–17.

Lipset, Seymour Martin, Martin A. Trow, and James S. Coleman
  1956 *Union Democracy.* New York: Free Press.

Litt, Edgar, and Michael Parenti
1973   *Democracy's Ordeal in America: A Guide to Political Theory and Action.* Hinsdale, IL: Dryden.

Little, Kenneth
1965   *West African Urbanization: A Study of Voluntary Associations in Social Change.* Cambridge: Cambridge University Press.

Loeser, Herta
1974   *Women, Work, and Volunteering.* Boston: Beacon.

Lovelock, Christopher H., and Charles B. Weinberg
1984   *Marketing for Public and Nonprofit Managers.* New York: Wiley.

Lowi, Theodore J.
1969   *The End of Liberalism: Ideology, Policy, and the Crisis of Public Authority.* New York: W.W. Norton.

Lowry, Ritchie P.
1982   "Social Investing: Doing Good While Doing Well." *The Futurist,* 16 (April):22–28.

Lyman, Richard
1975   "In Defense of the Private Sector." *Daedalus,* 104:156–159.

Lynd, Robert S.
1939   *Knowledge for What: The Place of Social Science in American Culture.* Princeton: Princeton University Press.

Lynn, Laurence E.
1981   *Managing the Public's Business: The Job of the Government Executive.* New York: Basic Books.

MacIver, Robert
1937   *Society.* New York: Farrar & Rinehart.

Mannheim, Karl
1940   *Man and Society in an Age of Reconstruction.* New York: Harcourt, Brace.

Manser, Gordon
1980   "Critical Environmental Factors Affecting Volunteering in the 1980s." In W. Rydberg and L. Petersen, eds., *Volunteerism in the Eighties.* Appleton, WI: Aid Association for Lutherans.

Manser, Gordon, and Rosemary Cass
1976   *Voluntarism at the Crossroads.* New York: Family Service Association of America.

Marshall, T. H.
1977   *Citizenship and Social Development.* Chicago: University of Chicago Press.

Marwick, Arthur
1980   *Class: Image and Reality in Britain, France, and the USA.* New York: Oxford University Press.

McAdam, Terry W.
1986   "Curricula for Nonprofit Management." In Michael O'Neill and Dennis
       R. Young, eds., *Educating Managers of Nonprofit Organizations*. San Fran-
       cisco: University of San Francisco.

McBride, William Leon
1969   "Voluntary Association: The Basis of an Ideal Model, and the 'Demo-
       cratic' Failure." In J. Roland Pennock and John W. Chapman, eds., *Volun-
       tary Associations* (pp. 202–232). New York: Atherton.

McCarthy, Kathleen D.
1982   *Noblesse Oblige: Charity and Cultural Philanthropy in Chicago, 1849–
       1929*. Philadelphia: University of Pennsylvania Press.

McConnell, Grant
1969   "The Public Values of the Private Association." In J. Roland Pennock and
       John R. Chapman, eds., *Voluntary Associations* (pp. 147–160). New York:
       Atherton.

McConnell, Grant
1966   *Private Power and American Democracy*. New York: Knopf.

Meister, Albert
1984   *Participation, Associations, Development, and Change*. Translated and
       edited by Jack C. Ross. New Brunswick: Transaction Press.

Miliband, Ralph
1969   *The State in Capitalist Society*. New York: Basic Books.

Miller, Arthur Selwyn
1969   "The Constitution and the Voluntary Association: Some Notes Toward a
       Theory." In J. Roland Pennock and John R. Chapman, eds., *Voluntary
       Associations* (pp. 233–262). New York: Atherton.

Miller, Arthur Selwyn
1976   *The Modern Corporate State: Private Governments and the American
       Constitution*. Westport, CT: Greenwood Press.

Miller, Lynne E.
1985   "Understanding the Motivation of Volunteers: An Examination of Person-
       ality Differences and Characteristics of Volunteers' Paid Employment."
       Journal of Voluntary Action Research, 14 (April–September): 112–122.

Miller, S.M.
1985   "Challenges for Populism." *Social Policy*, 16 (Summer):3–6.

Moore, Larry F., ed.
1985   *Motivating Volunteers*. Vancouver, B.C.: Volunteer Centre.

Morris, David J.
1982   *Self-Reliant Cities: Energy and the Transformation of Urban America*. San
       Francisco: Sierra Club Books.

Moyer, Mel, ed.
1984   *Managing Voluntary Organizations*. Toronto: York University.

Musolf, Lloyd
    1983   *Uncle Sam's Private, Profit-seeking Corporations: Comsat, Fannie Mae,*
           Amtrak, Conrail. Lexington, MA: D.C. Heath.

Naisbitt, John
    1982   *Megatrends.* New York: Warner.

National Center for Charitable Statistics
    1986   *National Taxonomy of Exempt Entities.* Washington, D.C.: INDEPEND-
           ENT SECTOR.

National Organization for Women
    1975   "NOW Task Force on Volunteerism." *Ms,* 3 (February):73.

Nielsen, Waldemar A.
    1979   *The Endangered Sector.* New York: Columbia University Press.

Nielsen, Waldemar A.
    1985   *The Golden Donors: A New Anatomy of the Great Foundations.* New
           York: E.P. Dutton.

Nisbet, Robert A.
    1962   *Community and Power.* New York: Galaxy.

O'Connell, Brian
    1978   "From Service to Advocacy to Empowerment." *Social Casework,* 59:
           195–202.

O'Connell, Brian
    1983   *America's Voluntary Spirit: A Book of Readings.* New York: The Founda-
           tion Center.

O'Connell, Brian
    1986   "The Value System Governing Nonprofit Management." In Michael
           O'Neill and Dennis R. Young, eds., *Educating Managers of Nonprofit*
           Organizations. San Francisco: University of San Francisco.

O'Connor, James
    1973   *The Fiscal Crisis of the State.* New York: St. Martin's.

O'Neill, Michael, and Dennis R. Young
    1986   *Educating Managers of Nonprofit Organizations.* San Francisco: Univer-
           sity of San Francisco (to be published by Praeger in 1988).

O'Neill, Michael, and Dennis R. Young
    1986   "Educating Managers of Nonprofit Organizations: A Background Paper."
           In Michael O'Neill and Dennis R. Young, eds., *Educating Managers of*
           Nonprofit Organizations. San Francisco: University of San Francisco.

Oberstar, Gloria Toivola
    1983   "Strategies of Single-Issue Interest Groups." *Policy Studies Journal,*
           11:616–625.

Odendahl, Teresa, and Elizabeth T. Boris
  1986 "Foundation Formation, Growth and Termination." In *Working Papers for the Spring Research Forum: Philanthropy, Voluntary Action, and the Public Good* (pp. 41–52). Washington, D.C.: INDEPENDENT SECTOR.

Odendahl, Teresa, et al.
  1987 *America's Wealthy and the Future of Foundations.* New York: The Foundation Center.

Ofshee, Richard, et al.
  1974 "Social Structure and Social Control in Synanon." *Journal of Voluntary Action Research,* 3 (July–December):67–76.

Oleck, Howard L.
  1980 *Nonprofit Corporations, Organizations and Associations.* 3rd ed. Englewood Cliffs, NJ: Prentice-Hall.

Oliver, Leonard P.
  1983 *The Art of Citizenship: Public Issue Forums.* Dayton, OH: Kettering Foundation.

Olson, Mancur
  1965 *The Logic of Collective Action.* Cambridge, MA: Harvard University Press.

Olson, Mancur
  1982 *The Rise and Decline of Nations: Economic Growth, Stagflation, and Social Rigidities.* New Haven: Yale University Press.

Olson, Marvin
  1982 *Participatory Pluralism: Political Participation and Influence in the United States and Sweden.* Chicago: Nelson-Hall.

Ortiz, Isidro
  1981 "Chicano Community Organizations and the Idea of Ethnic Coalitions: A Case Study." *Journal of Voluntary Action Research,* 10 (July–December): 85–98.

Orum, Anthony M.
  1978 *An Introduction to Political Sociology.* Englewood Cliffs, NJ: Prentice-Hall.

Ostrander, Susan
  1984 *Women of the Upper Class.* Philadelphia: Temple University Press.

Ostrander, Susan
  1985 "Voluntary Social Agencies in the United States." *Social Service Review,* 59:434–454.

Owen, David
  1964 *English Philanthropy 1660–1960.* Cambridge, MA: The Belknap Press of Harvard University Press.

Palisi, Bartolomeo
  1972   "A Critical Analysis of the Voluntary Association Concept." In David
         Horton Smith, Richard Reddy, and Burt Baldwin, eds., *Voluntary Action
         Research 1972* (pp. 39–50). Lexington, MA: D.C. Heath.

Palmer, John L., and Isabel V. Sawhill, eds.
  1984   *The Reagan Record: An Assessment of America's Changing Domestic
         Priorities.* Cambridge, MA: Ballinger.

Parsons, Talcott
  1966   "On the Concept of Political Power." In R. Bendix and S.M. Lipset, eds.,
         Class, Status and Power, 2nd edition (pp. 240–265). New York: Free Press.

Pateman, Carole
  1970   *Participation and Democratic Theory.* Cambridge: Cambridge University
         Press.

Pearce, Jone L.
  1980   "Apathy or Self-Interest?: The Volunteer's Avoidance of Leadership
         Roles." *Journal of Voluntary Action Research,* 9:85–94.

Pearce, Jone L.
  1982   "Leading and Following Volunteers: Implications for a Changing Society."
         Journal of Applied Behavioral Science, 18:385–394.

Pennock, J. Roland
  1979   *Democratic Political Theory.* Princeton: Princeton University Press.

Pennock, J. Roland, and John W. Chapman, eds.
  1969   *Voluntary Associations.* New York: Atherton.

Pennock, J. Roland, and John W. Chapman, eds.
  1974   *Participation in Politics.* New York: Lieber–Atherton.

Percy, Stephen L.
  1984   "Citizen Participation in the Coproduction of Urban Services." *Urban
         Affairs Quarterly,* 19:431–446.

Petersen, James, ed.
  1984   *Citizen Participation in Science Policy.* Amherst: University of Massachu-
         setts Press.

Peterson, Mark
  1985   "Ideology and Community Development: Friend or Foe?" Paper presented
         to the Community Development Society meeting, Logan, UT.

Phillips, Michael H.
  1982   "Motivation and Expectation in Successful Voluntarism." *Journal of Vol-
         untary Action Research,* 11 (April–September):118–125.

Pickvance, Christopher
  1987   "Central Government, Local Government, Voluntary Associations and the
         Welfare State: Some Reflections on Opposition to Recent Public Spending

Cuts in Great Britain." *Journal of Voluntary Action Research,* 16 (January–June):81–96.

Pifer, Alan
1975 "The Jeopardy of Private Institutions." In Bruce L.R. Smith, ed., *The New Political Economy: The Public Use of the Private Sector* (pp. 68–82). New York: Wiley.

Pifer, Alan
1979 "Responses to Edward H. Berman." *Harvard Educational Review,* 49:180–182.

Pines, Burton Yale
1982 *Back to Basics: The Traditionalist Movement that is Sweeping Grass-Roots America.* New York: Morrow.

Polsby, Nelson
1985 "Prospects for Pluralism." *Society,* 22 (January/February):30–34.

Powell, Walter, ed.
1986 *The Nonprofit Sector: A Research Handbook.* New Haven: Yale University Press.

Pranger, Robert J.
1968 *The Eclipse of Citizenship: Power and Participation in Contemporary Politics.* New York: Holt, Rinehart & Winston.

Putnam, Robert
1970 *Politicians and Politics: Themes in British and Italian Elite Political Culture.* New Haven: Yale University Press.

Raffi, Guy
1986 "Enjeux associatifs, enjeux de societé." In *Fonda Lettre d'information* #39. Paris: *Fonda.*

Raskin, Marcus G.
1971 *Being and Doing.* New York: Random House.

Reich, Robert
1983 "Industrial Evolution." *democracy,* 3 (Summer):10–20.

Rich, Richard C.
1981 "Interaction of the Voluntary and Government Sectors." *Administration and Society,* 13:59–76.

Riessman, Frank, ed.
1985 "Self-Help." *Social Policy,* 15 (Winter).

Robertson, D. B., ed.
1966 *Voluntary Associations: A Study of Groups in Free Societies.* Richmond, VA: John Knox.

Roelofs, Joan
1984/1985 "Foundations and the Supreme Court," 62, *Telos* (Winter):59–88.

Rogin, Michael
1967   *The Intellectuals and McCarthy: The Radical Specter.* Cambridge, MA: Massachusetts Institute of Technology Press.

Rooff, Madeleine
1957   *Voluntary Societies and Social Policy.* London: Routledge and Kegan Paul.

Rose, Arnold
1954   *Theory and Methods in the Social Sciences.* Minneapolis: University of Minnesota Press.

Rose–Ackerman, Susan, ed.
1986   *The Economics of Nonprofit Institutions.* New York: Columbia University Press.

Rosenbaum, Nelson
1981   "Government Funding and the Voluntary Sector: Impacts and Options." *Journal of Voluntary Action Research,* 10 (January–March):82–89.

Rosenbaum, Nelson
1982   "Currents." *Journal of Community Action,* 1 (January/February):3–4.

Rosenbaum, Nelson, and Bruce L.R. Smith
1983   "Composition of Revenues and Expenditures in the Voluntary Sector." In *Working Papers for the Spring Research Forum: Since the Filer Commission* (pp. 229–260). Washington, D.C.: INDEPENDENT SECTOR.

Ross, Robert J.
1979   "Primary Groups as Social Movements: A Memoir and Interpretation." *Journal of Voluntary Action Research,* 6 (July–December):139–152.

Rothschild–Whitt, Joyce
1979   "Conditions for Democracy: Making Participatory Organizations Work." In John Case and Rosemary C.R. Taylor, eds., *Co-ops, Communes and Collectives* (pp. 215–244). New York: Pantheon.

Rydberg, Wayne, and Linda Peterson, eds.
1980   *A Look at the Eighties: Crucial Environmental Factors Affecting Volunteerism.* Appleton, WI: Aid Association for Lutherans and VOLUNTEER: The National Center for Citizen Involvement.

Salamon, Lester M.
1983   "Nonprofit Organizations and the Rise of Third-party Government." In *Working Papers for the Spring Research Forum: Since the Filer Commission.* Washington, D.C.: INDEPENDENT SECTOR.

Salamon, Lester M.
1984   "Nonprofit Organizations: The Lost Opportunity." In John L. Palmer and Isabel V. Sawhill, eds., *The Reagan Record: An Assessment of America's Changing Domestic Priorities* (pp. 261–285). Cambridge, MA: Ballinger.

Salamon, Lester M.
1987   "Of Market Failure, Voluntary Failure, and Third-Party Government:

Toward a Theory of Government–Nonprofit Relations in the Modern Welfare State." *Journal of Voluntary Action Research,* 16 (January–June): 29–49.

Salem, Greta W.
1978 "Maintaining Participation in Community Organizations." *Journal of Voluntary Action Research,* 7 (July–December):18–27.

Saloutos, Theodore, and J. Hicks
1951 *Twentieth Century Populism: Agricultural Discontent in the Middle West 1900–1939.* Lincoln: University of Nebraska Press.

Savas, E. S.
1982 *How to Shrink Government: Privatizing the Public Sector.* Chatham, NJ: Chatham House.

Schattschneider, E. E.
1960 *The Semisovereign People.* New York: Holt, Rinehart & Winston.

Scheier, Ivan
1982 *Exploring Volunteer Space: The Recruiting of a Nation.* Boulder, CO: National Information Center on Volunteerism.

Schervish, Paul G., Andrew Herman, and Lynn Rhenisch
1986 "Toward a General Theory of the Philanthropic Activities of the Wealthy." In *Working Papers for the Spring Research Forum: Philanthropy, Voluntary Action, and the Public Good* (pp. 219–229). Washington, D.C.: INDEPENDENT SECTOR.

Schindler–Rainman, Eva
1981 "Toward Collaboration—Risks We Need to Take." *Journal of Voluntary Action Research,* 10 (July–December):120–127.

Schindler–Rainman, Eva, and Ronald Lippitt
1975 *The Volunteer Community: Creative Uses of Human Resources.* Fairfax, VA: NTL Learning Resources Corp.

Schindler–Rainman, Eva, and Ronald Lippitt
1980 *Building the Collaborative Community.* Riverside: University of California Extension, 1980.

Schmitter, Philippe C., and Gerhard Lehmbruch, eds.
1979 *Trends Toward Corporate Intermediation.* Beverly Hills, CA: Sage.

Schwartz–Nobel, Loretta
1981 *Starving in the Shadow of Plenty.* New York: G.P. Putnam's Sons.

Seldon, Arthur
1980 *Corrigible Capitalism, Incorrigible Socialism.* London: Institute of Economic Affairs.

Sennett, Richard
1978 *The Fall of Public Man.* New York: Random House.

Sharkansky, Ira
  1979   *Whither the State?: Politics and Public Enterprise in Three Countries.* Chatham, NJ: Chatham House.

Sharp, Elaine B.
  1979   "Citizen Organization in Policing Issues and Crime Prevention." *Journal of Voluntary Action Research,* 7 (January–June):45–58.

Sills, David
  1968   "Voluntary Associations: Sociological Aspects." In David Sills, ed., *International Encyclopedia of the Social Sciences* (Vol. 16, pp. 363–376). New York: Macmillan.

Sills, Patrick, Hugh Butcher, Patricia Collis, and Andrew Glen
  1980   "The Formation and Forms of Community Groups." *Journal of Voluntary Action Research,* 9:189–202.

Simon, Herbert A.
  1957   *Administrative Behavior,* 2nd ed. New York: Free Press.

Skloot, Edward
  1983   "Should Not-for-Profits Go Into Business?" *Harvard Business Review,* 61:20–25.

Slavin, Simon
  1986   "Different Types of Nonprofit Managers." In Michael O'Neill and Dennis R. Young, eds., *Educating Managers of Nonprofit Organizations.* San Francisco: University of San Francisco.

Smith, Bruce L. R., ed.
  1975   *The New Political Economy: The Public Use of the Private Sector.* New York: Wiley.

Smith, Constance E., and Anne Freedman
  1972   *Voluntary Associations: Perspectives on the Literature.* Cambridge, MA: Harvard University Press.

Smith, David Horton
  1973   "The Impact of the Voluntary Sector on Society." In David Horton Smith, ed., *Voluntary Action Research 1973* (pp. 387–399). Lexington, MA: D.C. Heath.

Smith, David Horton
  1978   "The Philanthropy Business." *Society,* 15:8–15.

Smith, David Horton
  1981   "Altruism, Volunteers, and Volunteerism." *Journal of Voluntary Action Research,* 10:21–36.

Smith, David Horton, ed.
  1973, 1974   *Voluntary Action Research 1973, 1974.* 2 vols. Lexington, MA: D.C. Heath.

Smith, David Horton, and Jacqueline Macauley
  1980   *Participation in Social and Political Activities.* San Francisco: Jossey–Bass.

Smith, David Horton, Richard Reddy, and Bruce Baldwin, eds.
1972 *Voluntary Action Research 1972.* Lexington, MA: D.C. Heath.

Smith, David Horton, and Jon Van Til, eds.
1982 *International Perspectives on Voluntary Action Research.* Washington, D.C.: University Press of America.

Spiegel, Hans B.C.
1982 *Love Thy Neighborhood: Essays on Neighborhood Development.* New York: Citizens Forum/National Municipal League.

Stasi, Bernard
1979 *Vie Associative et Democratie Nouvelle.* Paris: Press Universitaires de France.

Stinson, T.F., and J.M. Stam
1976 "Toward an Economic Model of Voluntarism: The Case of Participation in Local Government." *Journal of Voluntary Action Research,* 5 (January–March):52–60.

Stone, Clarence N.
1982 "Social Stratification, Nondecision-Making, and the Study of Community Power." *American Politics Quarterly,* 10:275–302.

Streeck, Wolfgang, Philippe C. Schmitter, and Alberto Martinelli
1980 "The Organization of Business Interests." Discussion paper, International Institute of Management, Berlin.

Streeck, Wolfgang, and Philippe C. Schmitter
1985 *Private Interest Government: Beyond Market and State.* London and Beverly Hills, CA: Sage.

Strickler, Gay
1986 "Volunteerism: How Democracy Limits It." In *Proceedings of the Fourteenth Annual Meeting of the Association of Voluntary Action Scholars.* University Park, PA: Association of Voluntary Action Scholars.

Stubblefield, Harold, and Leroy Miles
1986 "Volunteer Administration as a Career." *Journal of Voluntary Action Research,* 15 (October–December):4–12.

Suhrke, Henry
1983 "Self-Regulation Within the Philanthropic Sector." In *Working Papers for the Spring Research Forum: Since the Filer Commission* (pp. 433–449). Washington, D.C.: INDEPENDENT SECTOR.

Sumariwalla, Russy D.
1983 "Preliminary Observations on Scope, Size, and Classification of the Sector." In *Working Papers for the Spring Research Forum: Since the Filer Commission* (pp. 181–228). Washington, D.C.: INDEPENDENT SECTOR.

Titmuss, Richard
1963 *The Gift Relationship.* London: Allen & Unwin.

Tobin, Gary A., ed.
   1985 *Social Planning and Human Service Delivery in the Voluntary Sector.*
         Westport, CT: Greenwood Press.

Toscano, David J.
   1981 "Employee Ownership and Democracy in the Workplace." *Social Policy,*
         12 (May/June):16–23.

Trecker, Harleigh
   1980 "Crucial Environmental Factors in the 1980s: Implications for Volunteer-
         ism." In W. Rydberg and L. Petersen, eds. *Volunteerism in the Eighties.*
         Appleton, WI: Aid Association for Lutherans.

Truman, David S.
   1951 *The Governmental Process: Political Interests and Public Opinion.* New
         York: Knopf.

U.S. Small Business Administration
   1986 *Unfair Competition by Non-Profit Organizations with Small Businesses.*
         Washington, D.C.: U.S. Government Printing Office.

Useem, Michael
   1984 *The Inner Circle: Large Corporations and the Rise of Business Political
         Activity in the U.S. and U.K.* New York: Oxford University Press.

Van Til, Jon
   1980 "Critical Environmental Issues Affecting Volunteerism." In W. Rydberg
         and L. Petersen, eds. *Volunteerism in the Eighties.* Appleton, WI: Aid Asso-
         ciation for Lutherans.

Van Til, Jon
   1982 *Living With Energy Shortfall: A Future for American Towns and Cities.*
         Boulder, CO: Westview Press.

Van Til, Jon, Robert P. Culleton, and Dorrie Margolin
   1982 "Toward Coproduction in the Human Services." Camden, NJ: Rutgers/
         Camden Forum For Policy Research and Public Service.

Veblen, Thorstein
   1934 *The Theory of the Leisure Class.* New York: Modern Library.

Vladeck, Bruce
   1986 "The Practical Differences in Managing Nonprofits." In Michael O'Neill
         and Dennis R. Young, eds., *Educating Managers of Nonprofit Organiza-
         tions.* San Francisco: University of San Francisco.

Walker, J. Malcolm
   1983 "Limits of Strategic Management." *Journal of Voluntary Action Research,*
         12 (January–June):39–56.

Wallace, Anthony F.C.
   1961 *Culture and Personality.* New York: Random House.

Walzer, Michael
1983   *Spheres of Justice: A Defense of Pluralism and Equality.* New York: Basic Books.

Warren, Donald I.
1980   *Helping Networks: How People Cope With Problems in the Urban Community.* Notre Dame: University of Notre Dame Press.

Warren, Donald I., and Rachelle Warren
1985   "U.S. National Patterns of Problem Coping Networks." *Journal of Voluntary Action Research,* 14 (April–September):31–53.

Warren, Robert M., Mark S. Rosentraub, and Louis F. Weschler
n.d.   "Urban Service Delivery and a Community Services Budget: Public Spending, Private Actions, and Coproduction." Unpublished paper.

Warriner, Charles K.
1965   "Four Types of Voluntary Associations." *Sociological Inquiry,* 35: 138–148.

Warwick, Donald P.
1975   *A Theory of Public Bureaucracy.* Cambridge, MA: Harvard University Press.

Webb, Adrian
1979   "Voluntary Action: In Search of a Policy? *Journal of Voluntary Action Research,* 8 (January–June):8–16.

Weisbrod, Burton
1977   *The Voluntary Non-Profit Sector: An Economic Analysis.* Lexington, MA: D.C. Heath.

Whyte, William F.
1986   "Philadelphia Story." *Society,* 23 (March/April):36–44.

Widgery, David
1986   "Saint Bob." *New Society* (May 23).

Wilber, Charles K., and K. Jameson
1981   "Hedonism and Quietism." *Society,* 19 (November/December):24–28.

Wilmeth, Marlyn W., and J. Richard Wilmeth
1979   "Lesser Angels and Minor Profits: The Supporting Group Behind One Professional Opera Company." *Journal of Voluntary Action Research,* 8 (July–September):21–32.

Wilson, Rick
1981   "Citizen Coproduction as a Mode of Participation: Conjectures and Models." *Journal of Urban Affairs,* 3 (Fall):37–50.

Wolch, Jennifer R.
1986   "Voluntarism and the New American Political Economy." In *Working Papers for the Spring Research Forum: Philanthropy, Voluntary Action, and*

the Public Good (pp. 469–482). Washington, D.C.: INDEPENDENT SECTOR.

Wolfenden Committee Report
1978   *The Future of Voluntary Organizations.* London: Croom Helm.

Wolff, Robert Paul
1968   *The Poverty of Liberalism.* Boston: Beacon.

Wolin, Sheldon S.
1960   *Politics and Vision.* Boston: Little, Brown.

Wolin, Sheldon S.
1981   "The New Public Philosophy." *democracy,* 1 (October):3–5.

Wolin, Sheldon
1983   "Editorial." *democracy,* 3 (Summer):2–6.

Wolpert, Julian, and Thomas Reiner
1985   "The Not-for-Profit Sector in Stable and Growing Metropolitan Regions." *Urban Affairs Quarterly,* 20:487–510.

Wood, James R.
1981   *Leadership in Voluntary Organizations.* New Brunswick, NJ: Rutgers University Press.

Wortman, Max
1981   "A Radical Shift from Bureaucracy to Strategic Management in Voluntary Organizations," *Journal of Voluntary Action Research,* 10 (January–March):62–81.

Young, Dennis R.
1983   *If Not for Profit, for What?: A Behavioral Theory of the Nonprofit Sector.* Lexington, MA: D.C. Heath.

Zurcher, Louis A.
1967   "Functional Marginality: Dynamics of a Poverty Intervention Organization." *(Southwestern) Social Science Quarterly,* 48 (Dec.): 411–421.

Zurcher, Louis A.
1979   "Ephemeral Roles, Voluntary Action and Voluntary Associations." *Journal of Voluntary Action Research,* 7:65–74.

REFERENCES INDEX

SUBJECT INDEX

business and nonprofits, 138–41
criteria for voluntarism and, 193,
196
government and the third sector,
136–38
philanthropy, 143–47
tectonics and climate, 147–49
voluntary and informal sectors,
141–43
Sectoral maps, 77–81
Selby, Cecily, 176
Self-actualization, motivations of
volunteers and, 24–33
Self-help volunteering (self-help), 12
definition of, 45
democratic theory and, 53–54
in pluralist theory, 50–51
in social democratic theory, 52–53
Self-interest, vs. altruism, 32–33
Self-management, 107
Sensitivity
partnerships and, 159
in third sector, 178
Service volunteering
definition of, 45
democratic theory and, 53–54
in pluralist theory, 50–51
in social democratic theory, 51–52
"Shared commitment" principle, 96–97
Sliding fee scale, 200
Sloan Foundation, 204
Small Business Administration, 116,
138–41
Sociable Society, the, 121
Social democracy, 162–63
definition of, 41
maps of the third sector and,
81–83
professionalization of third sector
and, 210
theory of, 43–44
volunteerism in, 51–54
Social diversions, 66
Social economy, 91–163,167
contemporary voluntarism and,
113–32
France, 126–32

Great Britain, 120–26, 131–32
United States, 114–20, 131–32
new understandings and, 93–111
John Dewey, 93–96
Albert Meister, 104–11
political economy and voluntary
associations, 96–98
values, role of, 108–11
voluntarism, 98–104
partnerships and, 151–63
corporate responsibility, history
of, 152–54
successful collaborations,
159–62
sectoral boundary blurring and,
133–49
business and nonprofits,
138–41
government and the third
sector, 136–38
philanthropy, 143–47
tectonics and climate, 147–49
voluntary and informal sectors,
141–43
theory of, 100–4
Socialism, 105
institutional interrelations and, 95
"Socialist incubators," 66
Social justice, 196–97
maps of the third sector and, 82
voluntarism and, 15–16
Social movements
third sector management and, 175
volunteerism and, 32
Social Security Act of 1935, 115
Social services, 115–16, 137
coproduction of, 157–58
Social theories, voluntary action and,
57–70, 184–85
maps of the third sector and,
81–84, 85–87
Marx problem and, 63–67
Michels and, 59–61
paradigms, 184–87
Parsons problem and, 67–70
professionalization of third sector,
209–10